MY LIFE WITH MURDERERS

DAVID WILSON

MY LIFE WITH MURDERERS

Behind Bars with the World's Most Violent Men

sphere

SPHERE

First published in Great Britain in 2019 by Sphere

3 5 7 9 10 8 6 4 2

A CIP catalogue record for this book
is available from the British Library.

Hardback ISBN 978-0-7515-7414-2
Export ISBN 978-0-7515-7768-6

Typeset in Warnock by M Rules
Printed and bound in Great Britain by
Clays Ltd, Elcograf S.p.A.

Papers used by Sphere are from well-managed forests
and other responsible sources.

Sphere
An imprint of
Little, Brown Book Group
Carmelite House
50 Victoria Embankment
London EC4Y 0DZ

An Hachette UK Company
www.hachette.co.uk

www.littlebrown.co.uk

*For Anne, who has had to share so much of this
professional life with me and who has always
done so with grace and good humour.*

Note to Readers

I have had to change times, dates and places related to my conversations with some of the men whom you will encounter in the pages of the book. I have tried to keep these changes to a minimum but to have provided more specific details might have revealed their true identities, which was not the context in which these men agreed to be interviewed. These 'off the record' interviews are an inevitable part of the criminological world that I inhabit, and which is described in the pages that follow. In particular, I have had to change several details about 'Jimmy' (not his real name), whom you will encounter in Chapter Two.

If I use direct quotes, these come from my transcripts of the taped interviews that I conducted, or from my reflective diary entries, which I write up at the end of each research day.

I have also used pseudonyms for several of the prisoners and some of the staff that I have worked with but whom I could not track down to seek their permission to be part of this narrative. Again, but for a number of different reasons, I have also had to self-censor one or two details related to specific murder cases which I mention. Sometimes I have had to do this as I was involved in the case and, as a signatory to the Official Secrets Act, I am simply not allowed to use the information that I gathered; in other instances, providing too much detail would put at risk witnesses, or cause unnecessary distress to the families of the victims. Sadly, over the course of my career, I have also discovered that to offer too many specific details simply allows those who want to kill to learn how to do so more competently.

Introduction

'It is perfectly true, as philosophers say, that life must be understood backwards. But they forget the other proposition, that it must be lived forwards. And if one thinks over that proposition it becomes more and more evident that life can never really be understood in time because at no particular moment can I find the necessary resting place from which to understand it.'

SØREN KIERKEGAARD, *Notebook IV A*

I've always been able to get out of bed early in the morning.

This biological reality has meant that throughout my professional career, I have usually been one of the first people to get into work. I rather like that. It allows me to get a flying start to the day, which is especially important as the stresses, strains and disruption that have characterised most of my working life usually begin later. So, for personal and professional reasons, I really am a 'morning person'.

That day was no different.

It was 7 a.m. as I parked my car, grabbed my trusty backpack from the passenger seat and walked into the criminology department of Birmingham City University, making my way to the spacious office that had been mine for nearly four years. There was a flight of stairs to be managed before I could get to my desk and to a blessed hour of peace and quiet before the day began in earnest. As I reached the top of the stairs and was walking towards my office I spotted Rick, reading a memo pinned to a notice board. I knew Rick quite well and though there was nothing unusual about seeing him there per se, my experience of working in prisons made me suspicious that something a little more sinister was going on. It looked almost as if Rick was lurking in the corridor and I couldn't help but wonder what he was doing there at this time of the morning. Still, I acted as if everything was normal.

'Morning, Rick,' I said, as I passed him by.

He made no reply.

I walked on, shaking off my suspicions – maybe Rick just wasn't a morning person. I filed it as something to worry about later and took my thoughts back to the day ahead and the mountain of reports waiting for me on my desk.

Suddenly, without warning, I was hit over the head and expertly thrown to the ground.

'What did you say?' my assailant demanded, furiously kicking me as I lay helplessly on the floor. Time seemed to stand still. I don't remember much about those moments except that I was absolutely terrified.

Thankfully, as quickly and unexpectedly as the attack had started, it stopped, and I was alone in the now deserted corridor. I slowly got to my feet, checked how badly I had been hurt – miraculously, not too badly – and then hobbled the few metres to my office.

I put down my backpack, which I suspect had taken a few of the more serious blows of the attack for me, peeled off my jacket and slumped into my chair. After a few minutes I had composed myself sufficiently to pick up the telephone and call the Security Office.

Despite much of my working life taking place in prisons,

it may come as a surprise that this incident has been – touch wood – my one and only skirmish with direct, physical violence being inflicted upon me in my career and is, without embellishment, the one occasion which was potentially life-threatening.

In other words, this was my only skirmish with the type of violence that could all too easily have led to murder.

Murder!

The noun 'murder' seems both electrifying and all-encompassing. It provides a sneaky thrill and an air of certainty and so offers a confidence that a simple definition of murder, such as 'the unlawful and premeditated killing of one human being by another', subtly masks. We don't really register those dry legal words – 'unlawful' and 'premeditated'. These 'get out of jail free' qualifiers allow deaths which are legal – such as when a soldier or a police officer kills – and shatter the idea that murder is as straightforward as the description implies.

The same applies when we label someone a 'murderer'.

Murder, in my experience, is a slippery concept and murderers as diverse and different from one another as trees in a forest. Every murder – and the accompanying psychology – is different.

I should know.

I've spent my entire professional life working with violent men. Specifically, men who have committed murder and even that perennial, popular fascination, serial murder. I've drunk tea, or sometimes something stronger, with all sorts of killers; shared a joke with them in their cells; looked them in the eye and told them that they are liars or psychopaths; and helped to put a few of them behind bars, or, more typically, been part of the process that has kept them there.

Some of these men became my friends; others would love to kill me. Even now.

Homicide, infanticide, parricide, filicide; family annihilators, hitmen, spree, mass and serial killers; and not forgetting those offenders who use, or are prepared to use, violence to further their criminal careers, such as kidnappers, burglars or bank robbers – I've met them all at some point in my career. Along the way, they've helped me to come to some surprising conclusions about the phenomenon of murder and those men who commit these dreadful crimes.

Violence, like murder, is also a slippery concept. Violence does not need to be limited to the application of physical force and might simply involve the threat of violence, verbal aggression, or encompass psychological harms.

My conversations with men who commit lethal or violent crimes have allowed me unique access into the minds of murderers. My discussions with some of these men go back several decades and some are, even now, still ongoing.

Of course, with all of these historic and continuing conversations there are delicate ethical lines that need to be trod. With all my interviewees, for example, I make it clear that if they reveal to me an offence for which they have not been convicted I will have no option but to report that matter to the police. I accept that this might limit what they tell me but, on balance, I feel that this is a price worth paying to get them to talk at all. The fruits of my discussions with these lethal and violent men form the basis of what follows.

Before going any further I'd be remiss if I didn't address the issue of gender. This is a book about men who have murdered, or used violence against others. My focus on men is the consequence of a number of factors. First and most importantly, murder really is a young man's business. It is still relatively rare for a woman to commit this type of crime and, when a woman does kill, she will often use different methods – for example, if we're looking at serial murder, female serial killers will often use poison to dispatch their victims, whereas male serial killers usually bludgeon, stab, strangle or shoot.

And, while I describe violent men, it is important to acknowledge that I do not think of masculinity as one-dimensional. There are multiple masculinities, with various ways of performing masculinity and 'being a man'. Men are not 'programmed' in some way to be violent. It is not 'unmasculine' to be nurturing, loving and caring; I hope that I am one such man.

More immediately, I have never worked with female offenders and given that the book is about my working life with murderers and those who have used violence, the reason for my gender focus becomes more apparent.

In my experience, the general public imagine that lethal and violent men are monstrous, alien, 'others' to the extent that they should have horns on their heads and a long, pointed tail. If only it was that easy. What I have learned in nearly forty years of working within this field is how widespread the roots of violence are in our culture and therefore how seemingly 'ordinary' men can do dreadful things, often in the most banal of places and for the most ludicrous of reasons.

To illustrate my point, let me ask you a question about murder.

Of all the murders that get committed each year, what percentage get cleared up by the police? This isn't a trick question and, even though 'cleared up' can be slightly different to catching the actual perpetrator, if we take wrongful convictions into account, successful appeals and so forth, I simply mean that the police 'get their man'? What would you say? Ten per cent? Perhaps you might go as high as forty or fifty per cent.

In my experience of asking public audiences this question, it is rare for someone to suggest seventy, or even eighty, per cent.

These latter guesses would still be too low.

Year after year, the clear-up rate for murder hovers around the ninety-per-cent mark. That's right. Nine out of ten murders are solved and the perpetrator brought to justice. You may think that that is because of developments in DNA analysis and our growing national DNA database – the largest and oldest in the world – or maybe you think it's due to progress in forensic science; the growing expertise and persistence of the police; the stupidity of murderers; the publicity generated by the media or, bless you, the use of offender profilers. You'd be wrong. The reality of murder is that in over seventy per cent of cases where the victim was a woman, the perpetrator and the victim knew each other, and in just over half of murder cases where the victim was a man, the victim knew their killer. Husbands kill wives; boyfriends kill girlfriends; parents kill children, and friends kill each other. Two women a week are murdered in this country – killed by their partner or ex-partner – and countless others face the daily torture of domestic violence.

As a result most murders are self-solvers; you don't have to be Inspector Morse or Miss Marple to work out whodunnit. It is often the person reporting the murder to the police who is the culprit, even if a few still persist to the point of agreeing to participate in the inevitable press conference asking for witnesses to come forward.

To put this into a personal context, do you remember Rick and the attack on me?

Rick was a colleague of mine at the university. He taught sociology. Sadly, it transpired that he had a severe form of depression, which would become so marked and problematic that he had to leave teaching altogether and before he attacked anyone else.

Was this a bizarre, isolated incident? Perhaps. But aren't many violent incidents seemingly atypical and out of the ordinary? Who hasn't read reports of the shock of family, friends or neighbours after a violent incident, their descriptions of the perpetrator as 'a nice guy', a man who 'just wasn't the type who could have done that'? That's exactly how I would have described Rick.

The murderers that you will meet in the following pages will help you to understand both this everyday reality of the violence and murder that I have described and also its more extreme and unusual limits. However, in my experience, whether we are describing the typical or the abnormal, the hues of violence and murder are usually grey and rarely black and white – there can therefore be no single, grand narrative that explains murder.

We have to think more broadly about violence and murder and not settle for the easy, black-and-white answers that have all too often become the staple of popular entertainment.

The complex consequences of violence are obviously catastrophic and life-changing, and merely acknowledging that complexity is not enough for me. These issues are not simple, nor straightforward, for they deal with real human beings. Not only dangerous, damaged and disturbed offenders but the great harm that some men can inflict on their fellow human beings – all too often women and children.

Throughout my career I have never forgotten that the most important people that I have to deal with are the victims, if they have survived, or the families of those victims if their loved ones did not survive. I have cried unashamedly with the parents of children who have been murdered and tried, as best as I could, to help to get justice for those families whose son, daughter, parent or friend had been killed. I have often failed in these attempts. This too is devastating.

Some people may therefore find my focus on the perpetrators of violent and deadly crime insensitive, or at odds with what I have just described. However, I believe that it is only by attempting to understand the men who commit murder and, through discussing with them the circumstances in which they come to kill, that we can discover patterns of murderous behaviour and therefore, hopefully, prevent future violence. Over time I've learned that murder makes no sense when viewed as an isolated act of violence and that if we want to understand why men kill and prevent other men from doing the same, we need to examine the context in which murder happens. And, here's the thing: the murderer rarely interprets that context in the same way that you and I might. It is only by stepping into the murderer's shoes – no matter how ill-fitting – that we can begin to comprehend what might, at first glance, appear senseless.

This might already all seem too overwhelming and devastating but that is not my intention. In fact, I believe that what emerges from this professional memoir is optimism about people in general and many violent offenders.

So by all means enjoy what you are about to read. I would be disappointed if you didn't. However, enter the pages that follow with caution and also with a willingness to put old prejudices and certainties to one side. Above all, allow yourself the opportunity to think more broadly about the people and the circumstances which I describe and which, sadly, can have a deadly potential to affect us all.

CHAPTER ONE

The Scrubs, a Serial Killer and the Annexe

'It was as though in those last minutes he was summing up the lesson that this long course in human wickedness had taught us – the lesson of the fearsome word-and-thought-defying banality of evil.'

HANNAH ARENDT, *Eichmann in Jerusalem: A Report on the Banality of Evil*

I had a headache and was struggling to concentrate. Memories of the previous night, spent with Simon, Roddy and Antony, three of my university friends, in a trendy bar in Fulham, floated back and forth into my consciousness, jarring with the sights, sounds and, above all, the smells which now surrounded me in HMP Wormwood Scrubs.

It had been the small hours before I had got back to my rented accommodation in Hammersmith and I was now suffering the consequences.

I closed my eyes.

'No sugar! That's right, isn't it?' a voice asked, rather too loudly, as a mug of tea – or 'diesel' as it was called in Her Majesty's Prison Service – was placed on the wooden desk in front of me.

The voice that shook me from my slumbers belonged to Eric, one of C wing's senior officers and a fellow Glaswegian. He had decided very quickly, and mostly as a result of geography and misplaced patriotism, that I was 'worth saving', even if I was the prison's new assistant governor. In short, Eric had taken me under his wing. I was grateful not just for the tea but for his support in general. Prisons can be very lonely places, even if you're not one of the inmates.

I nodded an agreement and managed a rather weak, 'Thanks!'

Despite his being an ally, I knew that Eric's attempt at conversation wasn't meant to make me feel better; he was enjoying my discomfort and intended, not-so-subtly, to try and prolong my agony.

Outside my office, the prison was gradually coming to life and row after row of prisoners were slowly making their way to the central sluice area where they could 'slop out', before they went onto the ground floor landing to collect their breakfast. 'Slopping out' meant emptying the contents of their plastic chamber pot from the night before. My office was located beside the central sluice and so I had a front-row seat to witness this most obvious of the noxious and visceral daily rituals of life in our prisons in 1983.

I had recently graduated from Cambridge University with a doctorate about the philosophical origins of the American Civil War and had been recruited through the direct entrant scheme into the prison service. I was still adjusting to life behind bars, as it were.

'Never drink when you've got work the next day. I told you that! Didn't I?' Eric chided me as I took another sip of my tea. He had indeed explained this to me on several occasions. However, the impact of his wisdom had been somewhat blunted by the fact that his advice usually came about two pints into a drinking session together, just a few hours before we were supposed to start working. Eric was, as they say in English literature, an unreliable narrator.

'Anyway, pull yourself together. You've got receptions to see and one is a VIP.'

I put down the mug of tea and adjusted the knot on my old college tie, looking up at Eric once I had done so in the hope that my appearance would meet his approval.

'What do you reckon?' I asked.

'Every inch the yuppie,' said Eric.

I wasn't certain if that was a criticism, or a compliment. One of the ways that the prison staff had tried to make sense of who I was had been to latch onto the idea that I was a 'young, urban professional' – a yuppie. That might have been true of my Cambridge contemporaries, most of whom had gone off to work in the City and were enjoying Thatcherite excesses to the full. I knew that I wanted to travel in a different direction. I wanted to make a difference, rather than money; I wanted to help people. However, I soon discovered that my new colleagues needed to find a logic for my decision to become a prison governor that made sense to them and so I didn't discourage their misplaced analysis. I had actually tried to explain my career choice to them on several occasions but talk of public policy, idealism, hope, rehabilitation or redemption was always met with looks of pity, exasperation and much shaking of heads. So, yuppie it was.

It had actually been the former governor of Wormwood Scrubs, John McCarthy, who had helped me to decide upon this career path. John had resigned from the prison service in a wave of publicity in 1981, after writing a letter to *The Times* expressing his dismay at the overcrowding in the penal system and what he believed was the failure of the Home Secretary to do anything about it. He stated in his letter that he wasn't prepared to be 'the manager of a large penal dustbin'. Later, explaining his resignation further, he had also described how he was 'unable to come to terms with the present state of the prison service and the direction in which it is going'. This was John's coded message that the prison system had simply become reduced to warehousing people, rather than helping prisoners to rehabilitate. That was clearly a concern for me for, if McCarthy was right, I should really have been thinking about other career options.

At the time when John wrote to *The Times* complaining about overcrowding, the prison population was about 43,000. Today it is nearly double that number and even though there have been new prisons built, overcrowding remains a perennial problem.

I found his address and wrote to John explaining that I was now in two minds about joining the prison service, and he kindly agreed to meet me. John was warm and welcoming and the essence of his counsel over our lunch meeting was that I should make my own journey in life and come to the conclusions that best suited me, my values and aspirations. On the train journey back to Cambridge, a mixture of arrogance and naivety made me believe that I really could make more of a go of things than he might have been able to do during his career. Even so, John's advice is timeless, and I've also given it myself to many young people looking at their own career paths today. I did still have a few nagging doubts but the appeal of trying to make a difference to the lives of people on the furthest edges of our society was as strong as my naivety and arrogance. So, after much consideration, I decided to go for it. A few short months later I had moved from grappling with the abstract and academic to dealing with genuine questions of public policy and was faced with the all-too-real human beings who could be directly affected by the types of judgements and decisions that I, and others, might make.

In truth, very little of my academic training had prepared me for what I was now employed to do and even now I marvel that a doctorate in history and philosophy would lead to a career working with some of the most violent men in the country. However, my belief in rehabilitation and that *everyone* is capable of making positive change was going to be shaken to the core in the years that followed.

Not that Eric, the other prison officers, or even the prisoners seemed to care about the big philosophical concerns I was grappling with. To them I was just another 'suit' – prison governors wore their own 'civilian' clothes, rather than a uniform. To them the suits by and large got in the way and needed to learn who *really* ran the jail.

And who *really* ran the jail?

Well that would be the Prison Officers' Association (POA) and heaven help you if you lost their support. The POA could date its origins back to before the First World War and was made up of all the rank-and-file prison officers, senior, principal and chief officers, and they controlled the prison in a number of different ways. Most obviously they could (and often did) threaten to withdraw their labour and 'walk to the Gate', leaving the governors who remained behind with few, or perhaps no staff at all to undertake even the most basic of duties.

It was also the prison officers who controlled 'the detail', which determined how many staff were needed at particular times of the day. For a quiet life, governors would often turn a blind eye to the daily reality that there *never* seemed to be enough staff and so every prison had to run on overtime which, of course, attracted extra payments. Prison staff soon came to rely on working overtime to pay for holidays, new cars, or buying their homes and a new governor had to learn very quickly never to meddle in the detail, or challenge the amount of overtime that was being paid.

Governors, of course, were salaried and so did not work overtime.

In the 1960s, the POA had also become much more vocal

about what they thought punishment should be like and how prison regimes should be much tougher. This did not go down well with many governors who, typically, articulated a much more liberal approach to imprisonment and usually came from a very different social and educational background than most of the prison officers. Governors also tended to move on very quickly from one prison to another after gaining, or as a preparation for, promotion. This career trajectory would not be helped by having the POA undertake a vote of no confidence in that governor and so there was an incessant but hidden, low-level battle between the POA and management.

It was a battle which the POA usually won.

One small measure of their power was what I was wearing. It was only after a couple of months into my posting that I'd been allowed to wear my own clothes. For the previous eight weeks, I had been kitted out in an ill-fitting prison officer's uniform, so as to 'get a taste of what it is really like on the landings', according to the deal that had been struck between the POA and the prison service when they had introduced the direct entrant scheme. In fact, had there not been some staff shortages in the prison, I might have been in my prison officer's uniform for even longer.

But here I was, just ten weeks into my new job, finally dressed in my own clothes, and meeting my first VIP – whatever that meant here.

'VIP?' I said.

Eric threw a copy of the *Sun* down on my desk and nodded at the picture on the front page.

'Him!'

I drank a little more of my tea, staring at the picture and trying to recall everything that I knew about this case before I interviewed the prisoner, as I was required to do with all new receptions onto the prison's C wing. I still wasn't quite certain how I was supposed to react to the fact that this was now the sort of person I was responsible for managing. Repulsed or fascinated? Perhaps a combination of both?

Dennis Nilsen was indeed a 'very important prisoner'. He'd murdered at least 12 young men in London, in a killing cycle that lasted between 1978 and 1983. The press had other names for him, labelling him a monster, unable to comprehend his crimes, with lurid tales of cannibalism and necrophilia never far from the surface. Nilsen had only the day before been convicted of six murders and two attempted murders in North London, though the true extent of his crimes continues to be a source of confusion to this day. He had initially told the startled arresting officer that he had killed fifteen young men – twelve in Melrose Avenue, where he had access to a back garden, and three in Cranley Gardens, where he lived in the top-floor flat.

Most of his victims had been young, homeless men, many of whom were also gay. Nilsen would pick them up in local pubs, bring them back to his flat at closing time, ply them with more alcohol and, when they were suitably stupefied, strangle them to death. Sometimes he would revive them just before they lost consciousness, before strangling them again.

Although he denied it, forensics showed that after his victims were dead he would occasionally have sex with their inert bodies, prior to cutting them up and disposing of their remains. Disposal hadn't been too difficult in Melrose Avenue, where he would start a bonfire in his back garden, masking the smell of roasting flesh by burning old car tyres. It had proven more difficult in Cranley Gardens and this difficulty had been the source of Nilsen's discovery and downfall as he had been reduced to flushing body parts down the toilet. Not that he wanted to dispose of *all* the body parts; Nilsen sometimes liked to keep 'trophies' of the heads of some of his male victims.

Aside from the grisly nature of his crimes, the media interest had also been fed by criticism of the police and their handling of the case – fairly so, given that a number of young men had survived attacks by Nilsen and then reported the assaults.

Douglas Stewart was a twenty-five-year-old trainee chef who got chatting to Nilsen, a fellow Scot with a similar catering background, in the Golden Lion pub and was invited back for more drinks in Melrose Avenue. Once there, Douglas fell asleep in an armchair but woke up in the early hours of the morning in a darkened room and tried to stretch out. He realised that his ankles had been tied to the chair. He felt his tie being loosened and then knotted around his throat – Nilsen was strangling him. Douglas managed to aim a blow at his attacker's face and then struggled out of the chair.

There was a shouting match and Douglas accused Nilsen of trying to kill him. Nilsen suggested that if Douglas went to the police, 'They'll never believe you. They're bound to take my word for it. Like I told you in the pub, I'm a respectable civil servant.'

Douglas left Nilsen's flat and found a telephone box. He dialled 999 and waited for the police car to arrive. He showed the two police officers the red marks around his neck and explained to them what had happened. One of the officers stayed with Douglas, while the other went to interview Nilsen.

Douglas would later recall that, 'Nilsen denied everything I had told the police. He gave them the impression that we were going out together and it was just a lovers' quarrel in a homosexual romance.' As soon as the word 'homosexual' was mentioned, Douglas claimed, the police lost all interest and only got back in contact after Nilsen's subsequent arrest.

Even if the term itself had first been coined in the 1960s, we didn't really use the word 'homophobia' in the 1980s. It might not have been in popular usage, but it was certainly rife and there's no doubt that homophobia created a context in which it was possible for Nilsen to kill and then to avoid detection for as long as he did. Not that the media was overly concerned with homophobia. They were far more interested in cannibalism and necrophilia. It was obvious to everyone in the press that, as far as killers went, Nilsen was box-office gold.

However, buried beneath the sensationalism there was another description too: 'serial killer' – a term which had been created in the USA by the FBI and their Behavioural Science Unit in 1974, most probably by Robert Ressler, one of their profilers. By the early 1980s this description was in common usage in the USA and was about to become popular here. Upon first hearing the term, I'd done some research because, as amazing as it seems now, I'd never come across the description 'serial killer' before. A few of the papers I found in my reading had even quoted one FBI agent claiming that serial murder was a 'new phenomenon'. That I knew to be untrue and I wondered if he'd ever heard of Jack the Ripper.

My initial research had left me with more questions than answers. The little that I could find on serial murder seemed to be far from definitive. Two American academics had suggested an emerging typology of serial killers. Based on their interviews with convicted serial killers in American jails, they had divided them into four types: visionary (who would kill as a result of obeying the orders they believed that they were receiving); mission oriented (killing to rid the world of people they regarded as evil); hedonistic (killing for sexual pleasure); and, finally, power/control oriented (killing to establish dominance over their victims).

I could see problems with this typology but still I wondered what 'type' our new reception might be. Visionary, mission oriented, hedonistic or power/control oriented? His appearance in the photograph in the newspaper didn't afford too many clues – Nilsen wasn't much to look at. Tall, slim and wearing spectacles, he must have been in his mid-thirties. Even the detective who had arrested him some ten months previously had described him as 'Mr Ordinary' and that's exactly how he looked to me in the photograph. Mr Ordinary. Average. Normal. Banal.

What made him extraordinary was what he had just been convicted of. If I'd known that day was to be the day Nilsen would be arriving, I probably would have had an early night the evening before and I'd be lying if I said that, in that moment, I wasn't nervous.

'Ready?' asked Eric. I took a deep breath and nodded, and he shouted, rather too enthusiastically, 'Nilsen!'

Nilsen was a Category A prisoner – the highest prison security classification – and so was accompanied into my office by two prison officers. That made five of us, crammed into the tiny space for what was always the dullest of the formal meetings that I had with prisoners. This meeting served to establish that the inmate understood where they were and what the sentence of the court had been, and could tell me if they had any immediate personal needs. I would also allocate them to a work detail, based on the vacancies we had in the jail at that moment.

The objective of the meeting might have been dulling but I have to admit that that wasn't how I was feeling. I wasn't scared. The fact that Nilsen was accompanied by two officers and Eric, who was ever present, acting as a master of ceremonies, would have provided me with ample protection, should the need arise. No, I was excited. I wanted to meet the man who had killed his victims, cut up their body parts, burned them, or flushed them down the toilet. I wanted to know when the light in his head that connected him to the rest of humanity had been switched off and had left him in the morbid, murderous gloom. I wanted to ask him why and to try to make sense of what appeared to me to be senseless. I wanted to understand.

I surreptitiously put the copy of the *Sun* into my desk drawer and watched as Nilsen was ushered into my office. He spoke first and, in retrospect, this should have prompted me to think about how he liked to be in control. He was someone who asked, rather than answered questions.

'Are you a psychiatrist?' he demanded, blinking behind his glasses. One of the officers must have told him that I was 'Dr Wilson' – I often found it helped a little that my title confused offenders on first meeting me.

I shook my head, all too aware that the end of his trial had been dominated by questions of responsibility, personality disorders, abnormalities of the brain and the concept of free will.

Nilsen had been found perfectly 'sane' and so faced the full force of the law, even though he had claimed not only to have killed at least twelve young men but attempted to kill many more. That didn't sound like the behaviour of a sane man to me but over the years I would grow used to serial killers behaving in ways that, at first sight, appeared to run counter to their own best interests.

'I'm a doctor of philosophy,' I replied.

'Oh! Good. You looked too young anyway. So, we can talk.'

I smiled and then asked a few perfunctory questions, before I could really get into areas that fascinated me.

'Do you understand what sentence you have received from the Court?'

Nilsen nodded.

'Do you have anyone that we need to inform that you are here?'

'That's being taken care of by a friend,' replied Nilsen and, later, I wondered if he had meant his biographer Brian Masters, who had written to him whilst he had been on remand.

'We have no work at the moment but have a look at this form which will let you know the types of work which we usually have available and let your Wing Officer know what it is that you would like to do. I will then put you on the waiting list.'

Now was my chance.

I was about to ask about the murders, about sanity and

insanity, good and evil, sadism, cannibalism and necrophilia, when one of the prison officers accompanying Nilsen coughed.

'I have to get Nilsen down to see the doctor.'

With that he was gone, looking like a weedy geography teacher who would struggle to keep control of his GCSE class.

This wasn't my last and was certainly not my most insightful conversation with Nilsen. However it is this first meeting in the Scrubs that was important, despite its brevity. It would cement my interest and then growing expertise in the phenomenon of murder and serial murder, based on my future discussions with Nilsen and other serial killers and murderers that I would encounter inside. I would later find that ironic, as what these impending discussions convinced me of was that you cannot ever rely on a single thing a serial killer tells you.

Nilsen particularly had a strange relationship with the truth and it was through him that I grew to understand the narcissism, manipulation and dissembling behaviour that characterises serial killers and some murderers. In reality, they are far removed from the cultured, charismatic serial killers so beloved of film and TV series.

By the end of that day a joke had started to go round the prison.

It was that the new AG, by which they meant me, had just made Nilsen the 'drains red band'. Red bands are prisoners who can be trusted to get about the prison without being escorted by a member of staff. They literally wear a red band around their arm, which also contains their photograph. Every prison has several red bands who work almost as full a day as the staff and though drains weren't the work detail I would eventually allocate to Nilsen, the joke did accurately imply the gruesome means by which Nilsen had disposed of some of his victims and how he had been caught – by a Dyno-Rod engineer.

So Nilsen went off to see the doctor and then Eric suggested that we had had far too much excitement for one day and should therefore have another mug of tea, to help calm ourselves down. I readily agreed.

I didn't realise it at the time but over the years my work was going to bring me into contact with hundreds of other murderers and a number of serial killers too. Some would surprise me, most would depress me and, just occasionally, one or two would become my friends.

As I sipped my tea, I thought that I had best get on with learning the nuts and bolts of being a prison governor and – like my first meeting with Nilsen – I have no doubt that what I experienced and learned at Wormwood Scrubs had a major impact on the rest of my career.

Even the name of this first posting was typical of the jails where I was employed.

The prisons I worked in all have names that evoke the countryside. They sound rather lovely, bucolic and isolated, and although this might have been true at some point in their histories, it hardly reflected their contemporary geographic realities.

The Scrubs was built by convict labour between 1875 and 1891, on twenty acres of scrubland in west London. Despite the relatively isolated location which its name suggests, even at the time there were local objections to the building of the prison.

When I arrived at the Scrubs in 1983, a recent episode in the prison's history continued to exercise an undue influence on what happened within the jail, while a more historic incident served to create the context for the most significant development of penal policy in the country – and which would have an important bearing on my career. This historic incident was the escape of the spy George Blake.

In 1961 Blake had pleaded guilty to five counts in breach of the Official Secrets Act, and was subsequently sentenced to forty-two years' imprisonment, at the time the longest non-life sentence ever imposed on any prisoner.

Blake had worked for the Special Operations Executive and MI6 during the Second World War and was posted to Korea after hostilities had ended, where he was tasked with setting up a network of agents. He was captured by the North Koreans and imprisoned for three years. It was during his imprisonment that he was, unknown to his British handlers, turned into a Communist and on his return to Britain he started to leak information about British and American operations to the KGB. He was exposed as a double agent by a Polish defector but, by that time, it's estimated that Blake had betrayed at least forty agents – many of whom died.

Blake had initially been on remand at HMP Brixton, before being transferred to the Scrubs. He didn't stay there long. Blake escaped from the Scrubs in October 1966. He used a rusty iron bar to break a first-floor window at the end of the cell block, climbed out onto the roof of a small porch which covered the block's entrance and then dropped to the ground. The prison wall was only twenty yards away.

In a clearly choreographed move, a rope ladder was then thrown over the wall, which Blake used to make his escape. As he landed on the other side, he broke his left wrist and had to be helped to the car by his accomplices, who had all been fellow inmates with Blake in the Scrubs. Blake was eventually smuggled out of England to Russia just before Christmas 1966, having been hidden in various safe houses in and around London. As of 2017, Blake was still living in Moscow on a KGB pension.

The political impact of Blake's escape was immediate and produced something akin to panic in the Home Office, as it came in the wake of the separate escapes of the so-called Great Train Robbers Charlie Wilson and Ronald Biggs in the couple of years preceding. Roy Jenkins, Home Secretary at the time, attempted to placate the political storm that was brewing by appointing Lord Mountbatten to conduct an enquiry into prison security.

The report recommended that prisoners should be assessed according to the lowest level of security believed to be necessary to hold them in custody and suggested that all prisoners (although not women or young offenders) should be placed in one of four categories, according to the level of dangerousness that they would present to the public if they were able to escape.

Even through all the changes and improvements to internal and external security that have taken place since 1966, these security classifications have endured and have remained the basis on which prisoners are managed. Today, still, the categories run as follows:

Category A is the highest category of prisoner, such as Nilsen, one 'who must in no circumstances be allowed to get out, either because of security considerations affecting spies, or because their violent behaviour is such that members of the public or the police would be in danger of their lives if they were to get out.'

Category B are 'prisoners for whom the very high expenditure on the most modern escape barriers may not be justified, but who ought to be kept in secure conditions.'

Category C are 'prisoners who lack the resources and will to make escape attempts [but] have not the stability to be kept in conditions where there is no barrier to escape.'

Category D are the lowest category of prisoners, those 'who can reasonably be entrusted to serve their sentences in open conditions.'

All four classifications allow for subjective decision-making, which allows any decision to be influenced by factors other than security. For example, a member of staff might alter a prisoner's security level to establish a greater amount of control over that prisoner, or use security classifications to ease overcrowding.

However, a perennial point of discussion within the prison service is to do with the concentration, or the dispersal, of the highest security category prisoners. Is it safer and more effective to house all Category A prisoners in one place (like some kind of super-prison), or to disperse those offenders throughout prisons across the country? The dispersal system is the one we have in place, but we might like to consider whether the policy of dispersal did indeed lead to there being good order and better security so that prisoners did not escape.

The dispersal system was slowly introduced into the service from 1966 onwards but during the seventies there were four separate riots at new dispersal prisons. It was the most recent riot of dispersal prisoners on D wing at Wormwood Scrubs, in August 1979, that had an impact on my posting four years later. The report into how that riot had started and then how control had been regained by staff had only been published in 1982 and its conclusions were still being hotly debated when I arrived at the jail.

It had taken several days to regain control of D wing and order had only been re-established through the use of specially trained officers, known as the Minimum Use of Force Tactical Intervention (MUFTI) squad, which had been formed in response to previous riots. Initial reports suggested that no prisoners had been injured when the MUFTI squad regained control and it was only a month later, when the governor finally submitted a written report to the Home Office, that the true figure of fifty-three injured prisoners was revealed. The official inquiry into the riot suggested that there were:

Indications that members of the POA committee played a more intrusive role in the operational decision-making process than is appropriate, whereas some members of the management team, notably the Deputy Governor, the duty Medical Officer and the Assistant Governor in charge of D Wing, were either not involved at all or were inadequately consulted and briefed.

The effects of this riot were still being felt when I started: many of the staff that I worked with remembered it vividly. Eric was especially outspoken about it and felt that the dispersal prisoners on D wing had been given far too many privileges. As a result, the regime had become 'too soft' and so what if the MUFTI squad had, as he put it, 'cracked a few heads – it showed them who's in charge'. Frankly, this was the culture that still dominated the prison when I arrived and while I was and will remain eternally grateful for Eric's support, I also knew that I needed to form other alliances if I was to survive my posting to the Scrubs and start to make the kinds of changes that had attracted me to the job.

When thinking about this at the time, common sense suggested that I should attach myself to Ian Dunbar, the shrewd and approachable governor of the prison. However, common sense sometimes doesn't take into consideration the realities of the daily grind of trying to manage a 'penal dustbin'.

Dunbar had his hands full with dealing with the administration and bureaucracy of the Scrubs. He had to try to bring some order back into the jail in the wake of John's resignation, just a couple of years previously, as well as coping with the underlying and seemingly unremitting challenges of managing an often openly hostile group of staff.

I could tell that some days it wore him down.

I'd also been thinking hard about my place within the prison following my encounter with Nilsen. I realised that it would never be enough for me to be a straightforward jailer of the men that I was in charge of. I truly believed – and still believe – in the power of rehabilitation, and the only way to enact that is to attempt to understand the men that you're trying to rehabilitate. After a few weeks of ruminating on this, I went to Dunbar to ask his advice on who would make an appropriate mentor. He suggested that I talk with Robin Sewell, the prison's principal psychologist, and that, given my academic background, I should also 'try and get to know something about the Hospital Annexe and old Max Glatt'.

Glatt was a visiting psychotherapist at the prison and a pioneer of helping alcoholics and drug addicts. He had set up the very first NHS unit for the treatment of alcoholics in 1952 – rather than seeing addicts as nuisances, Glatt had recognised that they needed help and prioritised that need. His units operated as 'therapeutic communities', a term used to describe a hospital regime which was devoid of hierarchy and which allowed participants to take responsibility for their own actions, within a supportive environment. It was a description which I would get to know well. The goal was to combat the helplessness that comes through institutionalisation – and what could be more institutional than a prison?

The psychology department of the prison was located in a large port-a-cabin outside the main body of the jail. The psychologists did not have offices on the wings, which seemed to be both an acknowledgement that the prison was very overcrowded and therefore space was at a premium and, less charitably, yet another demonstration of the power of the POA to determine what happened inside the jail and who could be located there. Psychologists, like governors, were seen by many members of the POA to be part of the problem, not the solution.

After my chat with Dunbar, I headed straight to the

psychology department, fired up to start learning more about the prisoners at the Scrubs. I pushed the shabby door open and asked, 'Is Robin about?'

A woman's voice shouted, 'Hello!'

I had to contain my surprise – given the culture of the prison, I'd presumed that Robin would be a man. We got on immediately and pretty soon the psychology department became my favourite place to gossip about the prison and what had happened during the day. Eric was not so subtly being replaced.

Robin was old enough to be my mother and I think that she rather liked the fact that she could 'mother' me about how to manage my career. Perhaps she had also had a word with Dunbar but, in any event, she was enthusiastic in her role as my mentor. I chose not to look too deeply at why she also loved to call me her 'baby screw' and simply put it down to her sense of irreverent fun. There are various suggestions as to why prison staff are sometimes called 'screws'. Perhaps the most likely is that 'screw' used to be slang for 'key' and, of course, the most important custodial job that prison staff have is to 'turn the screw' – lock prisoners up.

But the work that Robin and Charles Clarke, the Annexe's psychologist, were engaged in was not about locking people up but instead a revolutionary new approach towards handling violent men within prisons.

The large annexe of the prison's hospital operated as a therapeutic community, just like the units that Glatt had set up previously. My initial questions were the obvious ones: Is the Annexe a soft option for prisoners who want to get out of the overcrowded mainstream prison? Do the prisoners change their behaviour? Does the Annexe work?

Charles answered all of these questions and more besides but also suggested that if I really wanted to understand the Annexe I should go and see it for myself and participate in some of the groups. It was a suggestion which was to have a huge impact on my career and my subsequent understanding of violent men, both in relation to how we should manage them when they are in custody and how we might help them change their offending. Everything about the Annexe was different to the main prison: first off, it was light and airy, rather than dark and gloomy; staff and prisoners talked to each other, rather than having one group shout orders which might, or might not be obeyed by the other group; and, most important of all, there seemed to be hope and optimism in the air, rather than a constant, low-level negativity which could turn to violence at any time.

I soon found a space in my working day to involve myself with the Annexe and, sometimes, I would also come into the prison on my day off just to participate in the groups.

At the heart of what happened in the Annexe was a form of talking therapy that took place in groups. As far as I understood things, talking therapy was part of and very much allied to psychoanalysis, and psychoanalysis led directly back to Sigmund Freud. Freud, of course, suggested that our minds were in almost constant conflict, with an unremitting tension between the 'superego' – our conscience – and the base impulses of the 'id', which operated on a 'pleasure principle'. That left the poor old 'ego' to try and mediate between the two.

It's not hard to criticise Freud. He developed his analytical method with a very specific group of wealthy clients but extrapolated more generally from his own and their rather privileged and unrepresentative worlds. He botched a number of his cases, especially those involving female clients, and often what he suggested seemed like mere speculation, rather than rigorous science. However, this fair criticism notwithstanding, what Freud did do was underscore that our conscious minds are the tip of the iceberg. In other words, that the majority of our feelings and thoughts, and especially our motives for behaving in certain ways, are largely hidden from us, and that often these motives are neither innocent nor benign. Talking about these things with a therapist might help to reduce an individual's emotional suffering and, if successful with people who have committed crime, might prevent other people from suffering too.

The Annexe allocated prisoners to a group containing between eight and ten offenders. This group would meet for an hour once a day to discuss their offending, their past lives and what might be happening within the Annexe. What was to be discussed was up to the group, sometimes reacting to seemingly trivial issues that had cropped up during the day. Why was someone always late for meals or for the start of the group? Why did some group members speak regularly, while others were perpetually silent? Why did one group member feel the need to belittle and demean another group member? Why did so-and-so always seem angry?

This small group would also be attended by a member of staff, which also revealed to me that there were other prison officers who, like me, wanted a career that looked beyond simply locking people up. Once a week, each small group fed back to a large Annexe meeting, where everything that had been discussed in each individual group would be outlined to the other groups and all of the staff on duty. As a consequence, there were, as Charles explained, 'no secrets in the Annexe'.

I'm not certain if that was accurate but the goal was that everyone should be open and honest about themselves, with each other and about why they had committed crime. In that way the therapeutic community could become a vehicle to see the values that these men had; their underlying morality; whether or not they had a conscience and, crucially, an ability to change.

At the first group that I attended, the eight prisoners introduced themselves by offering not only their name but also the offence for which they had been convicted. It was very soon apparent that I was with a group that dealt specifically with sex

offenders. For the first time, I knew my commitment to rehabilitation was going to be tested.

The label 'sex offender' is a catch-all term and can cover a wide
variety of behaviours. In that group I was among men who had
sexually abused babies and infants and others who had offended
against teenagers. The group accommodated other types of sex
offenders too. I knew what bestiality was, but these sessions
introduced me to the varied and seemingly endless predilections
of man: 'trichophilia'; 'hybristophilia'; 'pygophilia'; and 'saliro-
philia' are rather grand-sounding terms for some of our basest
desires. By all means look them up but I would suggest that you
don't do so whilst you are at work.

That first day it was 'frotteurism' that took front and centre – a
term I had some awareness of through my rudimentary French.

For those unacquainted with the word, frotteurism is the
name given to someone who gains sexual pleasure by rubbing
their groin area – most commonly with an erection – against a
non-consenting person as a way of gaining sexual satisfaction.
The 'frotteur' will seek out innocent situations where he is able to
quickly touch his victim's breasts, groin or bottom and then just
as quickly disappear before the unsuspecting victim realises that
something sexual has happened. Men are usually the frotteurs
and women are usually their victims.

During our group discussions, one of the men in the group,
Dean, explained that he had used the Northern Line of the
London Underground as his preferred offending location. Rush
hour was obviously the best time, as people would cram into
the carriages and have to travel cheek by jowl until they had
reached their destination. He would position himself beside a
woman that he was attracted to and, often choreographing his
movements to the swing and sway of the train, at first gently
bump into her, as if it was an accident.

Once he had normalised this occasional physical contact as

something which appeared to be accidental, his 'bumping' would become harder and more regular. Dean would have prepared by stuffing tissue into his underpants so that he could leave the station undetected, without any tell-tale stains on his trousers. He'd had been caught because too many different women, over too many days, reported someone similar touching them at roughly the same time of day to the police. An undercover policewoman had made the arrest and the Northern Line returned to normal.

There had been a few jokey, tabloid headlines that accompanied Dean's conviction – he was sentenced to two years – but these did not do justice to the suffering of his victims, or indeed the desire that Dean himself had to change his behaviour. He was as troubled as anyone by what he was engaged in; he was all too conscious that it was wrong. Dean wanted a 'proper relationship' and so he knew he had to stop, or be stopped, and now he wanted to use his time inside to change. His imprisonment had stopped him – at least while he was locked up – what about once he was released? How was he going to make lasting changes to his behaviour?

Talking with Dean revealed a number of issues which helped him and his group to make sense of his behaviour. In particular, over time and in fits and starts, he revealed the relationship that he had had with his eldest sister. It had been her who had first started to masturbate him when he was a child and, when he got older, she had continued to touch him inappropriately when she was certain no one else could see. It was a game to her, although that was not how Dean had seen things. For him, his sister's behaviour was about the power that she had had over him; a power to make him secretly sexual and available to her. Of course, the obvious questions that his group asked were: that if Dean did not like these behaviours why had he not told anyone previously, and why did he then impose himself on unsuspecting women?

The answer to the first question was more straightforward

than the second. Dean had told his mother about what his sister had been doing but she didn't believe him. This seemed to embolden his sister to engage more regularly in her sexual conditioning of Dean. Indeed, over the years, I came to understand how often female family members – mothers and aunts, as well as sisters and female cousins – introduced male family members into sexual activity.

The answer to the second question was much more complex, largely because Dean could only hesitantly acknowledge, in his answer to the first, that he had enjoyed what his sister had done. He liked the physical sensation of being 'wanked off', even if it was his sister rather than a girlfriend who was doing the wanking – and wasn't being masturbated by an older woman what all boys fantasised about? For Dean the boundary between what was appropriate and unacceptable had become inexorably blurred.

For Dean, frotting was a perverse way of replicating the circumstances in which he had first been introduced to sex but with him taking the initiative – as 'men should', he argued to the group – and showing the unsuspecting women who were his victims that he was sexually available. Frotting became behaviour that he could use to regain some feeling of power over his sexual desire for a woman.

Writing this makes Dean's story seem linear, logical and straightforward. It was not. What he said came with a great deal of shame and regret and only patient questioning extracted the details of his history. Much more work had to be done in getting Dean to understand how to go about establishing a healthy, consensual, sexual relationship with a woman.

One thing I discovered in this group was just how little sex offenders actually understood about relationships and sex. This was especially true of the paedophiles in the group. There was a world of difference between two of the paedophiles who attended, Max and Eddie, even if both were described as 'nonces' by the staff and other prisoners. As with 'screw' there are various explanations as to the origin of the term 'nonce', but most seemed to think that it was a diminutive of 'nonsense', as in a 'crime that had been a nonsense'. Literally, a crime that made no sense.

Max was in his seventies and had been sexually abusing babies and infants for as long as he could remember. It didn't take long to discover that Max had been abused by his father and his uncle when he was a child. In fact, virtually all of the paedophiles I have worked with were sexually abused as children. Over the years, Max's offending had escalated and now, while he was still interested in babies and infants, he was also only turned on by sadomasochism.

Consider that for a moment. Babies and infants, and S&M. It hardly bears thinking about. I started to realise that an individual offender's rehabilitation had to be carefully balanced against the harm that he had caused to his victim(s) and what he might be prepared to do again in the future. Nor was this calculation a predictive science with a carefully calibrated formula that could be applied equally in every case.

Max had been in prison many times before and so he knew to ask for 'Rule 43 Own Protection' at his introductory governor's interview, out of fear of what might happen to him if the other prisoners found out what he had been convicted of. The 'ordinary, decent criminals', as Eric ironically called them, were just like the letter writers to the newspapers who knew what should be done: *Castrate them! Cut off their balls!* The problem was that Max's most recent offences had been committed after he had been chemically castrated.

Eddie, on the other hand, was in his early twenties and about my age. He was a welder by trade and had got his girlfriend pregnant. When she had gone to the hospital to give birth, everything unravelled as the nurses discovered that she was only fourteen.

There are huge differences between Max and Eddie's offending, but both were labelled as paedophiles, as if that catch-all description in itself was enough to help to understand and then change their behaviour.

Actually, as I would discover, it was only Max who really wanted to change his behaviour, or at least consistently expressed a desire to do so. As far as Eddie was concerned, he was adamant that he had done nothing wrong. It was Eddie who fixated on discussing the age of consent historically in England and what it might still be in Canada, or South Korea. It was Eddie who took comfort in the oft-exploited sexual fantasy of schoolgirls in their school uniforms, which could at that time be seen on what were then called 'saucy' holiday postcards, or in the popular, mainstream comedy programme, *The Benny Hill Show.*

'What exactly did I do wrong?' Eddie would ask, believing his sexual tastes to be normalised throughout society.

Despite Eddie's reluctance to reflect fully on his behaviour, being part of this group made me realise that the Annexe was no soft option. Every day these men had to be prepared to expose themselves to some of the most painful moments of their lives and to describe the guilt and shame that they carried with them. Why do that if they could instead just sit in their cells all day reading the paper, or listening to the radio? Some of course might have done so because they thought that attendance of a therapy group might improve their chances for gaining parole, but the vast majority seemed to me to genuinely want some form of self-healing.

The big question is, of course, whether the Annexe worked: whether it changed their behaviour. Clearly it changed their behaviour while they were on the Annexe. These men did not pose control problems. They did not want to assault staff, or each other; they did not attempt to take their own lives or self-harm; they did not try to go on the roof, or riot. The evidence as to whether they changed in the longer term was more mixed but how realistic was it to expect that a year's intervention would be able to overcome a lifetime's worth of problems? There was no aftercare once inmates had left the group; they were simply expected to get on with their lives as best they could.

Even if I couldn't definitely answer the 'does it work' question in relation to whether or not these prisoners stopped offending once they were released, the groups gave me confidence that there were strategies that could be used to, at the very least, begin to tackle deeply ingrained and problematic behaviour that had led to crimes being committed. In fact, my exposure to group work in the Annexe gave me confidence in my thinking about a number of issues, which lasted throughout my career.

First, that difficulties in childhood can have a lasting impact and that our first relationships – for good or for ill – have an enduring influence on how and with whom we form subsequent relationships. Children really do need to have constant, loving and supportive relationships, if they are to acquire a sense of security and a positive understanding of the world. Second, that we have a bizarre compulsion to repeat early difficulties in our childhood when we are adults. We play them out over and over again, and often condition others to play the roles of other significant people in our lives, who may have caused those very difficulties in the first place. Finally, that a great deal of our unconscious is designed to protect us from guilt, shame and feelings of inadequacy and that the defence mechanisms that we might use can often be seriously unhelpful and damaging to ourselves and to other people.

It also made me realise that we cannot deny our existence as biological beings: we are all genes and hormones; flesh and blood that gets managed by our heart and by our brain. It is neither automatons nor programmed robots who commit violent crime but individual, organic beings who do reprehensible

things in response to feelings of humiliation, shame and perceived or actual threats to their sense of identity; threats to their
sense of self.

Freud would have been proud of me, although I knew someone
that wasn't. Eric wanted me to stick to being a yuppie, rather
than getting caught up in all that 'mumbo-jumbo, Annexe shite'
as he put it, before adding for good measure, 'They're all just
scabby hoodlums'. Over time I came to realise that while some
people – officers as well as the wider public – want offenders to
be rehabilitated, they only want them to change as far as to be
able to make amends and no more than that. They don't want
ex-offenders to be successful and certainly not more successful
than they perceive themselves to be.

It was at my next posting that I would begin to solidify my
theories about the importance of childhood experiences on adult
lives and it was also there that I would make a life-long friendship with a murderer.

CHAPTER TWO

Young Offenders Who Kill

'I'm a human being and I've got thoughts and
secrets and bloody life inside me that he doesn't
know is there, and he'll never know what's there
because he's stupid. I suppose you'll laugh at
this, me saying the governor's a stupid bastard
when I hardly know how to write and he can
read and write and add up like a professor. But
what I say is true right enough. He's stupid, and
I'm not, because I can see further into the likes
of him than he can see into the likes of me.'

'SMITH', Alan Sillitoe's *The Loneliness
of the Long Distance Runner*

I was only sent to Wormwood Scrubs to complete the introductory leg of my training as an assistant governor and
my first proper posting was to a youth custody centre called
Huntercombe, situated in Oxfordshire. This posting came with
a four-bedroomed house in a medieval village called Ewelme
and free membership to Huntercombe Golf Club. This was all
very privileged, especially after life at the Scrubs, and seemed
to hark back to a much earlier, pre-war era. Indeed, there were
still signs of the war almost everywhere I looked, including,

most movingly, the graffiti scribbled on the ceiling of the village pub by young Battle of Britain fighter pilots. Huntercombe had originally been used as an internment camp during the Second World War but had been converted into a borstal in 1946.

Borstal is now a rather despised but largely mythologised form of imprisonment that was aimed at rehabilitating young offenders. There are a number of reasons for its falling out of fashion.

Popularly, it fell prey to the radical kitchen-sink dramas of the 1960s, in many ways typified by Alan Sillitoe's brilliant short story, *The Loneliness of the Long Distance Runner*, which was later made into a film. Smith – the 'Borstal Boy' quoted at the start of the chapter – is scathing about the paternalistic, public-school educated governor who tries to get to know him. Smith stages his own personal rebellion by intentionally losing a race against the local boarding school.

However, it was the 1979 film *Scum* that really put the nail in the coffin for the borstal system, at least in the public's consciousness. Following the bloody, institutional life of an inmate making his way to the top of the borstal's pecking order, the film is full of innumerable fights, graphic violence, a male-on-male rape and the victim's subsequent suicide. We also see constant racism, staff indifference and brutality, denting irrevocably any thoughts that the viewer might have had that the institution of borstal could rehabilitate its charges.

Quite apart from this popular trashing of the borstal's reputation, it also fell out of penological favour, largely because a borstal sentence was indeterminate. You were sentenced to a period of 'borstal training' which, depending on the individual borstal 'lad', could last anywhere from a few months to two years. There was an inherent unfairness that two people sentenced for the same offence could end up serving very different sentence lengths, depending on how staff viewed their progress.

Borstals were abolished by the Criminal Justice Act of 1982

and replaced by Youth Custody Centres, now called Young Offender Institutions. This was not an easy transition, with an immediate tension between the majority of the prison officers who wanted youth custody to be much more carceral and punishing than borstal had ever been in reality. On the other side was almost everyone else, who were ill at ease with the vacuum of rehabilitation that had been left with borstal's passing. I arrived at Huntercombe just as borstal was disappearing and 'youth custody' had taken its place.

The governor in charge of Huntercombe at that time was a wonderful man called Ray Campbell and as I took up my post his advice to me was simple. Looking me straight in the eye, my personnel file lying open on his desk, he smiled and told me to, 'Just try and keep the best of borstal – that's all that you have to do.'

But what did that actually mean?

As if by chance, waiting for me in the drawer of my desk in my office at Huntercombe was a copy of *The Principles of the Borstal System*, which had first been published by the Home Office in 1932.

I flicked through its pages looking for inspiration. It starts by suggesting that, 'For the idle lad in his later teens the corner of a street is even more dangerous than the middle of a street for the aged and pre-occupied' and goes on to argue that 'borstal training is based on the double assumption that there is individual good in each and among nearly all an innate corporate spirit, which will respond to the appeal made to the British of every sort to play the game, to follow the flag, to stand by the old ship.' All of this was an appeal to team and country based on loyalty and comradeship.

Then, reflecting the influence of psychotherapy, it argues that the borstal lad should not be broken or kneaded into shape but encouraged to:

Stimulate some power within to regulate conduct aright, to insinuate a preference for the good and the clean, to make him want to use his life well, so that he himself and not others will save him from waste. It becomes necessary to study the individual lad, to discover his trend and his possibility, and to infect him with some idea of life which will germinate and produce a character, controlling desire, and shaping conduct in some more glorious end than mere satisfaction or acquisition.

The borstal regime in practice seemed to have been a mixture of muscular Christianity, work, education and sport, with the staff expected to get to know what made each lad tick. Small improvements in behaviour, sporting success or educational attainment were celebrated, which often was as simple as allowing the lad to wear a different colour of tie. The idea was that prisoners should to be treated as individuals and that prison should 'awaken the higher susceptibilities of prisoners, to develop their moral instincts, to train them in orderly and industrial habits' and finally, in what I think is a rather beautiful phrase, perhaps because it chimes exactly with what I felt, 'turn them out of prison better men and women, both physically and morally than when they came in.'

The interwar era might be viewed as the high point of the borstal system; it was certainly very successful. For every five young men that were sent to borstal, only one would reoffend, though by the time I reached Huntercombe the proportion of reoffenders had reached four in five. Despite work and training being offered to the lads, including City and Guilds courses in painting and decorating, catering, brick-laying, plumbing and motor mechanics, there was clearly a lot of work to be done in preparing them for life outside in the community.

One aspect of the system was very much in my favour – my

love of rugby meant that much of my life at this time was dominated by playing the sport. News of this had filtered through the prison grapevine from the Scrubs so that my natural allies at this posting were the two physical education instructors, David Price and Brian Humber. Brian had once been a county cricketer and David, although a footballer by background, had grown to love rugby. It was David and Brian who trained the lads and organised the Huntercombe teams. Despite their initial suspicion that one of the governors wanted to play sport, the barriers between us were soon broken down and I became an integral member of the Huntercombe side.

The lads had a training session each Tuesday and Thursday and a match on Saturdays, which would be played at home or away. The lads obviously preferred to play away, especially as we would buy them a pint after the game. Given that I was only a few years older than the lads, the teams that we played regularly mistook me for one of the prisoners, much to the delight of David and Brian and many of the lads too.

The lads would test out the limits of their relationship with me, especially during training sessions when they would tackle me in, how should I put it, robust and uncompromising ways. At first, there were one or two who would take a special delight in delivering to me a 'hospital pass', exposing my ribs to the oncoming tackler. Only my speed and an ability to sidestep saved me from serious injury on a few occasions. However, quite quickly, the team got used to a governor playing in the side and this in turn allowed me to form relationships with them and get to know them as individuals. They began to spread the word amongst the inmates who did not play sport that, 'The governor's all right'.

It was on the rugby pitch that I first met Jimmy.

Jimmy played full-back for the team. He was fast, fearlessly tackled everyone that came into his path and, when we had the opportunity to attack, it became obvious that he had a head for rugby – he knew when to pass, or when to hang onto the ball and make a dash for the touchline. It was clear that he had played before. I'd only spoken with him informally once or twice about rugby before I took a look at his prison file.

Frankly, I was surprised to find out that Jimmy had committed a murder. He had done so when he was fifteen. Even more surprising was his thin prison file – the files of all of the other lads bulged with the details of their previous convictions – and the remarks made by the judge when he had passed sentence, describing Jimmy as 'cold and calculating'. That was not how I would have characterised him. To me he seemed rather shy and self-contained.

Jimmy was now nineteen and could spend a further two years at Huntercombe, at which point he would either be released back into the community or moved into the adult penal system. I realised that I would be one of the people who would help to make that decision. Perhaps Jimmy knew that too and so, at first, he was wary of talking to me. However, as I had to write quarterly progress reports about all the inmates, it was inevitable that I would come to discuss the murder that he had committed and debate whether or not he might prove to be a risk to other people if he was released.

As with all my charges, I liked to have an idea of their background prior to their incarceration but the slim file provided me with little information that was useful about Jimmy's life before Huntercombe. There were some pre-sentencing probation reports and a solitary newspaper cutting describing a 'Public School Boy Sentenced for Murder'. The first half of that headline at least explained why Jimmy was so good at rugby, but the newspaper narrative only really provided the bare bones of his story.

What I managed to glean was that Jimmy was the middle

child from a professional, middle-class family. He had an older brother and a younger sister. He was the first in his family to ever get into trouble with the police and it was clear that the relationship with his parents had broken down long before the murder took place. Jimmy had been expelled from his boarding school, having been caught one too many times drunk in the dormitory and, after innumerable wasted chances, he was asked to leave. His parents had taken him back, but Jimmy couldn't settle. No doubt behind the scenes there were recriminations and accusations and a sense of shame about what had happened. After a few weeks Jimmy had moved in with an aunt but, when that relationship broke down too, he had drifted about and was seemingly sleeping rough at the time of the murder.

Being homeless and sleeping rough makes young people vulnerable, as I had discovered with Nilsen's victims. However, it wasn't Jimmy who was to end up dead.

Jimmy was still drinking heavily when he met his elderly male victim in a pub. According to his report of the evening in question, he'd been invited back to spend the night on the sofa, rather than sleeping rough. The pair had continued to drink after closing time and, once home, the elderly man had made a pass at Jimmy. He rebuffed the pass and had then calmly walked into the kitchen, where he found a knife. Jimmy returned to the sitting room where he plunged the knife into the elderly man's heart, killing him instantly. Jimmy had then fallen asleep on the sofa and only made his escape the following morning. It was this behaviour that had prompted the 'cold and calculating' comment from the trial judge.

The elderly man's sister had found him dead when she visited later in the day and reported the murder to the police. It didn't take them long to track down the young man that he had been seen drinking with the previous night and Jimmy quickly admitted that he had killed his victim. He had later tried to plead self-defence, but no one believed that the elderly man had actually posed any threat to Jimmy and he was convicted of murder.

I thought about Dennis Nilsen, as there seemed to be echoes of his case, especially the heavy drinking and the homelessness of his male victims. Of course there were differences too – most obviously who had died.

Four years on from the murder, what I could much more easily establish was what Jimmy had been doing with himself in prison. He had resumed his academic studies, had gained three A-levels and was hoping to start an Open University degree. When he was released he wanted to go on to a Further Education College, or university. He'd gotten into one or two fights with other lads – mostly through their mistaken belief that Jimmy would be an easy target; played a great deal of sport; had been sober for four years, and staff, especially the education staff, thought of him as a calming influence within the prison.

His parents had not visited him inside.

It didn't seem that Jimmy had been offered any counselling and nor did it appear that any work had been done with him about the circumstances of the murder itself. There was no psychology department at Huntercombe that I could have referred him to. The little that we did know came from his trial and was therefore partial. The need to prove the accused's guilt controlled the narrative of what had happened on the night of the murder. We had to rely on Jimmy's version of events that the elderly man had made a pass at him. Was that necessarily true? Perhaps Jimmy invented the sexual advance as a means of creating a defence for himself?

There were many other possible scenarios. Perhaps Jimmy had simply seen the opportunity to rob the elderly man, or had made a pass at him, in the hope of being paid for sex work, but had killed his victim when he himself had been rebuffed? Or perhaps this whole dreadful incident was just about a young man's confusion with his own sexuality?

These were important questions for me to consider, even with two years of his time at Huntercombe still left to run, as they indicated the risk that Jimmy might pose in the future. I also tracked down a rudimentary risk assessment that had been completed on him, so as to clear the way for him to play rugby outside the youth custody centre. I quickly formed the impression that his last four years in custody had served to normalise what he had done, and everyone had quietly accepted without challenge that he had killed an elderly gay man, who had made an inappropriate sexual advance. To David and Brian and most of the rest of the staff, Jimmy was a 'good lad who keeps his head down', end of story.

Violent behaviour often does emerge in adolescence when there is rapid emotional change and poorer self-control, which is usually coupled with physical growth. This can sometimes lead to there being confusion about self-image and my prior exposure to the work of the Annexe at the Scrubs made me suspicious of unquestioningly accepting Jimmy's version of events. I believed that there was work to be done here, whether or not the inmate was a stand-out rugby player. He might indeed be a 'good lad' but I needed to be certain that he wouldn't kill again.

My first step was to explain to Jimmy that as I had to write parole reports about him, I wanted to see him for an hour in my office each Wednesday afternoon. I'd chosen the time with care, as on Wednesday afternoons there were no education classes and ostensibly Jimmy was on what was known as 'free association'. In reality this meant that he would be lounging about on his bed listening to the radio.

My aim was to try and discover two things. First, why had Jimmy started to drink? Of course most young men start to experiment with alcohol (and indeed with other substances) at this time in their lives but Jimmy's use of alcohol was persistent and destructive. This wasn't the first foray with alcohol that comes with adolescence, or even those many forays which come with recreational use, but seemed to me to be at best excessive and at worst abusive. He was drunk when he committed the murder. That was the second area that I wanted to question Jimmy about. I needed to satisfy in my own mind the question of why Jimmy had murdered his elderly victim. Was this a one-off, dreadful act of aberrant behaviour by a young, drunk, immature man, or something that might be repeated when he was released as an adult? Was Jimmy really, in the words of the trial judge, a cold and callous killer? If that was the case, I had to find out what would stop him killing again.

Jimmy was ambivalent about these Wednesday meetings. On the one hand I think that he liked the attention but, on the other, he found my questioning of him intrusive and painful.

Very few of the lads that I worked with at Huntercombe were like Jimmy. In fact, 'very few' should perhaps be better read as 'none'. Jimmy came from a middle-class background and this fact alone meant that he stood out. Youth custody swept up working-class boys who were largely illiterate, school excluded and unemployed, as it sadly still does today. Jimmy may have been expelled from his boarding school, but he had used his time in custody to earn himself three A-levels. That achievement in itself was unusual, as most of the lads that I dealt with found it difficult to read or write.

Jimmy was also white. One in three of the lads at Huntercombe in the 1980s were black and the growing awareness that prison sentences were being imposed disproportionately based on race was only just becoming a pressing discussion point within public policy. Even today black people are still three times more likely to be arrested than white people, even though ethnic minority groups are more often the victims of crime.

At Huntercombe it was still common for the staff to argue that 'black people commit more crime', which wasn't true, or that 'black people commit more violent crime', which wasn't true either. In fact, Jimmy was the only lad at Huntercombe who had been sentenced for murder, although that had been all but forgotten by the staff. In one sense, given his offence, it was odd that Jimmy had been sent to us at all, although through my discussions with the governor, I was advised that he had been sent to us because we were regarded as the best place to help him to develop his talents.

The staff also seemed to be perpetually worried that we should disperse the black prisoners that we had throughout the youth custody centre, so that they couldn't 'congregate'. There was a fear that if too many of the black lads were allocated to a particular unit they would come to dominate that wing. This argument was never applied to the majority of the lads who were white.

As well as my being a governor, I also took over the role of Race Relations Liaison Officer for Huntercombe and was constantly having to challenge these types of arguments. It was not an easy role to perform, especially as it meant that I was also constantly challenging the low-level racist humour that was inherent in prison culture. 'It's just a joke' was the usual refrain but my failure to tolerate it meant that the staff just stopped using these types of jokes in my company; I knew that they hadn't completely disappeared.

I was very aware that I didn't want to be seen to be giving preferential treatment to Jimmy – a white, middle-class, boarding-school boy who had committed murder. So, I went out of my way to explain to staff that as Jimmy had been sentenced under Section 53 of the 1933 Children and Young Persons Act, which meant that if he had been an adult he would have received a life sentence, I was required to answer particular questions about him regarding granting him parole that demanded greater than normal scrutiny. Even so, I also made space on Wednesday afternoons for any of the other lads who wanted to see me during their free association time. Many of them did but mostly their worries were about what they were going to do after their release, as opposed to Jimmy who, hypothetically at least, might not get released at all.

Throughout some twelve months of our sessions together, Jimmy stuck resolutely to the story that he had told in court. He had been drinking heavily and the elderly man had made a pass at him, at which point Jimmy admitted that he had been confused and ashamed by the sexual advance. I didn't know it at this time, but I would find those two factors of shame and alcohol were generally key in the lives of the murderers I worked with. In my experience shame and the notion of 'losing face' are often a prelude to the violence of young men. Killing the elderly man had allowed Jimmy to regain some control over the situation.

We got to this point quite quickly and to the fact that he wasn't gay.

Over the next few months I asked Jimmy about the time that it took between the pass being made and going into the kitchen to find a knife. What was he thinking about when he picked up the knife? Did he intend to kill the elderly man? Jimmy freely admitted that he had intended to kill him and that the idea of 'self-defence' was only something that had been put to him by the duty solicitor after he had been arrested.

This part of the story which emerged in our sessions was confirmation of the narrative that I had already read, although it was clearly offered to me in much greater depth. This gave me some confidence. I usually trust stories that don't get embellished, or which change vital facts. I distrust details which are suddenly remembered, like rabbits being pulled from a hat. However, I still wasn't satisfied. Something – and I didn't know what that might be – wasn't adding up. As our sessions progressed, I started to form an impression that Jimmy was trying to present himself almost as being virtuous, rather than as a killer. Something was being repressed in his version of events. Why had he not called the police when he woke in the morning? Why had he not left the town where the murder occurred? It was almost as if he had wanted to be caught; that he wanted to be punished.

I kept pushing in my questioning of Jimmy but then realised that I had become so focussed on the murder that I had failed to ask him about his drinking.

'Jimmy, why were you drinking so much?'

'Don't we all? You have a pint after the rugby too!'

That was true and, reflecting the culture of both rugby clubs and Youth Custody Centres at the time, no one thought anything of sharing a pint with the lads after the game. Some might find this scandalous but, if I am honest, I still think that it helped to narrow the distance between 'them' and 'us' and served to remind us all of a shared and common humanity.

'But why did you start?'

Jimmy said something anodyne, flippant and evasive. A sixth sense suggested that I should continue to probe but, rather than asking something direct, I suggested to him, 'Would you mind if I wrote to your parents?'

The impact that this question had was immediate and elec- trifying. Jimmy almost pleaded with me not to do so, saying they did not want any contact with him. I wondered if this extreme reaction was caused by the fact that it replicated what his school had done.

'I'm not writing to them to complain, Jimmy. You've done really well. I just want to ask them some questions to help me with my parole report.'

I can't say that Jimmy was pleased, and nor did he give me permission. However, I felt that there were legitimate questions to ask and, anyway, I didn't need his permission to write a letter to his parents.

As it transpired, their reply helped me to unlock Jimmy's secrets.

The letter I received back from Jimmy's father was typed and effusive. The unrestrained gratitude that it expressed indicated that, far from wanting to break ties with Jimmy, the story was much more complicated. It was soon clear that it had been Jimmy who had broken ties with his family and in reality they were desperate to have him back within the fold. What came across strongly was that Jimmy had always been a much loved and valued member of the household. I got the impression from the letter that the pain that was being expressed to me in writing was not just about the murder but also about the fact that Jimmy now no longer wanted any contact with his family.

The letter also responded to my question about Jimmy's abusive drinking. It had all started simply enough and when he had first been caught, it was regarded as something that could be dealt with by way of a warning as to his future behaviour. Jimmy's father indicated that he now regretted a line of conversation with Jimmy about 'not amounting to much' and urging him to 'be more like your brother', who had been the former head boy of the school Jimmy had been expelled from and was now a very successful banker.

The warnings about drinking weren't heeded and Jimmy's father gradually became even more insistent that Jimmy was 'wasting his life', especially compared to how much his brother had achieved and how much 'the whole family was disappointed in him'. About the murder, the letter offered nothing new but ended with a hope that I might be able to persuade Jimmy to allow his family to visit.

I'm not now certain what I was expecting but the letter was far more positive than I had imagined it might be. I began to wonder if the root of the problem might be Jimmy's worry that he could never match the success of his brother and so had spec-tacularly sabotaged his chances of success. What better way of not competing than getting yourself locked up? Was this why he had hung around in the town after the murder?

I also knew that I now had another problem. How could I convince Jimmy to invite his parents to visit?

The letter had arrived on a Friday and so our next scheduled meeting was the following Wednesday. However, we had a rugby match in Wallingford that Saturday and I thought that the opportunity to talk a little might present itself after the game, in a more relaxed and informal environment.

We were due to play Wallingford's third team but, little by little, the local teams had got to know that we were quite good and so they slipped second team and sometimes first team players into their sides. It was a hard-fought match and Jimmy played exceptionally well. Even so, we lost; everyone was a bit down. The lads showered, changed into their white shirts and grey flannels, and put on their prison ties, then made their way into the bar area. David and Brian had promised them one pint before we travelled back.

Jimmy was sitting with some friends at a table discussing the match and I took the chance to join them.

After a few minutes I found an opportunity to quietly tell him of his father's letter and his family's desire to come and visit. Jimmy looked off into the near distance. I was about to speak again when we were interrupted by the captain of the Wallingford side who wanted to say a few words and to make a presentation. He made a gracious speech about how well we had played and then said that, as far as their team was concerned, the Man of the Match was the Huntercombe full back. There was some polite applause and the captain then shook Jimmy's hand and presented him with a club tie. Jimmy looked pleased, embarrassed and humbled. He was now also surrounded by

people and I knew that I'd have to wait until Wednesday to speak
to him again.

This type of kindness was repeated in every club we played
against and says much for the sport of rugby. People suspended
their judgement of the lads and accepted them for who they now
were, even if one or two would slide up to you at the bar, look
furtively around until they were sure that no one was listening
and ask, 'So, what are they in for?'

At our next Wednesday meeting Jimmy had obviously been
thinking quite a bit and had come along prepared for a fight, adamant that he didn't want his family to visit. I quickly realised that
I would be banging my head against a brick wall if I continued
to press and so returned to asking questions about the murder.

Jimmy sighed and shifted uneasily in his chair and then
started to stare out of my office window. He seemed to me as if
he was about to go back onto autopilot – answering my questions
in a perfunctory if not in an aggressive way.

'You've never really told me what you were thinking when you
left the sitting room, went into the kitchen and picked up the
knife,' I continued, undeterred by his lack of interest.

Jimmy stopped staring out of my window and looked at me
for the first time in our session.

'That this will sort it forever.'

'Sort what? What's "it"?'

There was a silence. I decided to use some new information
from his father's letter to try and fill in the gaps. Was that fair?
Was I abusing my position? I calculated that a man had lost
his life and if I was to be convinced that Jimmy was ever going
to be safe to release back into the community, I needed to be
satisfied that I really did understand the context in which he
came to kill.

'Is this about your brother?' I asked.

Silence.

'Were you afraid that you couldn't live up to the standard that he had set and so deliberately made sure that you couldn't compete?'

Then Jimmy did something totally unexpected. He laughed, although not in an arrogant way. He was laughing because my suggestion was ridiculous to him.

'I love my brother, I love my family. Competition wasn't the issue.'

A dam seemed to have burst, and Jimmy added for good measure, 'I would have won. Hands down. Easily.'

I tried to take all of this in and reassemble the information that he had provided to accommodate it into some sort of logic. If I understood him correctly, what was being repressed was not that Jimmy couldn't compete against his brother but that he *could* and within that competition he would be the one who was successful. His was not a fear of failure but of success. What then for the family that he loved? How would they cope with the adjustment to their thinking that his father seemed to have been expressing in his angry recriminations? Above all, how would his brother manage? In his own immature way Jimmy had sought to resolve all those seething, unconscious questions by 'sorting it forever'. Forever. The result was drinking to excess to render any competition void; being expelled from school; murder and cutting all ties to his family. In Jimmy's adolescent, unconscious mind he was making sacrifices to everything and everyone that he held dear.

The tragedy was that an elderly man needlessly died in the process.

Does all of this ring true? From that day in my office at Huntercombe to even now as I type these words, I still try and make sense of what Jimmy said, going over in my mind how credible his explanation might be. I try and walk in his shoes and see his story in the context of what he had experienced and how he had come to view himself and the most important people in his life. Even so, I know that I could never have taken the life of the elderly man who had shown him kindness, although that does not diminish what Jimmy might have thought and therefore how he had behaved.

I remain more certain about one thing – as a 'murderer', Jimmy was as far removed from Nilsen as night is from day.

Above all, what Jimmy's story taught me was that what we tell young people about who we think they are and what they might be capable of – how we label them for good, or more likely for ill – plays a central role in who they will become. Those labels become internalised until they create the boundaries of their personalities and the springboards for their behaviour. That behaviour, when mixed with alcohol and immaturity, can have tragic consequences. However, those tragic consequences – those dreadful, aberrant, violent acts – are not the sum total of their personality, or what they are capable of as they mature.

You don't believe me?

Imagine being perpetually judged for the worst thing that you did in your own childhood, of never being allowed to forget and to move on to be the person that you have become. Would that act define you as a person? *Should* that act define you as a person?

And it's here that I want to introduce Erwin James, a very different boy to Jimmy, even if he is also a murderer and served some time in a borstal. He actually describes borstal as a 'gladiator school' – a form of imprisonment that allowed only the strong to survive. I would meet Erwin much later in his prison career and, since his release, I continue to see him on a regular basis. However, it is his childhood that I am interested in here and how this created the context in which he came to take the lives of two men. For too many children like Erwin, that space in human existence which we call 'childhood' becomes a time that has simply to be endured and survived and which can, all too easily, create the context for some appalling behaviour.

What sort of background did Erwin have?

Erwin is always reluctant to say that he had a 'poor childhood' but he acknowledges that his parents were young and economically struggling teenagers, who had hitchhiked from Scotland to Somerset in the hope of getting a better life. This shows some determination, although it would appear that they couldn't overcome the difficult starts that they had had to their own lives. Erwin describes his parents as coming from backgrounds characterised by violence and alcohol and he describes their lives as 'dysfunctional'.

Alcohol played a major role in Erwin's father's life and it was a drink-driving incident that led to his mother's death, when Erwin was just seven years old. From that moment on, Erwin's life slowly spiralled out of control, as his father attempted to come to terms with his own demons. By the age of ten Erwin describes how he was 'running wild, sleeping rough and I didn't really know where I was supposed to belong in the world.' He then suggested that, 'As my frustration with a life without purpose increased, my recklessness and lack of concern for others intensified.'

Above all, Erwin could never really resolve if he loved or in fact detested his father – a long-distance lorry driver, who seemed to come into Erwin's life, cause chaos and then disappear again.

Like his father, Erwin started to drink heavily, which in turn led to petty crime, stealing and a number of incidents of violence. He rarely attended school and he gained no educational qualifications. Inevitably he came to the attention of the police. He did the 'short, sharp, shock' of a Detention Centre sentence and then, when that failed to change his behaviour, a borstal sentence two years later.

That didn't have much of an impact either and he would go on to commit two murders when he was twenty-five, at which point in his life he was sleeping rough, alcoholic and offending in the

company of a co-defendant called William Ross. Immediately
after the murders, Erwin fled to the French Foreign Legion and
it was two years later in 1984 that he handed himself in, after his
father had visited him in Corsica where he was serving; this, in
turn, had alerted the authorities as to his whereabouts. Like his
father, he had also created chaos and then disappeared.

Erwin killed Greville Hallam, a former actor and theatrical
agent, who was robbed and strangled in his flat in London in
September 1982, and then Angus Cochrane, who was mugged
when he was visiting London and who died of his injuries a few
months later. He committed these murders in the company of
his co-defendant and both seem to have done so when they were
drunk and desperate for money to buy more alcohol. Add to
this immediate context the reality that, for Erwin at least, these
murders emerge from a background that was already violent,
dysfunctional and peppered with petty crimes, which were often
committed for short-term gain and with little thought about the
consequences.

Erwin's story, much more than Jimmy's, better typifies the
types of lads who were sent to borstal and youth custody centres.
His lack of educational qualifications and the rootlessness and
recklessness that characterised his life were especially typical of
the majority of the lads that I would work with at Huntercombe.

Erwin's stability would only later come from his education,
which he started while in prison, and then from learning how to
write for newspapers. That he has gone on to have a career as a
journalist and author is unusual. The majority of the young men
that I worked with gained stability when they found work – often
a labouring or semi-skilled job which they had been trained to do
while in prison – and through the relationships that they were
able to establish once they were released. As they matured, they
would get married, have children and settle down, leaving their
offending history far behind.

That is certainly the lesson that I take from Erwin's childhood. His childhood was rootless, and he was permanently searching for the place where he really belonged. This wasn't just a physical place but a psychological one too and, more than likely, the place where he would be able to reconcile the ambivalent feelings that he has shared about his father.

Erwin's experience is therefore very different to Jimmy's. Jimmy knew where he belonged but in his own juvenile way felt that he had to deny himself all the comforts that came with that belonging. I always wonder if – for both of them – a friendly word from a teacher, or an interest in them from another significant adult, might have fundamentally changed the direction of each of their lives.

My Wednesday meetings with Jimmy continued until I was posted to Finnamore Wood, a small open youth custody centre that was a satellite of the much larger Huntercombe. By that point, they had lost much of their intensity. Slowly I realised that Jimmy was becoming more of a friend and I wondered to what extent I was becoming for him another version of his elder brother. After all, I wasn't too much older than Jimmy and we had similar backgrounds. Freudians would have called this process 'transference' and I worried that it served to dissolve the professional distance that should have existed between us. Obviously I felt that I now knew him much better and, above all, a few weeks after I left, with no further prompting from me, Jimmy invited his family to come and visit.

I was confident that Jimmy could make something of his life and would be successful.

Finnamore Wood was to be my first experience of being the governor, as opposed to the assistant or deputy governor, of the prison in which I worked. I was still in my twenties and barely out of university but, even so, I was thrilled to be given the chance to be in charge. My personal life was also changing, and it was whilst I was still governing Finnamore Wood that I would meet Anne and, shortly afterwards, we would marry and start a family.

Finnamore Wood (there's that bucolic name again) had started life as an evacuation camp during the war and could only hold just over one hundred lads, all of whom were accommodated in four wooden huts. It had a staff of some twenty people. Frankly, it was more like an outward-bound centre than a prison.

The lads who got sent there had very light convictions, mostly driving offences, being caught in possession of drugs, or failure to pay fines. I sometimes marvelled at the fact that they had been sent to prison at all, especially as they were usually sentenced to only three or four weeks. What were we supposed to do with them in that time? Well, we went for walks, played sport, ran half and full marathons for charity and did voluntary work in Marlow. On Sundays we would walk the couple of miles to the local church in Frieth, as the youth custody centre had no chapel. The parishioners rather liked seeing the lads and would make a fuss of them at the end of the service, offering biscuits and cups of tea.

Years later I would channel these experiences into a constructed factual reality TV series called *Bring Back Borstal*. It was not a critical success. I rather got the impression that the critics just couldn't imagine that borstals could ever operate in the way that we portrayed, with the lads participating in community fetes, attending church and doing local voluntary work. If only they had experienced Finnamore Wood and Huntercombe. These were places that really did have the power to rehabilitate the young men that were sent there.

I know that because, above all, I am still in touch with Jimmy.

Before leaving Huntercombe I wrote Jimmy's parole reports suggesting that when he reached twenty-one he should be transferred to an adult open prison, where he might be allowed to enrol at the local university. He actually didn't do that but instead took a design and engineering City and Guilds course and set up his own business once he was released. That business now employs over fifteen people and I still see Jimmy on a regular basis.

Three years ago when planning *Bring Back Borstal*, we arranged to go to the local pub for some lunch and catch up with everything that had been happening in our lives. Jimmy arrived at my house in his new Porsche, looking every inch the successful businessman. We drove to the local pub and ordered some food. After chatting about our families I thought it was about time to ask my favour.

I explained to Jimmy the premise of the series and wondered if he might like to appear. Of all the people I knew, his story was the one which best suggested how young people who commit crime – even murder – can go on to lead perfectly responsible and respectable lives after they have served their sentence. He could be an inspiration to so many other young people.

As soon as the question was out of my mouth, I knew he was going to say no.

Jimmy reminded me that, while his wife knew all about his background, his two boys knew nothing. They had just started at the local boarding school and he could well imagine what life would be like for them if their peers discovered that their father had been convicted of murder. So, no, Jimmy didn't want to appear.

Fair enough, I thought, and I remembered another passage from that first book which had outlined the aims of borstal, *The Principles of the Borstal System*. While rejoicing in all the achievements that borstal could boast of, if the system truly worked it meant that the world would hear nothing of its successes: 'Such lads pass into the merciful obscurity of the average honest citizen, and are widely loth to speak overmuch of the fire through which they have passed.'

CHAPTER THREE

The Prison as a Therapeutic Community

'Those who know what it is to be violent have
an understanding of the sort of motivations
and attitudes which are relevant to the violence
of other people. They can understand how
the other violent person may have felt and can
confirm this by asking questions which would
not occur to a non-violent investigator. When
these results are discussed in a wider group, it
increases the understanding of all concerned,
including that of the investigators themselves.'

T. C. N GIBBENS, *Violent Men: An
Inquiry into the Psychology of Violence*

The orderly officer was just finishing his report, advising me
about what was happening in the prison and what I had to
remember to do that day. As he finished, he turned to go but then
almost immediately turned back again.

'Oh, one last thing,' he said, smiling, 'you have a governor's
application.'

'An application?' I queried, as this was very unusual for HMP
Grendon. Under the prison rules, inmates had the right to
make an application to see a governor of the prison every single

day with a request or, more typically, with a complaint, but at Grendon the usual procedure was for the prisoner to discuss this request or complaint with his therapy group.

The orderly officer nodded and added, 'Cook on G wing. I'll see you there at 11.30,' and with that he was gone.

This made a little more sense as G wing was the sex offenders unit and the only wing in the prison that, at that time, did not operate as a psychodynamic therapeutic community. It was instead trialling treatment groups for sex offenders and some of the lessons from these groups would be harnessed to form the basis of the national Sex Offender Treatment Programme (SOTP) which would eventually be introduced throughout the prison system.

Though I knew Cook all too well by reputation, I hadn't yet met him – that seemed set to change at 11.30. Meanwhile, I took the opportunity to start my morning rounds.

HMP Grendon had opened in September 1962 and remains the only prison in England and Wales that functions wholly as a psychodynamic therapeutic community. It acts as a national resource to the prison service, as a means of working with some of the more challenging prisoners in the prison system. That's a polite way of saying that they have usually committed crimes of violence, including murder, and that they are often the types of prisoners who whilst in custody will fight other prisoners and staff, take hostages, riot, smuggle drugs or, in other ways, disrupt the smooth working of the prison in which they are located. I had been at Grendon for a couple of months, after my time at Finnamore Wood had ended when the opportunity to move on had presented itself in 1988. Given my interests and my experience at Wormwood Scrubs and the Annexe, I had asked to be posted to Grendon, even though I would not be the governor in charge. Grendon was run by a much more senior prison governor – at that time, a man called Michael Selby. I had only been working in the prison service for five years but Grendon felt like the natural home for me, given my interest in how to rehabilitate offenders.

Through its therapeutic approach, Grendon has consistently been able to reduce the future rate of reconviction by prisoners, who spend at least eighteen months there, by as much as a quarter. This success is achieved through the fact that – as with the Annexe at Wormwood Scrubs – Grendon devotes all of its resources to having prisoners talk about their offending, so as to better understand what prompted it, alongside teaching them new ways of living within the prison. Everything is geared towards working in small groups, and having violent prisoners ask questions of one another produces some astonishing results. The reasons for this are complicated but boil down to the fact that, as one of the prisoners put it to me, 'You can't con a con, especially a con who has committed crimes just like yours.'

The goal in all of this is to get the prisoner to 'own his offence'. In other words, to take responsibility for it and the damage that this offending has created. Thereafter, through learning how to live and work in the prison without resorting to violence and with respect for the needs and wishes of others, including those of the staff, this new way of behaving begins the process of rehabilitating some of the most dangerous men that I have ever encountered.

As part of my rounds, I wanted to pop into the prison's gymnasium and have a word with Paul, the gym red band, to see if he had time for a game of badminton during the lunch break. There was a difference at Grendon in how the red band system worked compared to other prisons: each wing voted as to why someone should be given a red band, based on their offending history and how they had been progressing in therapy, as opposed to the staff choosing. The most popular job in the prison was to work in the gym and therefore to get the vote to be the gym red band really suggested something about how well that person had been doing in therapy.

Almost a decade earlier, Paul Brumfitt had not been someone that I would have wanted to meet up with in the gym, or anywhere else for that matter. He had a criminal record that went as far back as 1968, when he was just twelve years old, but it was an eight-day killing spree in 1979 that had led to him receiving a life sentence.

Following an argument with his sixteen-year-old girlfriend, Brumfitt broke into a house in Heswall in Merseyside, holding the terrified, pregnant woman who lived there at knife-point. He attempted to strangle her, tied her up, raped her and then battered her unconscious with a table lamp. He then left the house, stole a car and headed to Tilbury, where he walked into a tailor's shop to buy clothes. When the tailor asked for money, Brumfitt hit him over the head with a claw hammer, killing him instantly. He stole £450 from the till and then, using a false passport, fled to Denmark on a ferry which landed in Esbjerg. In Esbjerg he befriended a bus driver called Teddy Laustrup and the two went for a drink in a local bar. After several drinks, they returned to Teddy's house with two women that they had picked up in the bar. When the women left, Brumfitt drunkenly admitted to Teddy that he was a one-man crime wave, prior to hitting him over the head with a table lamp and then strangling him with a telephone wire. Brumfitt then caught the ferry back to England and was arrested when he landed in Southampton.

At his trial, the judge had told Brumfitt that, 'You are suffering from a psychopathic disorder, a permanent disability of the mind which results in abnormally aggressive and seriously irresponsible behaviour.'

This wasn't unusual for Grendon. Many of the inmates had elevated scores on Hare's Psychopathy Checklist (Revised) (PCL-R). As a result, the prisoners were usually dangerous and often disturbed and damaged; we would now call them 'psychopaths'. Almost every prisoner Grendon accepted at this time had been convicted of serious offences against another person. Almost all had received at least one previous conviction. The offending behaviour of these prisoners was chronic and severe, and a substantial number had histories of institutional misconduct at other prisons. In other words, they generally had made a nuisance of themselves.

In short, I didn't agree to play badminton with every prisoner at Grendon!

I pushed open the door to the gym and was immediately greeted by the senior officer in charge.

'Is Paul about?' I asked.

The officer shouted 'Paul! The governor wants a word.'

The gym at Grendon was quite small, partly because it also contained a stage where each Christmas the staff and prisoners would perform a pantomime. Beneath the stage was a cellar, where the gym equipment was stored.

A tall, thin but muscular man with sandy hair emerged from deep beneath the stage.

'Were you shouting to me?'

'It was for me, Paul,' I said. 'Do you want to play badminton at lunch?'

'Yeah. OK. I'll let them know on the wing.'

Lunch plans decided, I headed down to finish the morning round and hear Cook's application.

Everyone who studied at Cambridge in the late 1970s and early 1980s knew all about Peter Cook, who was usually called 'The Cambridge Rapist'. His activities still haunted the place when I matriculated, and I subsequently met enough people who had lived in the city at the time to understand the impact that he'd had there. Cook was also sometimes called 'The Hooded Rapist', because of the leather hood that he wore when carrying out his attacks. In fact, he liked to dress completely in black leather when offending. This detail caught the imagination of some members of the public and just a few years after his arrest, Malcolm McLaren and Vivienne Westwood would reproduce images of the hood that Cook wore on T-shirts.

This use of Cook's criminal activities by McLaren and Westwood was a stark reminder for me that offending, even serious offending, could be used by various industries in very different ways. For many it simply became a form of entertainment – a way of being thrilled and appalled at the same time; for others it was a means to sell newspapers; to justify demands for more resources; or, it could become an engine to advocate for longer sentences, greater powers and even re-election.

Cook's targets were female students and between October 1974 and April 1975 he committed six rapes, wounded two other women and committed an act of gross indecency on another. At the time of his attacks he was forty-six and working as a delivery driver. He was caught on 8 June 1975, after he had stabbed his ninth victim, a young woman, at the Owlstone Croft nurses' hostel in the city and was seen cycling away from the scene disguised as a woman and wearing a long, blonde wig. He was later found to be in possession of more women's clothing and make-up.

I sat in an office on G wing and looked through Cook's file. He was by then well into his fifties and didn't seem to present any behavioural problems to the staff. He spent most of his time sewing dresses for the dolls that he collected and which he bought with his prison wages. He had also recently decided that he now wanted to be called 'Janet'. A memory of the housekeeper from the TV series *Dr Finlay's Casebook* floated into my mind.

The orderly officer joined me to prepare for the meeting, before going to find Cook just before 11.30 a.m.

A few minutes later there was a knock on my door and a

small man with straggling grey hair and long fingernails entered the office, with the orderly officer standing – almost towering – behind him. It was difficult to imagine that this bizarre, elderly-looking man had been the source of all the fear in the city I knew so well.

'You wanted to see a governor, Mr Cook. What can I do for you?'

'I've been told I need your permission,' he said, in a high-pitched, whiny voice. The orderly officer was smiling behind him; clearly he was aware of what was coming next. I was still in the dark but the look on the orderly officer's face put me on my guard.

'Permission for what?' I asked.

'I want to become a woman and I need you to agree to me having HRT. That's what the psychiatrist has told me.'

I wish I could now say that his question had then prompted a serious discussion about physically transitioning from male to female and that I questioned him about whether he really did not identify with the gender assigned to him at birth. Perhaps I could have explained how serious this is and therefore how it needs to be thought through carefully, as transitioning takes time, has psychological consequences and costs a great deal of money.

I didn't do any of that.

I sat dumbfounded for a few moments, trying to make sense of the Cambridge Rapist now wanting to become a woman. Did this explain the long, blonde wig that he was wearing when trying to escape and all the other female clothes that were found in his possession? But how then should we also understand the black leather that he wore, with all the inherited, cultural and hyper-masculine iconography that leather conveys? Perhaps he just liked dressing up and playing with his identity? Perhaps he was now over-identifying with his victims, to the extent that he wanted to have his offending penis removed and, in that way, he imagined, he could become a woman and atone for his crimes? Cook had never discussed any of this with me and, as far as I am aware, nor had he expressed remorse for his crimes with any other member of staff.

Nor could I tell him to discuss all of this with his group, as G wing didn't operate in that way. The procedure on G wing was very similar to how things operated in every other prison, in that prisoners could ask to see the governor and then expect the governor to provide some form of definitive answer to any query that they might have. As I was thinking through how to reply, Cook asked me another question.

'Oh, and I also want your permission to breastfeed my dolls.'

The surreal had just become even more dreamlike.

'No,' I replied. 'I'm not giving you permission to do that.'

I actually don't know how I could have prevented him from doing this, but it did seem to me that I wanted to ground our conversations in some form of reality, or at least how I perceived reality. Later, when I had had time to reflect on what had happened, I was struck by the vehemence in my voice when I had answered this second question and wondered if my emotional and instinctive reaction was simply that I had just had enough of Cook, even if it was only our first meeting. In these albeit brief exchanges he had seemed to be, at least, self-indulgent and lacking in any self-reflection. I wondered if he had just been seeking attention.

I spent a few more minutes discussing with Cook how he would have to have written confirmation from two psychiatrists agreeing that he should be allowed to transition from male to female and, until that occurred, he could not be given permission to start HRT. I also advised him to think very carefully about making this decision and that there was much more to being a woman than growing his hair and fingernails, calling himself Janet and speaking in a higher-pitched voice.

As tempting as it was, I stopped myself from giving him a lecture about all the harm that he had done to the women that he had offended against and the fear that he had instilled in many, many more. That might have been a perfectly human reaction but it would also have been self-indulgent on my part. In the years to come I wouldn't always exercise such self-restraint.

As far as I am aware, Cook had not gone through any gender reassignment at the time of his death in 2004.

It was also whilst I was at Grendon that I started to write for the *Prison Service Journal*, *PSJ* for short. I suggested to John Staples, the editor and also the governor of HMP Full Sutton, that given the public's fascination with and continued media interest in 'evil', it might be time to commission a special edition of the *PSJ* on the subject. Though he initially agreed, the interview that I conducted was deemed too controversial by the prison service and so all that Issue 89, the *PSJ's* special edition on evil, has from me is an almost blank page at the very start, in which I explain that my interview had been banned.

However, there *was* an interview and it was one that didn't take more than a telephone call to set up.

A friend worked as a governor at HMP Whitemoor and, in response to my request, he told me that Dennis Nilsen – it was Nilsen that I wanted to interview – was absolutely delighted that I wanted to speak to him; especially, as he had put it, as 'he doesn't get out very much any longer.' This type of arch humour was a Nilsen hallmark.

I hadn't come into contact with Nilsen all that often at the Scrubs after our first illustrious meeting, but it was that first meeting which had stuck with me. Why should that be? Perhaps it was simply that I had been unable to ask the questions which I had wanted to ask of him and was therefore still trying to understand how he could have repeatedly killed and then done what he had done with the bodies of his victims. And perhaps my desire to interview him again was simply a reflection of the fact that I now felt better equipped to ask these questions. Many reading this will not find that a satisfactory answer, but I believe that all humans have an inbuilt desire to solve mysteries and that was what Nilsen remained for me – a mystery.

So, a few days later, I found myself in an interview room in Whitemoor, once again sitting opposite Dennis Nilsen, and discussing the nature of evil.

At this time Nilsen was also still speaking to his biographer Brian Masters, although that would change. He afterwards sent me a document in which he suggested that, 'Masters is like an old music hall act with only one joke – me.' In fact, in the months following our meeting at Whitemoor, Nilsen sent me a number of other documents, giving each titles such as *Orientation in Me: A Trick of the Light* and *Brain Damage: The Missing Element.*

But that was all in the future.

The interview room that my friend had organised was usually used by solicitors when they were interviewing prisoners who were facing further charges. It had been painted pink and grey which, according to the latest research, were the colours that cre-ated a sense of tranquillity and therefore could calm potentially stressful situations. There was, however, a panic button under the desk, just in case the colour scheme failed. A faint smell of tobacco from the previous occupants hung in the air. One of the officers went off to fetch Nilsen from his cell and I used the time to mentally go through a list of questions which I wanted to ask him and which I had prepared by re-reading all the notes from his trial. I also moved the furniture around in the room so that my seat was closest to the door. I pushed the desk against the wall and made certain that the chair that Nilsen would use was at the far end of the room. It wasn't that I didn't trust the colour scheme, or the panic button, but I knew that this layout would allow me to get out of the cell quickly, should the need arise.

Unlike our first meeting, I wasn't excited or even nervous. This time I felt that I was doing my job.

A few minutes later I heard the officer and Nilsen outside; the officer knocked and pushed the door open. I thanked him and motioned with my arm that Nilsen should sit down.

Neither of us spoke; for a few moments silence filled the air.

Sitting opposite him, I was struck once again by how unassuming Nilsen looked – how ordinary, how much more like a man than a monster. It took me back to those early days at Wormwood Scrubs, although this time I was determined to control how the conversation was going to run. I started the interview by thanking him for agreeing to speak to me and asked him the question that he was expecting.

'So Mr Nilsen, do you think that you are evil?'

'Yes. But what is evil?' he replied.

'Killing fifteen young men?' I suggested.

I had forgotten all about the confusion that existed as to the number of people that he had killed. It gave Nilsen an opportunity to sidestep the question.

'I gave a provisional total killed to the police of fifteen or sixteen. Having committed myself to a number I just stuck to it lest the police thought I was deliberately messing them about.'

'So, how many people did you kill?' I asked.

'I invented three victims to maintain this continuity of evidence. I stuck with fifteen from pure ego. Fifteen is higher than twelve. The "long-haired hippy", the "skinhead" and the "anonymous Irishman" are pure inventions to complement the figure fifteen. I did not kill them as they never existed. This somewhat diminishes me as a notorious property.'

This is pure Nilsen. In just a few sentences he had tried to make himself appear to be helping the police, by lying about the numbers that he had killed to allow them 'continuity of evidence'; then he rather undermined that supposed motivation by stating that it was actually about his own ego; and finally imagined that killing twelve people was somehow less abhorrent than killing fifteen, to the extent that he was a less 'notorious property'.

I have also no doubt that his answer was deliberately framed to avoid answering my initial question. In his summing up at the trial, the judge had raised the question of Nilsen being evil and had suggested to the jury that, 'a mind can be evil without being abnormal'.

This irked Nilsen.

I asked him again about being evil and he mumbled something incoherent but later sent me the following reply which he thought 'better answered my question'.

'As the flashbulbs flashed and the wolves howled and in the universal public consciousness I joined the ranks of the damned alongside Crippen, Heath, Haigh, Brady, Hindley and Sutcliffe,' his letter started. He continued that he did not see himself in that way at all and, in our discussions, he suggested that the murders that he had committed were 'out of character' and that 'the catharsis of arrest and its relief helped me to regain my normal profile of morality'. He also thought that he had 'embraced my guilt – I did not shy away from it in denial'. He also resented the way that the three psychiatrists who had appeared at his trial had used him 'as the raw material to be slotted into pet theories'.

Yet again the same confusion in his thinking shines through, as well as his own narcissism. He wants to be given our credit for acknowledging that he did commit murder but does not seem to be able to understand how killing at least twelve young men demands our judgement and opprobrium and leaves him outside of normal society. He may indeed have regained his normal 'profile of morality' after his arrest, as if that fact in itself somehow excuses what he has done before his arrest. We should remember too that Nilsen did not himself go to the police and confess to these murders and, when a number of his young victims escaped his clutches, he denied attempting to do them any harm. Without the intervention of a Dyno-Rod engineer, I have no doubt that Nilsen would have continued to kill.

But how then does he explain *why* he killed, especially if he refuses to countenance the 'pet theories' of the psychiatrists who examined him?

As would become my habit, I asked Nilsen to describe the first murder to me. Over time I would come to understand how important this first murder is to the serial killer, as it pushes them out of their fantasies about killing and into the dreadful reality. It is also the murder when they are least experienced as killers and so they will often make mistakes. These mistakes usually leave clues, which the police can later use to track down the culprit. In fact, I sometimes wonder if we stop murderers from becoming serial killers because they aren't very good at the start of a budding killing cycle. I have no way of proving this one way or another and clearly this did not happen in Nilsen's case. This is what he said about the first murder:

By Christmas of 1978 I was completely isolated and dejected. I would walk Bleep [his dog] in Gladstone Park, drink to excess and watch TV. That was the extent of my social life. I had lost the stability of a flatmate. I had no sex and nobody to talk to. On the 30th of December after a good drink at home, I staggered out desperate for someone to talk to. I walked to the Cricklewood Arms and picked up a young Irishman. We went back to the flat after the pub closed and continued to drink at Melrose Avenue. We both stripped naked and slept on the mattress on the floor. Very early the next morning I strangled him with a neck-tie and after he was unconscious I drowned him by putting his head in a bucket of water.

All of this fitted with the hypothesis of the psychiatrist at his trial – Nilsen 'killed for company'.

'But that still doesn't explain why you wanted to kill him,' I replied. 'You had been desperate for someone to talk to and having found someone you then shut him up – permanently.'

Nilsen blinked behind his glasses and I suddenly became aware that he had only agreed to speak to me because he wanted someone to talk to. His joke that he 'didn't get out much any longer' rang a warning bell in my ears. I think Nilsen sensed that I had just become a little nervous and he smiled at me, perhaps because he now felt some power over me, or perhaps, just perhaps, to put me at ease. Whatever his intention, his smile made me even more nervous. However, he did then try to answer my question.

'I was just lying there with this young, smooth Irish man and I felt happy with him lying there warm by my side. I had felt miserable all Christmas break but with him beside me I felt good. I panicked that he would wake up and then leave and I would be plunged back into loneliness. I wanted him to stay. I wanted him to stay forever. I couldn't face him going and so I thought if I strangle him he couldn't leave.'

'But he would be dead,' I said. 'That warm body that you craved would be cold.'

'But his young naked body was now totally at my disposal. With his death he became a central prop in my fantasy. I liked to think that someone else had killed him and that I was looking after him. I had this ritual of washing, dressing and stripping his body and in this ritual how I handled his dead body became a manageable substitute for my own passive body. I was sort of carrying my own naked body and could enjoy it and its absolute passivity.'

This type of rationalising is unusual in my experience of talking with serial killers. If they talk at all – and usually they are silent and uncommunicative – they studiously avoid describing the murders that they have committed and simply find ways of obfuscating and talking around the subject. So whether we should believe him or not, Nilsen should be given credit for at least addressing the question of why he killed.

I would go as far as to say that it was in his answer to my question that I believe that we get a glimpse of why Nilsen killed and, far from simply wanting someone to talk to, we begin to see the common reality of a desire to dominate and control that all the serial killers that I have worked with share. Nilsen went further and also admitted to me that he would prop the dead body up on the bed and that he continued to have conversations with it for several days.

'What else did you do with their dead bodies?' I asked.

'Not necrophilia,' he lied and, while he admitted to having cut up this first body and all the others that would come later, he insisted that he 'did not keep "trophies"'. Even so, and again contradicting himself, he also suggested that, 'I would have liked to have kept their penises', if he could have found a way of properly storing them.

As he explained this, he looked at me to see if I was shocked. I was, but hoped that I was able to disguise what I was feeling. By this stage of my career I had started to perfect a way of talking with violent men that seemed intimate and almost private and which helped them to talk much more freely than they might otherwise have done. Nor had he engaged in cannibalism, he insisted, although he then advised me that 'when you slice through human buttocks the slices of meat look just like rump steak, with the colour being slightly lighter than in beef.'

There's a great deal going on here, including the deliberate attempt to shock by both describing slicing through human flesh and his casual use of sexual language. However, he was also by this time aware of Thomas Harris's novel *The Silence of the Lambs* and the character Hannibal Lecter and, almost as if he was trying to make himself a more notorious property and reinvent his brand, he suggested that 'these serial killer books have got a lot to answer for.'

That might be so, but it was also clear that Nilsen wanted to dominate and direct. Far from passivity defining his personality, Nilsen wanted to be in charge. This is perhaps why he chose careers that gave him a frisson of power, such as the army and the police. As a result, when his careers in these disciplined and disciplinary forces ended, the people that he met and killed were merely used to serve as replacement props in his fantasies of power, control and authority; props, moreover, that couldn't challenge, or talk back to him to give him their own point of view. Indeed, within his ritual of washing, dressing and stripping, Nilsen spoke to me about using mirrors to watch himself holding onto his dead victims and sometimes fondling them too, so as to be better able to view himself in the role that he preferred to play.

Power, control and fantasy. This is a potent brew and one that would ferment in the backgrounds of every serial killer that I met or worked with.

The interview, of course, had to end at some point but Nilsen wasn't going to let me leave without a fuss.

'Do you have to go?' he said, reaching over the desk and touching my hand as I got up to leave. It was his final gesture of trying to exert power over me. Both a come-on and also a deliberate allusion to killing for company.

As I left Whitemoor my head was spinning and I had to stop twice on the drive back to Grendon. I remember returning to my house and wondering if Nilsen could ever cope with therapy, or indeed if therapy would ever be able to cope with Nilsen. I also gradually came to accept that people like Nilsen – whether they engaged in therapy or not – could never be released back into the community. They might indeed be rehabilitated as individuals, in that they wouldn't commit further offences, but for a small number of offenders society still needed to have a way of expressing its total and utter disgust for what they had done by being able to exclude them for ever. It was therefore through Nilsen that I realised that I could never be a prison abolitionist, because we will always need prisons to house a small number of people who commit offences such as his.

I discussed all of this and what had happened during the interview with Dr Roger Cruickshank, one of the psychiatrists at Grendon and another fellow Glaswegian. We had struck up a natural friendship and would spend many hours discussing Freud, therapy and offending behaviour together in Roger's office, which he had decorated with rugs, beautiful ceramics and oil paintings by Scottish Colourists, especially the work of William Crosbie. If there ever was a more civilised room within a prison I failed to find it and it was in these incongruous surroundings that I shared the details of my discussions with Nilsen.

'He fancied you!' Roger said, giggling into his cup of coffee, before considering more seriously Nilsen's use of mirrors and how Freud thought about the mirror as a metaphor for the mind. 'Of course the first mirror was water,' said Roger, 'and Ovid says that Narcissus asks of his reflection when he sees it for the first time, "Am I the lover or the beloved – the one who wants or the one who is wanted?"'

Roger took another sip of coffee and then suggested that Nilsen's use of the mirror to provide a distorted view of himself was similar to his joining the army and the police. He was confused about who he was and therefore how he wanted to express who he was and what that expression might reveal to others. Was he the one that wants, or the one who wants to be wanted? He could resolve that confusion only when the young men that he had picked up were dead, because then he was safe in the knowledge that they would be unable to shatter the image of himself that he had created and cherished.

'But if that's the case, why did he let some of these young men go?' I asked.

'Remember he was drunk,' replied Roger. 'He probably didn't mean to.'

We sat in silence for a moment.

Roger looked at his watch.

'I've got a small group in ten minutes. You coming?'

Though I sat in on therapy at Grendon, I rarely sat in the same group as Roger. The therapy wings were structured in much the same way as the Annexe at the Scrubs, although at Grendon the culture of therapy seemed to permeate the whole of the prison. Therapy guided everything that happened within the walls of the jail. Grendon's four therapy wings were organised around a number of guiding principles: responsibility, empowerment, support and confrontation.

Responsibility refers to how the regime is constructed to get the prisoner to accept individual responsibility for his offending and the victims that he has created, as well as fostering collective responsibility for the functioning of the small group and his wing. Next, every member of the community is empowered to have a direct say in every aspect of how the prison is run, including having the power to vote fellow prisoners out of therapy if they break any of the three cardinal rules that guide behaviour – no violence, no sex with another prisoner and no use of drugs. Support is offered from the staff to prisoners who are engaged in therapy and, finally, there is direct and candid confrontation of anyone who attempts to minimise their offending history or the harm their actions have caused.

This last principle of being candid and confrontational with offenders who minimise their offending behaviour has come to characterise much of my own professional work and can be glimpsed in the interview that I also conducted with Nilsen.

What has to be remembered here is the profile of the prisoners that Grendon accepted. Prisoners who had committed very serious offences against others, prisoners who were dangerous and disturbed, and who had caused severe problems in other prisons, were now expected to live their institutional lives at Grendon without resorting to violence, using drugs or engaging in situational sexual relations. Prisoners could even vote for their fellow inmates to be thrown out of the prison and back to the prison where they had last been locked up.

Of course it takes prisoners some time to become comfortable with a prison being operated in this way. A few years after I left Grendon, Elaine Genders and Elaine Player, at the time two Oxford academics, published their research that they had started when I was a governor at the prison about the prisoner's 'therapeutic career model'. This model had five stages: recognition; motivation; understanding; insight; and, finally, testing. These five stages reveal the prisoner's journey within therapy. Initially what has to be done is to have the prisoner recognise the problems that need to be solved and then become motivated to change. Slowly the prisoner will come to understand the interconnectedness and related aspects of their lives, often based on childhood experiences and relationships, and this becomes the basis for insight. In this context and at this stage, insight simply means identifying the solutions to the problems that they have had, and the final stage is about testing out these solutions by putting into practice new ways of coping. This final stage does not emerge until after about eighteen months in therapy.

Indeed it was usually possible to identify how long a prisoner had been in therapy just by listening to what they said and how they discussed things in their small group. There was a world of difference between someone who was only six months into therapy and a prisoner who had been at Grendon for over two years.

Three quotes stood out to me in the group therapy meeting I went to that day, each of which typified the kind of violent men I was working with.

I knew that I could fight and when I did I got respect. In fact it was the only thing that I was good at and so I just kept on fighting.

I knew there was going to be trouble almost as soon as we went into the club. I saw him at the bar and just thought, 'There's no way you're going to fuck with me tonight.' He came over and before he could say anything I glassed him. I didn't really mean to kill him.

My mum used to tell me to grow up and be a man, just like my dad. I always thought that she was disappointed I wasn't more like my dad. He was in and out of prison all of his life. I remember being taken to see him once. It was strange. I felt close to him – that I loved him – but he was hardly ever around. I suppose that's what my son will say about me too.

The first point to note here is that none of these quotes relates to an instrumental violence, by which I mean violence that is used to achieve a specific, recognised objective, such as facilitating a robbery. In other words, instrumental violence is 'rational' because it allows the perpetrator to make some type of gain. That isn't what is being described.

The opposite of instrumental violence is what is known as 'expressive violence' and this is a less rational expression of personality or identity. Expressive violence is about anger, often in response to an insult. We should not presume that there is always, or ever, a clear distinction between the two but I find the distinction between instrumental and expressive violence helpful in trying to understand why some men will be violent.

The mention in the second quote of attacking someone's face was typical of other stories I had heard. The face is the most obvious representation of our self in relation to others; it is the visible manifestation of our identity. Think about how we have come to use that word 'face': casually, metaphorically, culturally and descriptively. We live in a face-to-face society, where we want to and often have to put on a brave face; we have a 'face off' before playing certain sports; we would never want to lose face and, even if there are sometimes comforts in being another face in the crowd, most of us would still prefer to be thought of as a friendly and familiar face within our community. Those at the top of the criminal tree are sometimes known colloquially as 'faces'.

Both the first and the second quotes offer us a window into understanding how the sense of face operates in practice. The first quote describes how fighting became a means by which this particular offender won respect and, not unnaturally, in the absence of other more conventional ways for him to do so, he became good at being violent. In his case he also sold that skill by becoming a bouncer and then an enforcer for a local, organised crime gang. In a memorable phrase, Professor Steve Hall calls men like this 'criminal undertakers', as they sell their propensity for violence as a commodity to the highest bidder so as to 'undertake' – in other words, to 'get things done'.

What isn't described here are the benefits for some men of being a criminal undertaker. They drive fast cars, they wear flashy clothes, and they are seen, by some, as being sexually attractive. All of this gives them status. Even in prison this type of offender is regarded as being a 'face' to be respected.

The second offender is describing something slightly different, even if he attacks the face of the man that he killed. What this quote does not reveal, and which was explained in the group, is that this attack was the culmination of a long history of antagonism between the two men, which stretched back to their schooldays. Ironically, the perpetrator was usually seen to be the weaker of the two, so was often on the receiving end of a beating. What made this occasion all the more potent and deadly was the presence of a crowd of witnesses in the club, which served to heighten his feelings of shame and humiliation of having been a victim in the past and the threat of being so again in the present.

He also revealed to the group that his girlfriend was in the club that night and, no doubt, her presence helped to heighten his sense of not wanting to feel, or to be perceived to be, weak.

The final quote is different again but also reveals another, related aspect that goes hand in glove with humiliation and shame: rejection. This offender had an unhealthy relationship with his mother and his desire to please her by being more like his imprisoned father was prompted by his fear that she would cast him off if he failed to live up to her expectations. 'Being a man' and 'growing up' for him became inextricably linked with offending, no matter that his father was rarely present in his life. His fear of rejection by his mother was more far powerful than the desire to be a better father to his own son and so, in this way, offending passed from one generation to the next, with every likelihood that it would continue to do so.

These quotes of what violent men said about being violent are mere glimpses through the window of therapy on that particular day. After all, talking about their offending in a therapy group was what they were required to do on a daily basis. These snapshots are indicative of the stories that they told over a long period of time and would be repeated by others throughout the course of my time in prisons. And what do these snapshots all add up to? For me, that violence is usually an attempt, sometimes a brutal, bloody and savage attempt, to regain face, restore pride and stave off feelings of humiliation. This is therefore about inadequacy and what is missing in a person, for it is almost as if violent men lack a nonviolent repertoire of behaviour – they commit violence, in other words, because they don't know what to do instead.

Here, my thinking about violence brings me back to Paul Brumfitt.

I was never in a therapeutic relationship with Paul, we just played badminton together over lunch. We'd usually do this twice a week and, inevitably, I got to know him well. Having read his file, I knew all about the offences that he had committed – what he had done was truly appalling. Paul acknowledged this to me too but the formal responsibility to work with him about the murders that he had committed lay with the other prisoners and therapists on his wing.

Even so, on a couple of occasions, I discussed Paul's offending with the wing psychologist. He had a similar sense of the case to my own. The trigger for the killing spree had been the end of Paul's relationship with his sixteen-year-old girlfriend, his feelings of humiliation and rage about that rejection, perhaps made all the more intolerable for him by her relative youth, since at that time he was twenty-four years old. He needed to regain a sense of who he was but was chaotic and out of control. I almost got the impression that he killed to show his former girlfriend who was boss. His murders seemed unplanned, instinctive, spontaneous and ill-thought through. He had attacked his victims with table lamps, or strangled them with telephone wire, rather than bringing weapons to the crime scene. He was drunk when he stupidly admitted his crimes to his final victim and was very easily caught on his return to England.

All of this would later echo with the sense that I made of why Erwin James had murdered.

By the time we started our badminton sessions Paul had been in therapy for three years and nothing about his behaviour within the prison suggested any substantive cause for concern. Indeed, quite the reverse. I remember one member of staff describing him as the prison's 'head boy' and he was someone that we would happily introduce to visitors to Grendon, so that they could gain an insight into therapy from the prisoner's point of view. Frankly, Paul was one of our stars whom I thought demonstrated everything that could be achieved within a therapeutic community. I had left Grendon before his parole application had been completed but if I had been asked I would have enthusiastically supported Paul moving on from Grendon into open conditions, with a view to him eventually being released.

The next time that I heard anything about Paul was in 1999.

I was in my office at the university, reading the *Independent* when I caught a headline saying 'Convicted Murderer Killed Again After Release'. A photograph of Paul appeared beneath the headline. Brumfitt had been charged with, and later would be convicted of, murdering a teenage sex worker called Marcella Ann Davis at his home. After killing Marcella he'd dismembered her body and attempted to burn her remains in a scrapyard that he rented. Three weeks after Marcella had disappeared, he'd also raped a second sex worker at knifepoint. This is bad enough but this second victim probably had a lucky escape, as it seems likely that Brumfitt was about to start another killing spree.

I felt sick and shaken and re-read the newspaper report time after time in the hope that it might be describing another Paul Brumfitt. It wasn't. Our 'head boy' – our therapy 'star' – had failed in the most appalling way.

From press reports it was possible to piece together what had happened to Brumfitt since leaving Grendon.

He'd been moved to open conditions and in total served fifteen years of his life sentence, before being released in 1994.

He'd found work as a gardener straight away and was employed doing general maintenance for Dudley Borough Council. Crucially he'd also married his prison visitor (prison visitors are volunteers from the community who visit offenders in prison who don't get visits). They had separated in late 1998, which had prompted Brumfitt to move out of the marital home. Their separation was probably the trigger to history repeating itself.

The Detective Chief Inspector who led the investigation into Marcella's murder described Brumfitt as an 'evil, calculating man' and, using the perfect vision that comes with hindsight, Edward Crew, Chief Constable of the West Midlands at the time, criticised the decision to release Brumfitt 'to wander the streets to kill again'. He went further and maintained that, 'It seems inconceivable to me that a man who has previously been convicted for a litany of offences for which he received three life sentences can still be allowed to wander around our streets.'

Crew's comments are disingenuous and I wrote to tell him so, given that parole for offenders who have committed murder is a long-standing and widely accepted feature of our criminal justice system. They were also inaccurate, as Brumfitt hardly 'wandered' around the streets but had found a home within the community where he had settled and was holding down a job for the local council. He was also on 'life licence' and so would have been in regular contact with a probation officer. The Parole Board also issued a statement noting that, 'The support for releasing [Brumfitt] was unanimous and in some instances enthusiastic. All stated unequivocally that the risk of Mr Brumfitt reoffending was minimal.'

Even so, to describe what had happened as tragic hardly captures how devastating all of this was, particularly for Marcella's family and for Brumfitt's other victim. It was also bad news for Grendon and for the faith that the Criminal Justice System had in therapeutic communities and the work that could be done there with violent men. Brumfitt was a 'false positive' – someone who appeared to have benefitted from therapy and had changed for the better but who, in fact, was still violent and capable of committing murder. Given his previous offences, it might even be more accurate to now call him a serial killer.

Brumfitt's failure reveals that being successful in therapy is no guarantee of leading a crime-free life when released, but I cannot allow his spectacular failure to diminish the work that is done at Grendon. There will always be 'false positives', especially given the scale and type of offending history of the prisoners that Grendon receives. I feel it underscores the extraordinary work done at the prison because, thankfully, those failures and 'false positives' are extremely rare, and figures produced by several different researchers since the 1980s continue to show that if a prisoner spends at least eighteen months at Grendon he is far less likely to re-offend when released and, if he does re-offend, it will be for a less serious crime than the one for which he was originally sentenced.

However, Brumfitt's case reminds me that protecting the public has to be the first priority of our criminal justice system and that any failure to do so can have deadly consequences.

I wrote to Brumfitt, as well as to the Chief Constable. I wanted to speak with him about what had happened, partly to try and understand if we could begin to better appreciate how we might identify other 'false positives' in the future. If I am honest, I also wanted to tell him how angry I was.

Brumfitt replied to me at the university saying no to an interview. As he put it, he 'couldn't face me.'

Chapter Four

Special Units, Riots and the Murder of a Toddler

'Collective violence is also an important strand of English history'

JAMES SHARPE, *A Fiery & Furious People:*
A History of Violence in England

 By April Fool's Day 1990, I had moved from Grendon to the newly built HMP Woodhill in Milton Keynes, where I had been asked to develop two special units to manage disruptive prisoners. Further north, a twenty-five-year-old prisoner called Paul Taylor, whom I had never met, was nearing the end of his two-and-half-year sentence for cheque book fraud at HMP Strangeways in Manchester. On that day, he decided that he wanted to attend the service in the prison's chapel which, as chance would have it, was being recorded on tape. When the Reverend Noel Proctor was in the middle of his sermon, Taylor stood up.

TAYLOR: I would like to say, right, that this man has just talked about the blessing of the heart and a hardened heart can be delivered. No, it cannot; not

with resentment, anger, bitterness and hatred being
instilled in people.

[General noise, over which in background a prisoner can be
heard shouting:]

PRISONER: Fuck your system; fuck your rules!

[Applause]

PROCTOR: Right lads, sit down.

But the prisoners did not sit down. Instead, they chose to over-power the prison officers supervising the service, taking their keys, and then swept out of the chapel and onto the landings beyond, unlocking the doors of their fellow inmates.

They were to remain in charge of the prison for twenty-five days.

The riot spread quickly throughout the prison. The end result was that 147 staff and 48 prisoners were injured. An officer and a prisoner subsequently died after being attacked by these 'ordinary, decent criminals', as Eric, my old SO colleague at the Scrubs, would doubtless have described them.

The damage done to HMP Strangeways, which had been designed to hold 970 prisoners but at the time of the riot actually housed 1,647, was estimated at £60 million. The total costs of the riot, including the refurbishment of the prison, costs for staffing, the subsequent inquiry and resulting court cases, eventually reached £112 million.

During the riot pictures appeared in the press and on TV screens of prisoners holding court on the roof day after day, where an ever-decreasing number who were holding out had sought sanctuary, smoke from the fires still smouldering in the prison wafting in the background. This hard core of prisoners left on the roof would periodically shout their various demands down to an eager group of journalists who had gathered below.

Prison staff and, by implication, more senior prison officials and politicians responsible for the management of the prison service in the Home Office, appeared powerless, disorganised and incapable of regaining control. Worse still, rioting spread to HMPs Bristol and Cardiff, two overcrowded local prisons, and then to a number of other prisons.

The subsequent independent public inquiry concluded that while there had been specific reasons for the riots in different jails, six key reasons were common factors to every prison that experienced problems. These reasons were:

- Physical conditions and in particular the fact that 'slopping out' resulted in poor sanitation
- Overcrowding
- Prisoners being locked in their cells for long periods of the day, 'banged up' with no access to exercise or association
- The quality of the food
- The attitudes of staff towards the prisoners
- An absence of justice – a feeling held by the prisoners that their legitimate complaints were not taken seriously by the staff.

We should particularly note the finding that staff attitudes towards prisoners were highlighted as a contributory factor in all the riots that took place and that an 'absence of justice' was the context in which these riots occurred.

Reflecting the culture that I had encountered during my first posting at Wormwood Scrubs, Strangeways was known as a prison which had been built on unchecked prison officer power. The criminologist Eamonn Carrabine, who studied the prison in some depth, observed that the prevailing culture was 'underpinned by a militarised hierarchy of masculinity and sustained violent interventions' into the lives of prisoners. One such intervention was the 'ghosting' of prisoners out of the jail in the middle of the night if they were proving, or perceived to be, troublesome. In other words, when the prison was locked up at night, staff would go to the cell of a particular prisoner who they thought was causing problems, remove him from his cell and then transfer him to another prison. He'd have no time to say goodbye to his friends or let his family know where he might have been moved to. Strangeways was also widely acknowledged to have a strong 'canteen culture' among the officers: a culture which celebrated hard drinking and promoted an associated authoritarian ethic of 'hard men' doing a hard job, which often involved physically confronting prisoners. Sometimes that physical confrontation was necessary and legal; often it was not.

In this brief description of the riot and of the political responses to it, one name is especially important – Paul Taylor. Taylor ignited the seething discontent beneath the surface of the formal culture of Strangeways and was to become the very first man to enter the special units I had helped to develop, just weeks after the riots ended. So understanding him was crucial to the management of the units that I had helped to create after my time at Grendon had ended. I needed to walk in his shoes to truly appreciate what might have motivated him to start the riot and, in effect, destroy the prison. However, I knew that that wouldn't be easy, for Taylor was not only the riot's instigator but also the last man standing, and so had had to withstand the various tactics that were developed to regain control of the prison.

For example, a number of psychological techniques had been deployed during the Strangeways riot to try to undermine the solidarity of the men who remained on the roof and to weaken their resolve: electricity lines were cut, cold water was sprayed onto the roof to make it slippery and loud rock music was played incessantly to make it difficult for the prisoners to sleep. One psychologist had also recommended that periodically one man in the Control & Restraint (C&R) Units, who had been deployed to the prison once the riots had started, should shout up to the roof, 'He's a beast, a beast' to unsettle group solidarity – 'beast', like 'nonce', was prison slang for sex offender.

The psychologist's message backfired. Rather than one member of the C&R team shouting this up occasionally, the whole of the C&R team chanted 'Beast, beast' in unison, banging their riot sticks on their shields as they did so for added effect. Far from undermining the group solidarity of the prisoners on the roof, it served to make them more dogged.

Every day of the riot, prisoners not on the roof would surrender to the teams of prison officers who staffed the C&R Units that were slowly taking back parts of the ruined prison, landing by landing, wing by wing. After the first day 700 prisoners had surrendered and just over a week later only thirteen prisoners were still refusing to come down from the roof, where they had taken sanctuary. By 25 April only five remained there, refusing to negotiate, and Taylor could often be seen using a traffic cone as a megaphone to address the journalists who had gathered – he was determined and resolute in what he was doing and the message that he seemed to be sending was a plea for penal reform, albeit expressed by this most unexpected of leaders and in the most unusual of circumstances. When on 25 April Taylor eventually agreed to surrender, the last prisoner to do so, he raised a clenched fist as a final gesture of defiance. He had been not only an instigator, but also a leader, who had shown persistence, nous and media savvy.

Taylor, along with others, would eventually be charged with the murder of Derek White, the prisoner who died in the riots, but at trial the group were found not guilty as it was established that White might have died from a pre-existing thrombotic condition. Taylor was found guilty of riot under Section 1 of the

Public Order Act 1986 and given a further ten-year sentence, extending his original sentence four times over.

Of course, that left a problem.

Where would be the safest place to imprison the man who had started the Strangeways riots and who had held out the longest before coming down from the roof? The answer was in the special units at Woodhill.

As should be obvious from what I've just described, prisons can be very dangerous places. Despite the fact that we think of them as being under the control of staff who manage the environment through, most obviously, locking prisoners behind their cell doors, the penal world is nonetheless one which is often characterised by violence. This problem of violence becomes all the more acute with an increasing prison population, reducing the amount of time available for staff to work constructively with prisoners.

Of late, our prison population has reached record levels: there are currently over 80,000 people in jail, with more young, elderly and female offenders being locked up than ever before and more life-sentenced prisoners in our system than the whole of Western Europe combined. This isn't because we are inherently more criminogenic than the French, Swedes, Danes, Italians, Spanish, Portuguese, Belgians, Luxembourgers, Swiss, Norwegians, Finns, Greeks or Germans but is simply the result of us choosing to imprison more of our people who offend than our European neighbours. We use prison, whereas they find other forms of punishment to manage the majority of their offenders.

Prison violence can range from hand-to-hand combat to fights where knives, bars, or homemade weapons are used; boiling water can be thrown in an opponent's face – sometimes with sugar dissolved in the liquid, to make it stick to the victim's skin. There are regular fires, sexual assaults and rapes, and my own research suggested that in some years the murder rate in prison could be double the murder rate in the community.

A small number of prisoners within the general prison population continually pose these problems. For various reasons they refuse to conform and set themselves to constantly challenge the good order and running of the jail. These are the prisoners, like Taylor, who riot, take hostages, try to get onto the roof to take part in demonstrations, assault staff or other prisoners and, on some occasions, will have killed while serving their sentences. These prisoners spend much of their sentence in segregation units because they cannot be trusted anywhere else. Surely we could do something more productive? As early as 1984 a special Home Office committee was recommending that particularly disruptive prisoners such as these should be separated from the mainstream prisoner population and located in three or four special units.

The first of these units for prisoners who were both disruptive and who also had a history of psychiatric illness opened in 1985 at HMP Parkhurst. In 1987 two further units opened at HMPs Lincoln and Hull, both with the objective of getting the behaviour of prisoners to improve so that they could be returned to normal locations within the dispersal system. The two special units at HMPs Lincoln and Hull were to be replaced by the units at the soon-to-be built HMP Woodhill in Milton Keynes, and that's where I arrived in 1990, fresh from my work at Grendon.

Rather unimaginatively, we called one of the units 'Milton' and the other 'Keynes', though one wag suggested that we should call them 'Jekyll' and 'Hyde'. Milton operated as an assessment unit and Keynes as the unit that receptions would eventually progress onto.

I wanted to harness my experience of working at Grendon and consult with the architect at Woodhill's design stage, to see if we could apply some principles that might allow us to design violence out of the buildings. Throughout the project, the goal was twofold: keeping the staff and the prisoners safe, while at the same time maintaining a humane and constructive environment that offered the possibility and the hope of change for the prisoners. From the outset of the various planning meetings that were held, two psychological principles remained uppermost. First, that the best indication of future behaviour is previous behaviour; and, second, that the best way to deal with violence is to avoid it.

The first of these principles does not imply that the past is the only indication of future behaviour. People can change but that change involves committing to therapy and, even then, it takes time. The prisoners that the special units were going to accept had never committed to therapy, or were often regarded as too dangerous or disruptive to even be given access to this type of intervention and regime.

In relation to the people that these units were going to house, I knew that we should presume that they would be violent if they were not managed appropriately and that therefore we had to do everything in our power to design violence out of the fabric of the two units. A mountain of research suggests that most violence occurs in environments that are hot, polluted and overcrowded and so, if we want to avoid violence, we can do a significant amount to reduce the likelihood of it occurring by managing the temperature, eradicating pollutants and manipulating the sense of space.

Bearing this in mind and applying these principles to Milton and Keynes, what we tried to do was give an impression of space – even though we were surrounded by a high prison wall and a series of internal walls which marked out the territory of the two units. However, in order to make the units feel less claustrophobic and prison-like, one of the internal walls was made from toughened but see-through glass. The glass also gave a view of the grounds and allowed a great deal of natural light to flow into the units, as opposed to the harsh, artificial, manufactured light that usually illuminated prison life.

We had other design principles up our sleeves too. Prisons are usually noisy places – doors and gates slam shut, key chains jangle, footsteps on the prisons' landings and corridors regularly disrupt any sense of peace and quiet. Of course, we couldn't get rid of the noise altogether, but we could do a great deal to camouflage it by designing a sound system to be built into the unit, playing music from the local radio station. This served to mask any sudden noise and helped to even out what prisoners and staff could hear. As far as pollution is concerned, we banned smoking from any common space: prisoners were only allowed to smoke in their cells, although this too would later be banned.

Milton and Keynes also had air conditioning, and this would later prove to be controversial. However, it allowed us to deliberately keep the temperature lower than was normal – not to the extent that it was abnormally cold but rather to ensure that it wasn't stiflingly hot. After all, when we are 'hot and bothered', we are all more likely to become 'hot-headed' and lose our temper.

None of these psychological and design principles would have worked without the right staff being in place, and the staff had to be given a great deal of training prior to the two units opening. It would be the staff who made these approaches and principles come to life and they would achieve this not only by implementing them on a day-to-day basis, but also through their own behaviour and interactions with prisoners – many of whom had long reputations of being hostile to staff, or had assaulted staff in the past.

This is not to imply that staff had to be soft or inappropriately lenient with the prisoners but rather that they had to learn how to draw behavioural boundaries and then develop the skills needed to police those boundaries, without using force.

Training staff to recognise that it was often possible to predict which prisoner would react violently and in which situations was the first skill that we worked on. If we knew that a prisoner was about to have a difficult visit from a family member or had to be re-interviewed by the police about further charges, we could take appropriate action to better manage that situation. Communication was the key here, and the need to remember who we were locking up. This involved sharing with each other information that we felt to be important in managing a particular prisoner and carefully noting changes in their behaviour: were they associating with different people; or, perhaps, had they become unusually quiet?

We also took the view that we would attempt to get the prisoners out of their cells and involve them in as much education, physical education and work as we were able to accommodate within the two units. This had the benefit of allowing the prisoners' day to be better structured, with distinct periods of activity, and also encouraged the prisoners to recognise that there were benefits from behaving well within the unit. After all, activities could be taken away as well as provided, depending on how the prisoners responded to what was on offer.

Would all of this succeed? Based on my work at Grendon, I believed that it would but clearly the stakes were high both personally and professionally. After all, the units were the logical and practical extension of my method of working with violent men and so, if that approach failed I too would have been viewed as a failure. What made things even more tricky was that much of this approach involved trusting prisoners to respond positively to what was being offered. There is an element of calculation going on here by both sides: a calculation that is based on the prisoner being rational and recognising that he is being given a chance and better off if he accepts it. A deal is being offered but would prisoners accept the deal, or betray the trust? Paul Taylor was our very first prisoner and, from the outset, he behaved impeccably.

We have to acknowledge that this was not only the result

of the staff training and all the design principles that we had employed, but also the fact that Taylor wanted to get his head down and finish his sentence as easily as possible. It would be wrong of me to underestimate Paul's own personal desire to get on with his sentence. In reflecting on the riots on the twenty-fifth anniversary in 2015, Taylor gave a number of interviews to the media about his role in them. He suggested that he was:

> ... glad that I took part in a protest that changed the course of history. The prison service were reluctant to implement any changes whatsoever until Strangeways happened. We shouldn't have taken the law into our own hands because it detracted from our root cause of the protest – conditions and violence towards prisoners by prison staff and the general condition of prisons.

This acknowledgement that Taylor and the other rioters shouldn't have 'taken the law into our own hands' was not a reference to the fact that they had rioted. Rather, it concerned the immediate object of their hostility after they had overcome the prison officers in the chapel and taken their keys – sex offenders who had been segregated for their own protection.

Taylor remembered that:

> I wanted to locate a particular prisoner [undoubtedly Derek White] who came in that week for the attempted rape of a six-year-old girl. We went onto the landing and we found the cell that he was in and we entered that cell. I did punch him two times and prisoners set about him with sticks. He was dragged from the cell and his face was pushed into the railings. Then he was picked up and thrown over the railings. He grabbed hold of the railings so intensely that it required hitting his fingers with a stick for him to let go.

In other interviews he gave he stated, 'My family suffered; I suffered. From that point of view it wasn't worth it.' It is impossible to say with any certainty if this type of insight and reflection came as a consequence of the units, or if perhaps Taylor's family played a more significant role in his reflecting on what he had done.

Even so, the periods of reform that come in British prisons usually follow in the wake of two different sets of circumstances. First, following riots when, as at Strangeways, prisoners decide that enough is enough and take action for themselves. It would be lovely to imagine that the grotesque daily routine of slopping out which characterised our prison system at the time would have disappeared as a result of enlightened public policy initiatives. It did not, and only came to an end in the wake of the direct action of Taylor and a number of other rioters.

The second set of circumstances which produce change in our prisons emerges after significant numbers of middle class, literate and influential people get imprisoned. The imprisonment of the Suffragettes and the conscientious objectors who refused to fight in the First World War was what produced reform in our prisons after the end of hostilities and helped to prompt a reduction in the prison population, so that the numbers being sent to jail halved between 1918 and 1938. This remains the longest sustained period of decarceration – the opposite of incarceration – in world history and our prison numbers would only grow again after the end of the Second World War. The reason for the power of this second set of circumstances is not so difficult to fathom: people who experience prison tend to be less likely to advocate for its use. Think of Winston Churchill, himself an ex-prisoner of war during the Boer War, who declared that, 'The mood and temper of the public in regard to the treatment of crime and criminals is one of the most unfailing tests of the civilisation of any country.'

Paul Taylor may have conformed within the units but the other prisoners that we housed behaved very much as we had predicted. They were nasty, aggressive, belligerent, conning and manipulative and, on some days, the threat of violence hung heavy in the air.

Most of the prisoners that we had to deal with had committed murder – sometimes multiple times and even after they had been imprisoned. We held prisoners like Lee Baker, Ferdinand Lieveld and Kenny Carter – a typical cross-section of the men we were in charge of.

Baker had murdered his two victims in 1986. He'd killed the mother of a former girlfriend and then had decapitated her body, before going out and shooting a man with a crossbow.

Lieveld, a physically imposing man, was also a murderer, having been convicted of stabbing two men whilst he worked as a doorman. He seemed to spend his days in the unit making towers of carved skulls from the coconut shells that he could get access to from the kitchens. He regarded these towers as pieces of art and wanted me to contact the auctioneers Christie's to get them valued.

Carter, a man initially sentenced for armed robbery, had cemented his reputation as a hard man with a conviction for the murder of his cellmate Darren Brook. Brook was serving his first sentence and evidence produced at court showed that Carter had bullied him mercilessly, both physically and psychologically. As the final culmination of this grotesque bullying, Carter coerced Darren into hanging himself, kicking away the chair to complete the job. People speculated that Carter had hoped to get more favourable treatment because of the emotional trauma he had had to endure from witnessing the 'suicide'.

However, the prisoner who caused me the most difficulty had actually been convicted of aggravated burglary, rather than murder. I will call him Pete; he is now serving another sentence.

Why Pete caused so many problems was largely to do with the fact that he seemed unreadable. Through working in close proximity with people who were capable of being violent, I had developed an acute sense of body language and other non-verbal clues as to what a person might be thinking and how those thoughts might motivate their behaviour.

There are usually lots of clues that someone is thinking of assaulting you and acting on those clues allows you to de-escalate the situation, or remove yourself from harm. People usually need an emotional run-up before becoming violent: the inflections in their voice alter and what they say changes; their bodies become larger, as blood flows to the muscles that they might have to employ; their posture becomes more direct, sharp and confrontational.

The problem with Pete was that he could mask all of this with consummate ease and so I was never certain if he was going to remain friendly, or turn hostile. Meeting with Pete was always an exercise in managing the tiny space of my office. In the same way I had rearranged the office when I last interviewed Nilsen, I would sit closest to the door, in a seat that was markedly higher than Pete's – that way it would take him slightly longer to get out of his seat and allow me a little more time to make my exit. I'd also always let one of my colleagues know when our meeting had been scheduled, so that they could observe what was happening in my office. If we had other intelligence, from monitoring his mail or telephone calls and which suggested that he was under some form of emotional pressure, there were times I would only agree to meet with Pete in the company of other staff. In these various ways, I ensured that he was never able to physically attack me, although he shared with me and others what he thought of me on a regular basis.

It was no surprise to me that Pete was the only prisoner who actively sought to routinely undermine the regime within the units. On one occasion he managed to climb onto the top of the exercise yard wall, cutting himself severely on the razor wire. He seemed to revel in the pain.

Nonetheless, we had no hostage incidents, no escapes, very few staff or prisoner-on-prisoner assaults in the units and no one ever attempted to get onto the roof. In that sense they were a success; frankly, I felt that we had achieved everything that had been asked of us.

However, here's the problem.

Giving prisoners, especially prisoners who had assaulted, taken hostages or rioted, access to a weights room, exercise, art, music and education classes is not necessarily viewed as being fair to other prisoners who have not been problems to prison management, or to members of the public who had never committed any crimes but who couldn't afford to join a gym, or who couldn't get a place at a local college for themselves or their children. As one politician told me in exasperation, 'They've even got air conditioning!' That, seemingly, was the final straw.

Ultimately the contradictions of trying to appease these competing forces meant that the two units developed away from these original principles. As it was explained to me by Michael Howard, home secretary at the time, 'We can't have the worst prisoners being given the best things,' and so, despite the fact that the two units had been a success, they eventually changed their regimes and developed in a different direction.

All of this was deeply frustrating and suggested that no matter the success of the units, political considerations would always take priority. I would soon find that out in other ways too and a pernicious mix of the personal and the political would eventually lead to my resignation.

It was during this time that I had to manage another infamous, self-publicising, violent prisoner.

Michael Peterson was born in 1952, to perfectly respectable, middle-class parents. However, by his early twenties Peterson was in prison, serving a seven-year sentence for armed robbery, with time then added to this sentence for attacking staff and other prisoners, and for taking hostages. Michael was eventually released, but since that date has spent only 131 days as a free man, having been imprisoned again in 1988 and then once more in 1992. His offences have ranged from armed robbery, GBH and wounding with intent to false imprisonment and threatening to kill. He has never been convicted of murder.

Many of his offences have been committed in prison where, as a consequence, he spends a great deal of his time in solitary confinement. He has been held in 120 different jails, as well as in special security hospitals. He has written eleven books, paints (after a fashion) and holds a variety of records for the number of push-ups that he is able to achieve within a specified time frame.

He is a prolific hostage taker.

In 1998, while located in HMP Belmarsh, he took two Iraqi hijackers hostage. He insisted that they call him 'General' and said that if the prison authorities did not agree to his demands he would start to eat one of them. His demands included a helicopter, two Uzi sub-machine guns and an axe. He has taken a prison governor, an art teacher and a prison librarian as hostages. He tied the art teacher up and dragged him about the prison for nearly two days.

He has many female admirers and regularly plays with his identity. Currently he is called Charles Salvador, a name he adopted in 2014 supposedly to honour his favourite painter, but he has previously been called Charles Ali Ahmed and Charles Bronson.

It was by this latter name that I knew him, and it was this name that was used as the title of a 2008 film that was loosely based on his life.

I'd seen a number of reviews about this film and heard a

variety of people debate the pros and, no pun intended, cons of the movie before going to see it myself. The film is keen to claim that it is 'based on a true story' but there is no way for the viewer to tell what is truth and what is fiction in the film. We are required to take on trust what is dramatised and so it contributes to the various myths that have grown up around Bronson and to which he has contributed, and all of which have undoubtedly added to his celebrity status. I watched the film in Milton Keynes – in a cinema no more than ten minutes' drive from Woodhill, the prison where I had got to know Bronson – which seemed to add a reality to me, even if what I watched on the screen was nearly always imagined and partial.

The two special units were, and still are, used to house the twelve most disruptive prisoners in England and Wales, although how they are now organised is very different to the way that they used to be run in the 1990s. However, here's the thing: Bronson was never located in either Milton or Keynes. Instead he was in solitary confinement in the segregation unit of Woodhill and, as is typical of him, he consistently resisted any attempt on our part to work with him so that he might have been able to move out of the segregation unit and onto normal location.

There was only one person who wanted Bronson to be in solitary confinement – Charles Bronson.

It didn't take us long to realise that Bronson didn't want to be on normal location because he couldn't survive there. By this I mean that being 'normal' was exactly what Bronson didn't want to be. He wanted to be extraordinary. His focus was centred on creating a sense of difference that normality would have stifled and killed. As his character says at the beginning of the aforementioned movie, 'My name is Charles Bronson and all my life I've wanted to be famous.' Only one of those statements is true, and of course 'famous' and 'normal' do not make good bedfellows.

Even if my primary accountability was to the prison's special units, I saw Bronson regularly enough in the segregation unit when I had responsibilities for the prison as a whole. The first meeting between us was perfunctory and I asked him if he was OK and if he needed any books. As I got to know him I felt able to be more personal and shared with him that I was concerned that he was locked up by himself and what that might be doing to his mental health. I might as well have been talking to the door. He didn't seem able to respond to this type of approach which involved me reaching out as a fellow human being, as opposed to simply speaking in my role as a governor talking with an inmate. It seemed to disrupt his sense of who he was and how he wanted to be perceived by others.

On my next visit, he was waiting for me.

I walked down the segregation unit corridor to the far end where Bronson's cell was located, accompanied by two escorting officers. As we reached his cell, the first officer put his key in the lock and pushed back the door. There, standing before us, was Bronson. He'd stripped naked and covered his entire body with black shoe polish. As we stood dumbfounded, looking at him and then at each other, Bronson broke the silence by threatening, 'I'm going to stab you with my moustache' – the ends of which he had fashioned into two sharp points – and he then told me and the escorting officers to 'fuck off'. We did.

Over time, we would negotiate internally about the merits of giving Bronson a radio, allowing him to have exercise in the yard, or perhaps the gymnasium, and giving him access to more books in return for good behaviour – in other words not assaulting any of the staff. However, it was at Woodhill that he took hostage the librarian who came to deliver the books that we had negotiated over, meaning the incident ended in a very different kind of negotiation and one which would see him being moved out of the prison.

What can we conclude about Bronson and what should we make of a sometimes very vocal campaign to have him released?

Bronson is the type of prisoner who cannot ever be trusted to accept the deal that is on offer; he will always betray you. He calculates that he would rather harm himself, in order to be able to live his life as he chooses – no matter the consequences for himself, or for other people. Is this rational behaviour? Of course not. Nor is it the product of some clearly thought-through ideological position about the role of the individual in society and the right of the individual to resist state authority in its various forms. He doesn't think like this at all. He reacts violently when he feels emotionally challenged because violence is always his default position when he is required to interact with other people. Sadly, I have no doubt that that would be exactly how he would react if he was ever released from prison.

The incident that I have described which saw the prison's librarian being taken hostage features prominently in the film. I was one of the governors who acted as Hostage Commander during that incident and I sincerely hope I was nothing like the rather suave, detached, chain-smoking, balding, bespectacled and calculating character played in *Bronson* who refused to take one of Bronson's pictures when it was offered. Of course the idea that he is some sort of undiscovered Jean-Michel Basquiat is all part of the glamorising and partial mythology that surrounds him and which is, frankly, totally undeserved.

Of course I might have been calculating, or appeared so to Bronson, but I am not bald or bespectacled and have certainly never smoked.

One aspect of Bronson – the man – that I think that *Bronson* – the film – does capture is how camp Bronson was. I was not the only member of staff who thought there was something sexual about all that stripping off to show us his muscles and his genitals. Bronson wanted to display his body and I believe he wanted to impress on everyone that he really was a 'real man'. Of course any underlying homoeroticism is not what the media want to hear of Bronson, especially as he has become a poster boy for unregulated hyper-masculinity.

In a scene towards the end of the film the suave, calculating, chain-smoking, bespectacled, balding governor tells Bronson that he fears for him dying behind bars. In truth, I did say that to him during one of our conversations. I still think that that is probably true. However, in the same way that Bronson chose to ignore my concern about his being in solitary confinement, so too he appeared to be completely unconcerned by my observation that he might in fact die in prison. Perhaps that's because Bronson knows that in the same way he can't survive on normal location, nor can he survive in the community. Out there in the real world he would just be another sad nutter that no one would ever want to live next door to, work beside or meet in the pub, never mind make a film about.

However, for all my discussion of Bronson, the Strangeways riots, Paul Taylor and the emergence of the special units, what really came to dominate the development of our criminal justice system and popular attitudes towards violence, murder and how to respond to this type of crime was the murder of a toddler in Liverpool. Even if I had nothing to do with the management of his killers, it seems to me that we cannot truly understand our ever-increasing prison numbers and our very British approach to the management of violence and violent offenders without some understanding of this crime, which continues to have repercussions even now.

On 12 February 1993, two ten-year-old boys, Robert Thompson and Jon Venables, were truanting from school. As the day wore on, they became increasingly bored and, almost as if they were egging each other on, they decided to abduct two-year-old

James Bulger while his mother was being served in a butcher's shop. The abduction was filmed by the shopping centre's CCTV system, capturing the now infamous images of James (he was never called 'Jamie') being led away to his death.

James was led on a journey of two and half miles through the town, Venables and Thompson battering him along the way. They were passed by at least thirty-eight witnesses, none of whom intervened effectively to save the small boy. As darkness fell, Venables and Thompson finally brought James to a railway line where they brutally kicked him to death and hammered him with bricks and an iron bar, before leaving his partially stripped body on the tracks, which was later severed by a train.

Venables and Thompson were arrested on 18 February and first appeared in South Sefton Magistrates Court on 22 February, outside of which were scenes of mob violence. Police feared there would be a riot. They were finally sentenced in November 1993, after which their tariff was set at eight years. This was later increased to ten years, and then, partly in response to a campaign in the *Sun*, increased further to fifteen years in 1994. Eventually – after various appeals to the European Court of Human Rights – the sentence was reduced to the original eight-year tariff and Venables and Thompson were subsequently released in 2001, although Venables has been in and out of jail ever since.

This outline of the case hardly captures how central the murder of James Bulger is in relation to the recent history of criminal justice in England and Wales, or how shocking it was to every parent in the country. Our own son was the same age as James and I know that his mum and I held his hand just a little bit more tightly in the months that followed the murder when we went out shopping together. At a political level James's murder was a turning point in penal sensibilities which saw prison sentences lengthen and prompted the numbers being sentenced to prison increase to their current levels. The reality is that the murder of a two-year-old boy by two other children sparked a debate in our country about a range of social and moral issues, including: single mothers; 'home alone children'; bad parenting; video 'nasties' and violent video games. It shaped the Criminal Justice and Public Order Act of 1994 – lowering, for example, the age at which a child could receive an indeterminate sentence – and created the Secure Training Order which allowed 12-to 14-year-old juvenile offenders to be locked up in newly created and privately run Secure Training Centres.

No matter how dreadful the murder was, there is also a case to be made that politicians used the Bulger murder for political ends, effectively creating a climate in which New Labour and the Conservatives both strove to be perceived as the party of law and order; a climate which exists to this day. Crucial here is the fact that Tony Blair was the shadow home secretary and had been influenced by a visit to the USA where he had come under the spell of Bill Clinton – a Democratic president who nonetheless supported the use of the death penalty.

Once again, political policy was going to see a trickle-down effect into our prisons, and not for the better. Reactionary, public-assuaging politics should never replace carefully thought-out policy developments, although sadly they often do.

In January 1993, a month prior to James's murder, Blair had argued that New Labour would be 'tough on crime, and tough on the causes of crime'. Following the murder, he stated that 'children should be taught the value of what is right and what is wrong'. More broadly, he told a Labour Party audience that:

The news bulletins of the last week have been like hammer blows struck against the sleeping conscience of the country . . . a solution to this disintegration doesn't simply lie in legislation. It must come from the rediscovery of a sense of direction

as a country . . . not just as individuals but as a community . . .
we cannot exist in a moral vacuum. If we do not learn and
then teach the value of what is right and what is wrong, then
the result is simply moral chaos that engulfs us all.

Not to be outdone, John Major, prime minister at the time,
went on record saying, 'I would like the public to have a cru-
sade against crime and change from being forgiving of crime
to being considerate of the victim. Society needs to condemn
a little more and understand a little less.' At the Conservative
Party Conference, home secretary Michael Howard delighted
his audience by reminding them:

> Let's make one thing absolutely clear: prison works. It ensures
> that we are protected from murderers, muggers and rapists –
> and it makes many who are tempted to commit crime think
> twice . . . this may mean more people will go to prison. I do
> not flinch from that.

As these sound bites of political sloganeering suggest, James
Bulger's murder became the battleground of a political culture
which was oppositional and confrontational. No one sought to
remind the country that in the mid-1990s figures produced by
the NSPCC suggested at least one child under the age of five was
dying at the hands of their parents or carers *per week*. This stark
reality did not have an impact on the policy process.

Here too I think that we have to acknowledge that our media
played an equal role in shaping how the murder was reported
and viewed and, by and large, their reporting of this case was
sensationalist and often irresponsible.

One way of seeing this case more broadly and which adds to
the argument that the murder of James Bulger fed into particular
political, popular and media cultures and was variously used by

those cultures, is to compare this murder with that of five-year-old Silje Redergard in Trondheim, Norway, just eighteen months after the murder of James.

Silje was murdered by two six-year-old boys who had her strip and then took it in turns to hit and beat her with stones and sticks, before finally stamping on her. They left her unconscious in the snow where she would later die of hypothermia. In contrast, there was no great outpouring of anger or outrage from the families involved, no cries for vigilante justice and no political manoeuvring by any politician to politicise the incident. Rather, it was treated as a tragic event – a terrible aberration – rather than an incident which was indicative of broader political or moral anxieties. There were no policy developments related to this incident in Norway and its prison population remained unaltered.

Of course, there are differences: the boys were younger than Venables and Thompson; Silje was an older victim and a different gender. However, these differences notwithstanding, there is still a case to answer that the murder of James Bulger was being used by different people, groups and industries, often with competing purposes in mind. As a result, the murder of James remains a significant – if not *the* significant – murder within English culture. How it was used by these different groups and industries may also help to explain the differences that remain between our prison numbers and those of our European neighbours. Our per capita prison population, for example, still hovers around 140 per 100,000 of the general population, whilst Norway's is about 65 per 100,000 of their general population.

More immediately, the murder of James was a game changer for the approach that I had adopted within the special units over the previous three years and meant that I never had the opportunity to try and bring aspects of therapy into the regime. The public appetite for the rehabilitation of offenders had shifted and prison was increasingly seen as an opportunity for punishment and retribution; an opportunity for politicians to maintain that they were going to get justice for victims by being 'tough on crime'.

Within the prison service, there was a general acceptance that the units had been successful in helping staff to manage disruptive prisoners and so, as is often the case, I gained promotion and was asked to take over prison officer and operational training for England and Wales in 1994. This offer came in the wake of two very high-profile escapes – an area in which the special units' record was spotless.

September 1994 saw the escapes of six Category A prisoners, five of whom were members of the Provisional Irish Republican army (PIRA), from HMP Whitemoor – where I had interviewed Nilsen just a few years earlier. That the prisoners escaped from the supposed confines of a special secure unit – a 'prison within the prison' – was especially damaging. They had managed to smuggle two pistols and associated ammunition into the prison and then made their way to the prison's perimeter fence with a 30-foot rope ladder, metal clamping devices, support poles, bolt croppers and a torch. A prison officer was shot in attempting to thwart the escape. After the escapes, a former civil servant described Michael Howard as, 'Running around like a headless chicken, apparently making policy on the basis of whatever was in that afternoon's *Evening Standard* editorial.' Never an effective way to instigate lasting and effective policy.

But there was more embarrassment to come. Just four months later, in January 1995, three more Category A prisoners, two of whom had been convicted of murder, escaped from HMP Parkhurst on the Isle of Wight. Their plan had been to steal a light aircraft after they had scaled the prison's wall, but this had been foiled and they remained at large on the island for six days. The damage had been done and created the same panic in the Home Office that the escapes of the Great Train Robbers and George Blake had in the 1960s, adding still further to the climate of protectionism surrounding attitudes towards the prison service.

It was the mid-1990s and in between these escapes and Tony Blair's election, I was tasked with training staff on the basis of what had become the new mantra for the prison service – 'security, security, security'. Despite being been promoted from Woodhill into this exciting new role I was also uneasy. I relished the opportunity to train new recruits but what was I training them to do? Gone were hopes that something positive could be done with the people we were locking up; our main objective was to focus our efforts on ensuring that they *stayed* locked up. My role was to implement the prison service's response to the new training requirements that were needed to guarantee 'security, security, security'. I spent my week driving between my offices in the two Prison Service Training Colleges in Rugby and Wakefield.

Given how often I was on the road, the work took me away not only from the type of interaction with prisoners that I favoured, but more practically from my family. We had a new baby too – a sister for our son. I started to wake up to the fact that this was not what I had joined the prison service to do. Increasingly I was representing the penal system and making it work with all of its flaws, rather than challenging how it went about its business. Underneath all my training the young, hopeful PhD student still wanted to make effective change, not cover up for the failings of politicians.

However, it was a trip to Albania, on behalf of the Council of Europe, that prompted my resignation.

I had been asked among other experts to help advise the newly democratically elected Albanian government of Sali

Berisha. Specifically, the Council of Europe wanted Albania's prisons to reflect democratic values, rather than those which had characterised imprisonment under the long, Maoist-inspired dictatorship of Enver Hoxha. Hoxha had been ruthless in his purge of any opposition to his rule. Prison and capital punishment had been central to his success in staying in power for over forty years.

I have to say that I wasn't expecting much from Albania at the time and my first glimpse of Tirana, the capital, was shocking. I initially thought that I was witnessing scores of dead children lying in the roads, until I realised that they were begging. By lying in the streets they hoped to stop any cars that might want to pass. If they were successful, they'd jump up and approach the driver hoping to get money. That was all right in theory but in practice the price of life in Tirana was cheap, and most of the people who owned cars were in too much of a hurry to bother too much about child beggars. Some didn't even bother to slow down.

Alongside the extreme poverty, there had been weeks of rioting in protest against a pyramid selling scam that had made some very poor people even poorer; democracy, which had only recently been re-established, was on a very slippery slope back towards anarchy; and the basic necessities of life, such as food and even water were either scarce and only available to the rich, or in the case of water, most probably contaminated. The water contamination meant that I had to brush my teeth in bottled water and I had to keep my eyes and mouth shut when I took a shower. This in itself was discomfiting but the visible scars of absolute poverty have left an indelible impression on me. I will never forget walking in the streets, being followed by both the Shik – Albania's secret police – but also by scores of pleading children hoping for money.

Nor can I forget looking out of my hotel window at the people looking in at me. I saw pain, disease, fear and envy, but what did they see? A chance? Or perhaps just hope that there might be some way out of the misery of their existence. I represented 'the West', whose images dominated the nascent skyline of the city in the form of advertising and which seemed to promise so much, or at least something better.

And yet something extraordinary happened when I visited Albania's prisons – I realised that they were better than ours.

Here's the thing about dictatorships. One day you might be the dictator's favourite, the next he will have fallen out with you for some reason and have had you banged up in the nearest jail. Albania's prisons might have been starved of resources but the brutal, political reality of life outside meant that there was no stigma attached to being sent to jail. There was a fluidity between the outside and what happened inside, which ensured that imprisonment was normalised.

Albania's prisons had schemes where inmates were employed in local shops and factories; flexible visiting arrangements, with families able to bring in food and spend most of the day with their loved ones; and, for those who couldn't read or write, compulsory education for several hours a day. The atmosphere inside was also much more pleasant, largely because the low-level, constant harassment that seemed to characterise many English prisons was largely absent. And yet I was supposed to come in and teach them the mantra 'security, security, security'!

And that was the final straw for my career within the prison service. Nearly fifteen years after my lunch with John McCarthy, I reached the same conclusion that he had. My resignation led to some supportive headlines in the *Observer* and later I would give an interview to Fergal Keane for his Radio 4 series *Resigning Issues* – I had been recommended to him as an interviewee by Ian Dunbar, my former governor at HMP Wormwood Scrubs.

I left the prison service soon after my arrival back in the UK and returned to academia, taking up my post at Birmingham City University in 1997. However, I still wanted to make a difference about what happened in our prisons. The only way I could do this was to continue my involvement with prison reform through various charities, especially New Bridge, The Friends of Grendon and The Howard League for Penal Reform. Indeed, these three charities were and still are particularly important in allowing me to continue to advocate for the types of reforms that I want to see in our prisons and in our public policy approach to imprisonment.

Only this time I was advocating from outside, rather than as an insider.

Chapter Five

Profiling Violent Men

'The range of opinions offered was staggering.
Some thought that it was the work of Al Qaeda
operatives. Others considered it a homage to
the 'Son of Sam' murders, to mark their twenty-
five-year anniversary. An even more exotic
suggestion was that it was a re-enactment
of a storyline in the television programme
Homicide. Computer nerds, addicted to shoot-
'em-up video games were also blamed. And,
inevitably, the Devil got in on the act. "This
has something to do with a satanic ritual" said
"holistic adviser" Zorel. "If you look at the map
and connect the dots, it looks like a cross upside
down, but people aren't realising it, not even
the police."'

Professor David Canter, describing
the Washington sniper case

Even if my formal work within prisons had ended, that didn't
mean to say that I had stopped working with violent men,
who would kill in all sorts of different circumstances. Some of
that work came out of contacts I'd made while in the prison

service. Given the types of offenders that we locked up in the special units, it was no surprise that detectives from various police forces were regular visitors. They would make the journey to the prison from all over the country in the hope of being able to interview one or other of our clientele and, through discussion with them, clear up some unsolved cold case.

Fat chance.

If the detectives even got as far as convincing the offender to come to the interview room, it was usually pretty obvious that the answers to any questions they had asked would be deliberately evasive and merely offered to lead the police a merry dance.

In time, I got to know one Detective Chief Inspector (DCI) pretty well, largely because we discovered that we both supported Northampton Saints. Over a cup of tea, we started to discuss the Saints and then the prisoner that he was about to interview for the third time. The first two interviews had not gone well. I suggested my own method that he might find more helpful in getting this prisoner to talk, based on my knowledge of him and how he had reacted to other members of staff, who seemed to be able to engage him in conversation. In fact, this different approach about how to discuss the crimes that offenders have committed, or are suspected of having committed, has become an enduring legacy of my experience of working with violent men. For good or for ill, my method is predicated on being able to suspend judgement about what the offender might have done and be willing to tell you about and so helps to create a dialogue – almost an intimacy – which, in turn, allows new information to emerge.

After he left, I thought no more about what we had discussed. My duties that day took me to another part of Woodhill but, later that evening, I was surprised to receive a phone call from the DCI. The approach that I had suggested had worked to the extent that the prisoner had been far more forthcoming than usual, although he still hadn't provided any specific information that might lead to an arrest. I was about to apologise for wasting the DCI's time, when he asked me if I would be willing to help to advise on a different case that he was currently investigating. It was all very informal, but this case was to be my entrée into the strange world of 'offender profiling'.

In the course of my career, I have constructed offender profiles in four live cases for the police, all in the early 1990s and at a time when I was still working directly with serious and violent offenders. Sadly, and unlike what is seen in most fictional cases of offender profiling, I can't pretend that constructing these profiles was a very successful experience. While in each of these incidences the offender was eventually caught, I'm still not at all convinced that my profile had any part to play in their detection. In fact, in at least two of these cases, I was completely wrong and suggested personal characteristics that simply did not fit with the reality of the perpetrator, after he had been arrested. And that, after all, is what is at the heart of the first wave of profiling that originated in the USA: the belief that you can tell something about the offender's characteristics, based on how the offence was committed, what happened to the victim and how, in the case of murder, the body may have been disposed of after death.

Profiling was pioneered by the FBI, who wanted to find a practical way of using the forensic information they were able to generate from crime scenes, to see if they could suggest something of the type of offender who had committed the offence from that evidence. So, in part using their collective experience of investigating multiple murder and sexual assaults, and through carrying out extensive interviews with thirty-six convicted murderers or serial killers, they began to assert that, in cases of serial rape or murder, the personality of an offender could be gleaned from a consideration of the following five areas:

the crime scene; the nature of the attacks themselves; forensic evidence; a medical examination of the victim; and victim characteristics. Above all, their central argument was that crime scenes and the people who created them were going to be either 'organised' or 'disorganised'.

The interviews which the FBI conducted have been fictionalised in the Netflix series *Mindhunter* and at the start of each episode in Season 1 is a dramatisation of a seemingly unconnected event involving a white, middle-aged man in Kansas. This is in fact a dramatisation of the activities of a serial killer called Dennis Rader and it was Rader who was to spectacularly dent this first wave of FBI profiling, undermining everything that had become accepted as fact when dealing with a serial killer. Rader's is an extraordinary case and when the opportunity to study him for a Channel 5 documentary arrived in 2015, I jumped at the chance.

The start of my trip was ominous. As I entered the lift of my hotel in Wichita, Kansas, two other people joined me. Both were dressed from head to toe in furry animal costumes although, luckily for me, despite being completely encased, they both spoke English.

I pretended not to notice how they were dressed. As all children are told, it's rude to stare.

'Which floor?' asked the largest who was dressed as, I think, a biker mouse.

'Eighth please,' I replied, and we then stood in total silence waiting for the doors to close, before heading north. The biker mouse's companion seemed to be a stoat, although it was hard to tell given that most of his fur was acid green. All I knew was that no trace of human being pierced either of their costumes.

Later I'd discover that there was a 'furry' convention booked into my hotel and so my days in Wichita would start and end with about a hundred people dressed as animals or, more exotically, as pseudo-animals, milling around drinking coffee in the morning, or beer at night. Even at the time, this seemed like a weirdly perfect motif for the blurred line between normality and oddness that had brought me to Kansas and one which resonated with the man that I had come to study.

My interest in Rader, who dubbed himself 'BTK' – bind, torture and kill – goes back a long way, partly because he is almost the perfect embodiment of both a serial killer and a psychopath. A church-going, Scout-leading, family man, he also had a life-long interest in bondage and sadism, which he indiscriminately inflicted on the ten people he murdered between 1974 and 1991, although he wasn't actually arrested until 2005.

Like my furry friends in the lift, Rader too was disguised, only in his case it was as a normal human. It was a disguise that he had almost perfected, even helping the police after he had been employed as a local compliance officer.

Little about Rader fits the 'typical' pattern of a serial killer. Most serial killers, for example, start small; they will have had a history of violent fantasies which will only very slowly get turned into reality. They usually begin by assaulting people and then, bit by bit, as their fantasies take over and become more demanding, they start to kill. Not Rader. His first victims were an entire family – the Oteros – whom he obliterated in January 1974.

Even during this first kill of Joseph Otero, his wife Julie, and Josephine and Joey, their eleven- and seven-year-old children, he was in almost total control of the crime scene. Normally we expect the serial killer's first kill to be somewhat botched and therefore a source of potential evidence. Not so for the Oteros, where Rader showed great ingenuity and complete control. He secured Joseph and Julie's compliance to the extent that they allowed him to tie them up, promising them that he just wanted their car and some money and then he would be on his way. Perhaps Joseph and Julie thought that if they didn't resist

Rader might leave more quickly, or at least not harm their two youngest children.

But Rader hadn't come for a car, or even for the Oteros' money: he'd come for Josephine. Josephine died slowly, bound in the basement of her home, with Rader watching her. His semen was later found on her leg. Rader liked to watch, to observe. No doubt that was also how he had first spotted Josephine whilst driving around in his car; fantasising about the moment that he could have power over her. The detectives who showed me the Otero crime scene photographs even pointed out that there were marks on the bedroom carpet where Rader had pulled up a chair to sit and watch Josephine's younger brother Joey struggle for his last breath.

'Geographically stable', as opposed to 'transient' serial killers, are usually caught quite quickly but, despite the fact that Rader killed entirely within Wichita and its environs, he escaped justice for over thirty years. He also took long breaks between his murders: there were almost eight years between his murder of Nancy Fox in 1977, which he described as his 'perfect hit', and Marine Hedge, his next victim, in 1985. Most of Rader's victims were adult women but he was also indiscriminate, killing an adult man as well as children.

Serial killers aren't supposed to stop killing until they are caught or die. Not Rader; he could turn his killing activities on or off again. This too is unusual.

We have come to accept the FBI idea that, for the serial killer, killing becomes a compulsion, propelling the serial killer ever onwards to more victims and often in increasingly bizarre circumstances. This might make it appear that they want to be caught. Nothing can be further from the truth, though by the time that justice finally catches up with them, they have grown so divorced from reality that they often don't realise how strange their behaviour has become. Sometimes this behaviour and the escalation of that behaviour is simply a response to their fantasies developing, as they first experience and then begin to become more skilled at killing. However, over time they also start to take more risks and can often change their *modus operandi* – the way that they kill – because they believe that it is no longer going to deliver what they want to achieve, or they have simply become better killers.

Rader regularly communicated with the police about his killings and also with a local newspaper called *The Wichita Eagle*. It was he himself who coined the name 'BTK'. He left a letter in an engineering book at Wichita Public Library in October 1974, in which he confessed to killing the Otero family, and sent a further letter to a local TV station four years later, again claiming responsibility for murdering the Oteros and three more victims: Kathryn Bright, Shirley Vian and Nancy Fox. In this second letter he demanded media attention. Communication in this way allows the killer to feel powerful; to be in charge; to be dominant. But then the communication stopped, reflecting a degree of self-control, rather than the impulsive fantasies of his kills. Wichita secretly hoped that BTK had gone away – that he had died, or been incarcerated for other crimes.

It was in 2004 that Rader got back in touch with the police, some thirteen years after his final murder of Dolores Davis in January 1991. He was prompted to do so because he was worried that, in his thirtieth anniversary killing year, others were being given credit for the BTK murders. Rader was less than pleased. His displeasure proved to be a mistake because the police were soon able to identify the location of the computer that he was using to write to them from – one in the Lutheran church where Rader was President.

During my time in Wichita, I drove to all the key locations and deposition sites and talked with the police, court staff and journalists who worked the case, as well as with Rader's former neighbours. I would later call this type of research a 'criminolog-ical autopsy'. From this work I could tell that Rader was almost the 'perfect' psychopath. Think of psychopathy as a personality disorder defined by a cluster of traits centred around three dif-ferent factors which, over time, have become ingrained as beliefs and behaviours.

First is their inter-personal style, which allows the psycho-path to be glib, grandiose, dishonest and manipulative; they are always arrogant and deceitful in their day-to-day dealings. Second, as far as their behaviour is concerned, psychopaths will be sensation-seeking, impulsive, reckless to the point of stupid-ity – seemingly having no thought for their own safety. Finally, psychopaths will have defective emotional responses so that they lack remorse for their manipulative, reckless behaviours and find it impossible to truly understand why it is that you might actually find their behaviour wrong. In short, they just don't get it; they operate in a totally different moral universe.

Rader could often be reckless in how he went about his mur-ders, despite seemingly planning them with care. For example, he later admitted that he was surprised to find Joseph Otero still at home during this first murder; he left semen at the Otero crime scene; and he had not expected the brother of his next victim, Kathryn Bright, to be accompanying her when she arrived home in April 1974. He shot Kevin – Kathryn's brother – but he managed to escape.

Rader was manipulative of his immediate family and of his community; arrogant in his demand for attention; grandiose in his belief that he would not be caught; and convinced that he had somehow befriended the police officer assigned to catch him. You can judge all of this for yourself. Rader's trial was tel-evised and so you can still see him in all his arrogant pomp on YouTube and view his jaw-dropping and insensitive performance in front of the judge and the families of his victims. He was at last publicly living the life less ordinary that he had always craved and which he could only previously achieve in private when he killed.

Yet, according to his son, Rader was also a 'perfect father' and Paula Rader described her husband to the police as 'a good man, a great father. He would never hurt anyone.' Indeed, that was the face that Rader liked to present to the community, to the Scouts in his troop and to the congregation of the church that he attended. Psychopaths like Rader often hide in plain sight and some disguises are just too difficult to see through, until it's too late.

In October 1984, two detectives from Wichita consulted FBI agents John Douglas, one of the originators of this first wave of offender profiling, Roy Hazlewood and Ron Walker at FBI Headquarters in Virginia about the case. After the Wichita detectives had taken the FBI agents through the case, the latter 'climbed into the head' of BTK and offered their opinion as to the type of person who was committing these crimes. As Douglas explains in his account of the case:

> We were going to toss out ideas about what sort of person might be responsible for those seven unsolved murders in Kansas, how police might track him down, and ways they could get him to crack once they had a possible suspect ... in many ways, our goal here felt similar to what musicians do when they get together and jam[.] The objective of the session was to keep moving forward until we ran out of juice, until we were tapped out. It was up to the two detectives from Wichita to take notes, jotting down elements they found helpful.

Douglas kicked off the session by suggesting that BTK was mid- to late-thirties, divorced, lower middle class and living in rented accommodation. Hazlewood thought that he would be middle class and articulate. Walker suggested that as BTK had never engaged in any sexual penetration, he would be sexually inadequate and immature, whereas Hazlewood thought that BTK would be a 'sexual bondage practitioner' and 'heavily into masturbation'. As a result, suggested Hazlewood, 'women who have had sex with this guy would describe him as aloof, uninvolved, the type who is more interested in her servicing him than the other way around'. Douglas, too, believed that BTK would have 'racked up a bit of sexual experience' and that his partners would be either 'many years younger, very naive, or much older and depend on him as their meal ticket'.

According to Walker, he would be a 'lone-wolf type of personality' although he could function in social settings but only 'on the surface' – a conclusion with which Douglas agreed, and which, for him, suggested that BTK wouldn't stay at any one job for any length of time because he wouldn't like people to have power over him. As such, he would not be a 'team player'.

Hazlewood thought that he would be a 'now person' who wanted instant gratification.

His IQ would be somewhere between 105 and 145. All three thought that he might have some connections to the military (unsurprising given military drafts for Korea and Vietnam for men in BTK's suggested age range) and Douglas suggested that he would drive a 'nondescript type of car – perhaps a sedan'. They also all thought that he would collect detective stories and be interested in law enforcement.

Finally, Douglas suggested that 'This guy isn't mental ... but he is crazy like a fox'.

So, after six hours, the FBI handed the Wichita detectives a blueprint for their investigation and, as Malcolm Gladwell ironically put it in *Dangerous Minds: Criminal Profiling Made Easy*, what they had to do was:

Look for an American male with a possible connection to the military. His IQ will be above 105. He will like to masturbate, and will be aloof and selfish in bed. He will drive a decent car. He will be a 'now' person. He won't be comfortable with women. But he may have women friends. He will be a lone wolf. But he will be able to function in social settings ... he will be either, never married, divorced or married, and if he is married his wife will be younger or older. He may or may not live in a rental, and might be lower class, upper lower class, lower middle class or middle class. And he will be crazy like a fox, as opposed to being mental.

In any event, Dennis Rader was a pillar of his local community; a happily married family man with two children; the president of his local Lutheran church, a Scout leader; and a reliable employee of the Sedgwick County animal services division. BTK, in other words, came nowhere near to what Douglas and his colleagues were suggesting.

Of course, when I constructed my own, tentative profiles I knew nothing of BTK and had simply accepted much of the first wave of FBI profiling on trust. However, I knew that I was uncomfortable with the approach, especially as my own interviews with Dennis Nilsen and other murderers had suggested to me that very little of what they said could be relied upon. Why therefore build an understanding of what they might do based on what they were prepared to reveal in interview? Thankfully, the discipline of offender profiling has developed from these American origins and in the UK has become much more scientifically robust. Some indication of these different approaches can be gleaned from what offender profiling is called in this country. For some it is 'crime scene analysis', for others 'psychological profiling' or 'investigative psychology'.

Whatever it is called, the British approach to offender

profiling has been keen to emphasise its academic, rather than law enforcement roots, and, above all else, its scientific robustness. Profilers in this country tend to work in applied settings such as secure hospitals, prisons or regional secure units, rather than within police stations. This type of professional background means that they have had long careers spent working with the types of offenders who will repeatedly kill. Their knowledge does not come from one-off interviews. So too, whilst the FBI tended to produce popular books about their offending profiling work, British profilers will typically publish their research in peer reviewed, academic journals. Often this work is filled with pages of statistical appendices, which will be harnessed to prove – or otherwise – the author's central hypothesis. The results would be largely impenetrable to someone who did not have a good grasp of statistical analysis. My own work about serial murder has appeared in journals such as *The Journal of Offender Profiling and Investigative Psychology, Criminal Psychology, European Journal of Criminology, The Journal of Forensic Psychiatry and Psychology* and *Crime Media Culture.*

Another way of thinking about all of this is to see the British approach to profiling as being 'bottom up' – built on evidence that emerges from the crime scene and from the subsequent investigation. On the other hand, the FBI approach is a 'top down' method, with Douglas and his peers offering local police the fruits of their wisdom.

The FBI's central finding was that crime scenes and therefore the people who have created those scenes are either 'organised' or 'disorganised'. This categorisation is worth unpacking. An 'organised' offender is one who uses a great deal of logic and planning, such as wearing gloves, or bringing a rope or handcuffs to incapacitate the victim. The organised offender is very much in control of the crime scene and, as such, few, if any, clues are left. It is also suggested that 'organised' offenders have a specific personality type. They will typically be intelligent, sexually active and competent, and are likely to have a partner. They will have skilled or semi-skilled jobs, and to all intents and purposes will appear 'normal'. It is also suggested that organised offenders follow reports of their crimes in the news and that they are often impelled to commit crime as a result of anger and frustration in their personal lives.

On the other hand 'disorganised' offenders do not plan their offending. Their crimes are sudden and opportunistic and, as such, the offender will use whatever comes to hand to help him commit his offence. For example, he will tie his victim up using her scarf or underwear; he will attack by using weapons he finds in the home or the vicinity of the offence. There is little attempt to conceal evidence, and often the victim's body is simply abandoned, rather than hidden. More than this, the 'disorganised' offender is said to live alone, or at home with his parents, and usually offends within his local area. He will be socially and sexually immature and will often have a history of mental illness. Finally, it is suggested that this type of offender commits his crimes while being frightened or confused.

These are the basic principles behind the descriptions 'organised' or 'disorganised'. Are they of any assistance when looking at crime scenes, or in considering more generally a linked series of crimes? I know that they helped me to form some broad suggestions in 2006, when a series of sex workers were killed in Ipswich.

At the end of October 2006, nineteen-year-old Tania Nicol went missing from the red-light area of Ipswich. A public appeal was quickly issued to the media asking for help to find the missing teenager. A few days later Kerry Nicol, Tania's mother, gave an interview to the press asking for anyone with information about her daughter's whereabouts to come forward, and leaflets were handed out on the bus that many believed Tania might have taken to meet with her clients in the red-light district of the town.

Just a few weeks later, in mid-November, Gemma Adams was reported as missing by her partner and the police launched a further appeal for information. At the local Ipswich and Norwich derby football match a few days later, the police handed out leaflets to the fans, appealing for help to find the missing girls. Ipswich's football stadium is in Portman Road which, along with Handford Road and London Road, makes up the heart of the red-light area of the town.

Nearly two weeks later, a water bailiff found a body lying face down in Belstead Brook as he went about clearing debris from the water, after a bout of heavy rain had caused flooding. The following day the body was formally identified as being that of Gemma Adams. That same day, Anneli Alderton disappeared and subsequently a murder inquiry was formally launched.

Three days later a second body was found by police divers at Copdock Mill and the following day it was confirmed that this was the body of Tania Nicol. The police admitted that there were 'obvious similarities' between the two bodies that had been found.

In mid-December the police announced that they were concerned about the disappearances of two other missing women – Annette Nicholls and Paula Clennell. The latter had even given an interview to the press after the first disappearances, saying that she understood all the dangers involved but that she was still going back out onto the streets to make money. The Assistant Chief Constable Jacqui Cheer warned all sex workers to stay off the streets. The following day police found two further bodies near the village of Levington, some five miles south of Ipswich, and it was announced that these were the bodies of Nicholls and Clennell.

On Tuesday 19 December police arrested Steve Wright. Wright lived in London Road with his partner and he was soon charged on 21 December with the murder of all five women.

Wright appeared in Ipswich Crown Court on 21 March 2007, where he pleaded 'not guilty' and his trial began.

These basic details of the case omit one crucial detail – the huge press interest in what was unfolding in Ipswich. Given the relatively short time span of events – just six weeks – the story grew very quickly from something of regional interest, to one which had national and international appeal. There was a serial killer active in the streets of Ipswich! It was almost as if the stories that people had got used to consuming as fiction had become fact.

I was commissioned by Sky News to work with their broadcast journalist Paul Harrison on the story, although initially I had been very reluctant to take on the job. I especially didn't want the serial killer to take centre stage in the story, with his victims merely being used as props to bolster his infamy. What I said I wanted was greater understanding for the victims and the dangers that they faced. Frankly, I had to be convinced by Paul that the story would be taken seriously by putting the disappearances of the women into the broader context of the routine violence experienced by sex workers and not sensationalised. In retrospect, given how quickly events unfolded, with women disappearing every few days and then their bodies being found, I don't see how it could not have been sensationalised. It really was sensational.

Paul had been the first national broadcast journalist to report from Ipswich on Friday 8 December, when police had found Tania's body at Copdock Mill, and two days later he and I made our first broadcast together on the case. By that stage I had been able to visit the sites where the first two bodies had been disposed of and get to know something of the area. This is the transcript from that very first broadcast.

PAUL HARRISON [PH]: Professor David Wilson, you've
    been to both locations, what are your impressions?

DAVID WILSON [DW]: There is a pattern emerging, it seems to me. Because I have been able to visit the disposal sites I would say first this is someone who has a good knowledge of the highways and byways. This is someone who feels quite confident about where he can stop his car to dispose of a body. And remember, because the first body was discovered accidentally, this is someone who has taken great care in terms of disposing of that body. So he's confident and organised. What we're seeing is an organised killer. In other words he goes through a great deal of planning. He carefully selects his victims; he finds a place to incapacitate them; and then, once he's killed them, he finds a way of disposing of them, so their bodies won't be discovered unless by accident. There's something else. He knows this area which either implies he lives here, has lived here, or works in this area. But for me the overwhelming factor is that nobody emerges as a double murderer as if by magic, or chance – this is obviously a pattern in his past. He probably used prostitutes in the past; he's undoubtedly hurt prostitutes in the past, and I would suggest that he's killed prostitutes in the past too.

PH: Looking at the bodies that have been found, there are similarities – most obviously, both naked. The police have also stated that there are no marks on the bodies to indicate a cause of death. Does that strike you as strange?

DW: Don't forget, we may not be being told all the details. We don't know if there was any forensic evidence at the scenes. Obviously placing the bodies in water is an example of how planned the disposal was. If I was in the police's position, I would be trying to discover

which punters used prostitutes in this area and gather
as much CCTV evidence as possible. I know people
keep using the word 'prostitute', but that tends to
stop the public from coming forward because the
term implies they deserved it – they asked for it; they
shouldn't have been behaving in this way. So the
police should be getting as much information from the
public as possible and from the other girls in the red-
light district.

PH: How common is this?

DW: There have been sixty murders of prostitutes in
England and Wales in the past ten years and only
sixteen arrests, so that gives you some idea of the scale
that we are talking about.

This first broadcast revealed a number of themes that I continued
to use throughout my time in Ipswich: the killer's obvious knowledge of the road network in the town and surrounding areas,
therefore the strong possibility that he was likely to live and work
in Ipswich; he would be a plausible punter and would have used
sex workers in the past. This latter theme suggested to me that it
was likely that some of the women selling sexual services in the
town would know his identity and that he had probably harmed
or killed sex workers prior to the incidents in Ipswich.

In later broadcasts I also queried why the killings had started
to happen at that time: had something happened in his domestic
or working life to trigger this wave of murders, or had he perhaps
just been released from prison? I thought that he was likely to
already be known to the police. More controversially, there were
a number of unsolved murders of sex workers in Norwich, about
forty miles from Ipswich, and I insisted that some of those murders appeared to be similar to the murders that were now taking
place. I even named some of the women who had been killed in

Norwich and, in particular, two young women called Michelle Bettles and Natalie Pearman.

I made these observations based not only on my familiarity with some of the original principles that lay behind the 'organised vs disorganised' findings suggested by the FBI but also on my experiences of working with violent offenders.

Here are some of the facts that influenced my thinking.

The killer had placed the bodies of his first two victims in water and this to me seemed like classic organised behaviour, given that it would destroy any forensic evidence. Indeed, the body of Gemma Adams had only been found because it had rained so hard that Belstead Brook had burst its banks and the water bailiff had been forced to unblock some of the debris that had floated into the river. In other words, it had been an accident that she had been found at all.

Was Adams the killer's first or second victim? I was always interested in discovering more about the first murder, which I presumed had been Tania Nicol's. Once again it pays to remember that one of the crucial developments in our understanding of serial murder is the importance of the first murder. This was one of the reasons that I suspected the killer had killed before. His disposal of the body of Tania Nicol was just too accomplished for someone killing for the first time. This looked to me to be the beginning of a new pattern of killings, not to killing in general.

The killer knew where he could stop his car and dispose of a body through his knowledge of the road network, which implied that he lived or worked in the area. The fact that he could drive also suggested that he was mentally competent and that he was plausible enough as a punter for a sex worker to get into his car without feeling threatened. She would be comfortable in his presence, which also explained why there were no signs of a struggle.

As time went on, there were later elements of his *modus operandi* which seemed to be disorganised, to the extent that I worried that the killer was almost reacting to what was being said in the media. Paul and I agreed that I'd better self-censor much more carefully what I was arguing, how I analysed what was unfolding and to what extent this might indicate the characteristics and background of the likely perpetrator.

It was gratifying when I was later told by one of the senior detectives working on the case how uncannily accurate my observations had been and how they corresponded with the views of the offender profiler that the Suffolk police had commissioned.

The police might have been impressed by what I was saying but members of the public still had to be convinced.

Given that my name was being used in the media and my email and telephone numbers at the university are freely available on the internet, I was inundated by members of the public offering me their hypotheses, such as:

Have you considered that the killer may be a woman who has been infected by some sexually transmitted disease that her husband caught while visiting a prostitute?

I think that you've got this right Professor Wilson, when you talk about the importance of the roads to this killer. And don't forget that there are ports at the end of the A12 and the A14 – Felixstowe and Harwich. I think that is significant for the killer must be a foreigner as I just can't see an Englishman doing this.

Is the fact that the first two bodies were found in water of significance? Is the killer trying to cleanse these women of their sins? I think that he is religious, and in the same way that Ian Huntley was never off the TV in Soham and he proved to be the killer of Holly and Jessica, don't you think that it is interesting that [names a cleric who had been regularly inter-viewed] is never far from a microphone?

Perhaps the killer still lives at home with his mother? He's probably very repressed because his mother hates sex and so he kills these young girls to win her approval.

Do you think that the KGB might be behind this? Ever since these bodies have been found Litvinenko has been taken off the front pages of our newspapers. [Alexander Litvinenko was a former KGB officer living in London who died on 26 November 2006, having been poisoned.]

I have no doubt that the people sending these emails were sincere in their wish to see the killer brought to justice. From my perspective, there are a number of themes that seem to dominate their contents and which in turn help us to gain an insight into what people imagine the perpetrators of murder and serial murder are like and the circumstances in which they will come to kill.

First is an underlying assumption about sex generally and sex work specifically. Sex work is sinful and needs to be cleansed. The correspondents did not speak about sex workers but instead about prostitutes. Prostitutes carried diseases which infected husbands, although there was no acknowledgement that these husbands were also willing clients of the sex workers. The first email suggests that the killer is a vengeful wife of one such hus-band. Why did this wife not attack the husband, I was tempted to ask? More generally it seemed that only men were allowed to be sexual. Women, in the shape of the mother who disapproves of sex and represses her son, play a non-sexual role as sex is viewed as only being part of the culture of men.

Second is the idea that the killer must be some type of 'other'.

He is certainly not going to be from the local community. He has to be a foreigner as, in the words of one of the above, 'I can't see an Englishman doing this'. So, he will come into the community from somewhere else and then disappear once he has murdered. There is even the beginning of a conspiracy theory being suggested here, with Russian agents committing the murders so as to prevent Vladimir Putin's name from being dragged through the mud. Serial killers have to be framed as alien 'others', rather than everyday members of the community.

Finally the emails suggested a lack of knowledge about the realities of murder and serial murder, as opposed to media presentations of serial murder. It was statistically unlikely that the killer would be a woman and nor did there seem to be too much awareness of Peter Sutcliffe – the Englishman better known as The Yorkshire Ripper who targeted sex workers in the 1970s and 1980s.

I would go further than this.

What seemed to drive these hypotheses was the love of a 'whodunnit', with a twist in the tale for added excitement. The serial killer was going to be the cleric, rather than someone known to the police through his previous offending history. It was almost as if my correspondents imagined that a serial killer could emerge overnight, fully formed, and suddenly, frighteningly and unexpectedly kill, despite having no history of violence or offending behaviour.

In any event, I hope that my correspondents weren't too disappointed. Wright would eventually be found guilty of the murders of all five women in 2008 and the following day he was sentenced to life imprisonment with a whole life tariff. In other words, he will never be released from prison.

I will leave it for you to judge if my profile fitted Steve Wright – a local man, living in the heart of the red-light district in the town. He was employed as a fork-lift truck driver and so had to use the back roads to get to and from his workplace. He was well known to the sex workers in the town and had been a regular customer of several, especially when his partner was working nights. He'd also lived and worked in Norwich, most notably as landlord of the Ferry Boat Inn which was at the centre of Norwich's red-light district and from where Natalie Pearman had disappeared.

Later, a number of sex workers in Ipswich and Norwich would describe to me how they did not like to have Wright as a customer, as he was often strange and difficult. A number described how he would pick them up dressed in a PVC skirt, wearing a woman's black wig.

However, Wright was caught not as a result of my profile, or indeed anyone else's, but simply because his DNA had been kept on the national DNA database. Wright had been arrested and convicted of stealing £84 from his employer in 2001. As soon as the police were able to find DNA from the killer on the bodies of some of the victims, they were able to catch their man.

As the police made abundantly clear at almost every press conference they gave, they were using a 'variety of experts' in helping them to catch Wright. Some of these experts worked for the Forensic Science Service (FSS), an executive agency of the Home Office, who were called in to help at the very early stages of the investigation. The FSS could offer assistance not just in relation to DNA, but also regarding firearms, clothing fibres, bite marks, footprints and blood spatter patterns.

As all of this suggests, the science that drives murder investigations has overtaken the intuitive art of offender profiling.

Does that mean there is no place for intuition, or what I tend to call, based on my training as an historian, 'imaginative leaps', into the crime scenes? I hope not.

What is clear is that no offender profile, no matter how it is arrived at, can identify a specific individual as the culprit in any given case. What profiles can do is suggest specific lines of enquiry; where the focus of the investigation might be concentrated; and demographic parameters for likely suspects, which should not be so broad as to make them meaningless.

I still maintain that a careful analysis of how an offender behaves when committing his crimes does allow inferences to be drawn as to their likely personal characteristics. Organised and disorganised do not separate like oil and water and, like other experts in the field, I believe that they should be seen as a continuum. That said, as concepts they still allow us to begin to make sense of what has happened and what sort of person might be responsible. However, no offender profile can ever be certain that 'X' is the perpetrator. A stubborn belief that they can has been partly created by the media and by the way that profiling and profilers have been presented and dramatised which, in turn, has helped to shape and influence the public's understanding of how murders are investigated.

The media's influence in these matters has been brought home to me in various ways, not least through my work at Birmingham City University.

Despite the staggering costs now involved, more and more young people want to come to university, and increasingly they want to study criminology, often in conjunction with psychology. These students will regularly describe to me the fascination that they have with violent crime, murder and serial murder, and many claim that they want to use their degree after they graduate to work with violent offenders. A persistent number are desperate to become offender profilers.

My own university now attracts two thousand applications a year – mostly from women – for just a hundred undergraduate places.

It seems ironic to question why this should be so. After all, I am myself still interested in what drives some people to commit crime and, of course, all these young people who apply to study criminology create a working environment that benefits me and also my colleagues. In that respect, I am very pleased that they do apply and in increasing numbers. However, that doesn't mean that I don't want to question why large numbers of people, and especially women, are so fascinated by violent offenders and serial killers that they would want to study and work with them. What is it about the gruesome crimes committed by serial killers that grips their imagination? We know that what they do is appalling but, somehow, some people don't want to – metaphorically – look away from what it is that they have done.

Most immediately, we might want to remember that when most people read about serial killers, watch programmes about them or study them, there is a safe boundary between the reader, viewer or student and the serial killers that they are learning about. In other words, there is a protective frame, so that any real danger is effectively non-existent. This interest is like watching a horror movie – it is frightening, but as you know it's not real you can enjoy the action on the screen.

Note these two different emotions – fear and enjoyment. We describe this ability of people to be able to take pleasure from two different emotions at the same time as 'coactivation' – something that we have all witnessed when cars slow down to get a better view of an accident on the other side of the motorway. I slow down too but I also know that when I am working with people who have killed, or with the families of their victims, I don't experience enjoyment, or even fear. Often I am simply depressed and saddened.

Yet another reason to explain the public's fascination with serial killers might be that we regard someone who kills repeatedly over time as mysterious and, as humans, we have a deep in-built need to solve mysteries. Someone who repeatedly kills appears bizarre to us and not quite human. Even if most of us have said in the heat of the moment 'I could kill you', thankfully we don't and therefore someone who repeatedly does is at the extreme limits of our human existence. Does being at that extreme make the serial killer a pariah? Or perhaps, for some, it serves to make serial killing seem almost aspirational. However, whichever way you look at it, we need to explain this murderous behaviour, which in turn allows us to feel that we can control – or at least predict – when this type of behaviour might occur again. Looked at from this perspective, studying violent crime, murder and serial killers and, more broadly, the phenomenon of serial murder is entirely rational. Indeed, this is what first prompted my interest in Nilsen.

It may indeed be rational to have an interest in serial killers but, in reality rather than fiction, serial killing is extremely rare and therefore the chances of having to deal with an actual case of serial murder are equally unusual. I usually have to whisper this but given that infrequency there really aren't that many jobs for prospective offender profilers.

This rarity does not extend to how TV, film, books, and the print and broadcast media use serial murder and serial killers. They seem to be everywhere. Serial killers appear in fiction or on screen in numbers that are grossly disproportionate to their actual significance. Jo Nesbø, for example, has had his fictional detective Harry Hole track down six serial killers, even if Norway – where his novels are set – has only experienced one such murderer, Arnfinn Nesset. Nesset was a nurse and later a nursing home manager, who was convicted in 1983 of murdering twenty-two of his former patients and potentially many more. He was released back into the community having served the maximum penalty available in Norway for any crime – twenty-one years.

The public talks that I give have offered me a wide exposure to many different groups of people, the length and breadth of the country and, in doing so, they have helped me to form some tentative answers to all of these questions about our collective interest in the phenomenon of serial murder.

One lecture has always stuck in my mind.

I always agree to give a public lecture at Birmingham City University's Open Day. I normally speak about serial murder and try to correct a number of the myths that have developed about these crimes, using the forum as an opportunity to get the audience to think a little more deeply about the circumstances in which murder is committed and how we have all become influenced by media portrayals of murder and serial murder.

As far as serial killing is concerned, I explain that I teach my students to think about this phenomenon in different ways. That rather than trying to 'enter the minds' of the killers, we might better understand their motivations if we consider the groups they target instead. If we acknowledge that most serial killers target gay men, sex workers and the elderly, at the very least this provides a basis for us on which to change public policy, so as to reduce the incidence of serial murder in the future.

A victim-centred approach to the phenomenon of serial murder would suggest that we should study serial killing and serial killers because in their actions we begin to understand better our culture, our values and our civic society. After all, why are the groups that are targeted so vulnerable to attack, while other groups – perhaps, simply for argument's sake, bankers, dentists or accountants – are rarely, if ever, the focus of the serial killer? Why are those who are poor and marginalised repeatedly victimised but not those who are seen as being successful? Of course, I am not advocating that bankers, dentists or even accountants should be targeted but merely drawing attention to the fact that it is significant who is and who is not repeatedly victimised by serial killers. In this respect serial killing emerges as the elephant in the sitting room of public policies that create a culture of 'them' and 'us' and a society where there is a widening gap between the 'haves' and the 'have nots'. In such societies it is presumed that some people don't have value for the development of that society and can therefore be cast adrift as challenging the status quo and unrepresentative, or as a burden on the state's resources.

I explain that it is these circumstances and those groups that are characterised in this way that serial killers target.

One prospective student listened intently to what I had argued and then threw her hand in the air when I opened the floor to questions.

'Yes?' I said.

'That's all very well Professor Wilson,' she said, 'But how many dead bodies do I have to see in my first year?'

Sometimes my message just doesn't make it through, especially when so much of my world continues to be shaped by much more powerful forces and particularly the media.

I should also say that this question was not the strangest that I have ever been asked at an Open Day. That prize would go the man who asked me why there were no heated towel rails in the halls of residence.

Plumbing really is beyond me, although not psychopathy – that other favourite staple of our contemporary media's interest in violent crime.

CHAPTER SIX

Psychopathy

'Noel, two labels can be applied to you, neither
of which describes me – you are a *Sunday
Times* bestselling author, and you've been
clinically diagnosed as a psychopath. Which
label has been more helpful to you in your life?'

David Wilson, *In The Criminologist's
Chair*, BBC Radio 4

It was nearly 9 p.m. I would normally have been reading at
home, with a glass of wine in my hand. However, that night,
I was in a theatre near to London's Kings Cross, being led from
a rather splendid dressing room to the stage by a floor manager
for a not-for-broadcast run-through for a new TV show. After
a few moments, I climbed onto the stage and Russell Howard
introduced me to the audience who had gathered for some of
Russell Howard's Good News. I was nervous. I was going to be
doing a rudimentary test on the audience to explain psychopathy. The audience seemed similarly unsure but there was some
polite applause anyway.

Everything went quiet and so I knew it was my turn to perform.
Thankfully, at that point, my lecturing experience took over.

'OK,' I said, 'I would like everyone in the audience to stand up.'

The two hundred members of the studio audience crammed into the theatre shuffled to their feet.

'So,' I continued, 'here's the situation. You've got £400 left in your joint bank account which has got to be used to pay the rent on your flat. However, last week you met someone in a bar and they've just telephoned you to let you know that they've got a great deal for an all-expenses, weekend break in Ibiza which costs exactly £400. Keep standing if you would go on the break, rather than pay the rent.'

About half of the studio audience sat down, leaving roughly a hundred people standing.

'OK,' I said, 'now of those of you who are still standing I have to tell you . . . '

A woman in the audience shouted out, '. . . we're psychopaths!'

Everyone laughed.

'No,' I continued, 'that's not what I have to tell you! What I wanted to give you was some more information. If you don't pay your rent this will be the fourth consecutive month that you won't have paid and your landlord has said that he will evict you if you don't stump up. Keep standing if you would still go to Ibiza.'

Again, about half of those who had been standing sat down.

'There's now another piece of information that I want to put to you. It won't just be you who is evicted but also your partner and your new baby. They'll be made homeless too if you go to Ibiza. Keep standing if you would still go on the weekend break.'

This time everyone sat down with the exception of one man who looked as if he was in his twenties and seemed to be slightly drunk.

Russell shouted, 'That's the psychopath!'

Everyone, including the young man, laughed.

Actually that wasn't correct either. I then explained that one feature of psychopathy is risk-taking, sensation-seeking, impulsive and irresponsible behaviour on the part of the psychopath, who never seems to change despite the problems that this type of behaviour has caused in the past. Psychopaths do not learn from their mistakes. This type of behaviour has become ingrained into their very being and is likely to have been a feature of the psychopath's personality throughout his entire life; it is in his nature. Ever since childhood, unless they were raised in very specific ways, psychopaths will have prioritised their own enjoyment over being responsible.

I admitted that this experiment didn't really allow us to consider the other two facets of psychopathy, at which point Russell asked if it was just 'a rubbish experiment'.

This time, I laughed too.

This was actually a pretty good outcome, as I had been reluctant at first to even appear on the show until I realised that this might offer me an opportunity to correct a number of popular myths about what psychopathy is and who a psychopath might be. 'Psychopath' has become one of the most overused but least understood criminological labels. I have lost count of the times I've been told by someone that they are certain that their ex-girlfriend or boyfriend is a psychopath and sometimes parents email me, worried that their teenage son or daughter might be turning into a psychopath.

But how did I get from governing prisons to appearing on popular entertainment shows discussing psychopathy? Even to me, even now, it is a strange leap but one that I am most grateful for. The truth is that the leap was made due to the very thing that has carried me through my prison career – my fascination with how offenders think and behave; my desire to understand what motivates them; and, in particular, my interest in psychopathy which had been created by the time that I spent at HMP Grendon.

Psychopathy is a personality disorder which current research suggests is characterised by a constellation of behavioural, interpersonal and affective characteristics. At the most basic level, this means that people don't turn into psychopaths – the psychopath has always been and, most probably, will always be this way. What people will often see first in the psychopath is their behavioural characteristics. In particular, what often attracts someone to a psychopath is their risk-taking behaviour. The psychopath says things which we'd never say, or behaves in ways that we'd never dream of emulating and so, at first, they can be fun to be around. They live for the now and are always in the moment but ultimately they will prioritise their own needs. Psychopaths don't really make lasting friends, which is why the scenario that I gave to the audience in my 'rubbish experiment' was about a recent acquaintance.

The second facet of psychopathy is an arrogant interpersonal style, which means that what a psychopath says is often glib and grandiose. At first what they say is meant to seduce you – the psychopath needs to get close to you to be able to better use you for their own ends. But be warned. A psychopath is ultimately parasitic, which means that the £400 in the joint bank account was likely to have been their partner's money. The grandiosity makes them appear extraordinary; it is meant to impress you and everyone else and, at first, it does. They've been everywhere, done everything and seem to know all the right people.

The final facet is the psychopath's limited and essentially damaged emotional experience and his responses. This is not someone who can walk in another person's shoes; the psycho-path does not show empathy (although they can sometimes fake it so that they appear to); nor do they take responsibility for their actions. It is always someone else's fault if things go wrong and, though they might have learned to mimic what it looks like to be sad or concerned about another person's well-being, they are only imitating those feelings. One way that they do this is to steal the language that you use to describe how you are feeling or what you think. In truth, they have no genuine emotional attachment to anyone but themselves.

The psychopath would have chosen the trip to Ibiza; he would have been in the moment. And, being in that moment, would create another moment. And another. I often compare working with psychopaths to continually putting out small fires. Just when you think that you've got one fire under control, another breaks out close by. Psychopaths are usually the most difficult people to work with therapeutically, although that does not mean that they are impossible to help, or that we should not try to help – no matter how exasperating this might be. I have no doubt the psychopath in Ibiza would have got into a fight and have then been arrested; he would have had to borrow money to get home.

It was no surprise that it was a man who had been left standing in the studio audience. While women can be psychopaths, the diagnostic tools which we currently have available to us suggest that it is a personality disorder which is much more likely to appear in men. About 1 per cent of the general population are thought to be psychopathic and 1 in every 150 men. And, while psychopaths do not need to offend, it has been estimated that perhaps as many as twenty-five per cent of the male prison population are psychopathic. There has been far less research about female psychopaths which renders direct gender comparisons difficult but the best evidence that we have suggests that for every ten male psychopaths, there is likely to be one female psychopath. Female psychopaths also tend to get in trouble with the police, just like their male peers.

Psychopathy is a disorder which will manifest itself from an early age. As children, psychopaths get into trouble at home, in school and at every other social gathering that they attend. Let's conjure up one such child – I'll call him Steve. Other parents warn their children not to play with Steve because Steve likes to start fights, or fires, or is cruel to animals – or all three. Steve is the kind of boy who takes the goldfish out of the bowl to see how long it can live out of water. Perhaps the hamster, rabbit, or cat mysteriously disappears, only later to be found dead somewhere in the back garden. Everyone suspects but can't prove that this was down to Steve. Steve may also still wet the bed, even though he has already started to smoke cigarettes.

Steve's parents are as exasperated by his behaviour as everyone else but they are at their wits' end about what they should do. They've tried everything, maybe including, on one or two occasions after some horrendous act, physically punishing Steve. It's all the more difficult because Steve's siblings aren't like this and are doing well at school and have a wide circle of friends. His siblings are 'normal'.

Why is Steve like this? Is it nature or nurture?

No one is completely certain but there are two working hypotheses that might go some way to help to explain psychopathy. First there is the hypothesis that psychopaths have a low fear of punishment. That's why Steve's parents punishing him doesn't ultimately change his behaviour. Second is the suggestion that the part of the brain that would help to inhibit violence is underdeveloped, or has been damaged in some way. Even now, that's why I often check to see if an adult has had some head trauma in his childhood, as there is often a correlation between some form of brain damage and psychopathy.

If Steve is brought up in a home that is loving and caring, that might also go some way to prevent the worst excesses of his behaviour becoming particularly problematic. Alternatively, if Steve's childhood is characterised by rejection, or physical, sexual or emotional abuse, his underlying personality would become much more marked and come to public attention much more quickly. If his parents are inconsistent in their approach to him or if they abandon him in some way, they would help to create the circumstances which would make his behaviour more difficult to manage.

I need to raise here the fact that there are considerable overlaps between Anti-Social Personality Disorder and psychopathy. People with APD are self-centred, impulsive and seem to engage in behaviours which disregard their own safety, or the safety of others. They lie, cheat and don't seem to be able to form genuine emotional attachments; they don't have a conscience – all reminiscent of the attributes which we would associate with psychopaths. That said, while there are overlaps, the two concepts are not identical. Most obviously, while psychopathy is thought to be comparatively rare, APD is much more common. APD is really a catch-all term, with only about one in every five people with APD scoring high enough to classify as a psychopath.

The German psychoanalyst J.L.A. Koch is usually credited with coming up with the term 'psychopath', which literally means 'suffering soul'. But even before Koch came up with the term, Phillipe Pinel had described a group of his psychiatric patients as having *'manie sans delire'* – insanity without delirium. In other words they had disordered thinking and feelings, without having a demonstrable illness. These were seemingly intelligent people but they were still consistently irresponsible and anti-social.

Koch insisted that we should assess an individual by considering his whole life history and not just one or two incidents that might have brought that person to the attention of the police, or to other agencies. In other words, it is the pattern of the person's whole life which is important. Think again about our hypothetical example of Steve and how there were clear problems even in his childhood that gave his parents and others cause for concern.

Of course, all of this feeds into the question of nature vs nurture but, as I repeatedly argue and explain to my students, it is neither one, nor the other but a messy combination of the two. We are all biological beings – we are all flesh and blood, hormones and genes – but, that having been said, we are not all simply programmed to behave in predetermined ways irrespective of how we have been nurtured, or the specific circumstances that we find ourselves inhabiting as adults. There is always going to be a combination of nature and nurture and what that combination might look like will be unique to each individual and might present itself in different ways and at different points in time. However, when thinking about violent men and as a general rule, it is always important to try and understand something about their lives before they might have come to the attention of the police, and the specific context in which they have been violent.

Though there have been various diagnostic tools for determining psychopathy over the years, it is Robert Hare's Psychopathy Checklist (Revised) (PCL-R) which is now the most common – a twenty-item scale for determining psychopathy, based on his work with psychopaths in prison settings. These twenty items are:

- Glibness
- Grandiose sense of self-worth
- Need for stimulation
- Pathological lying
- Manipulation
- Lack of remorse
- Shallow affect
- Lack of empathy
- Parasitic lifestyle
- Poor behavioural controls
- Promiscuous sexual behaviour
- Early behavioural problems

- Lack of realistic long-term goals
- Impulsivity
- Irresponsibility
- Failure to accept responsibility for own actions
- Short-term marital relationships
- Juvenile delinquency
- Revocation of conditional release
- Criminal versatility.

This is now the most commonly used tool to assess psychopathy and involves conducting a semi-structured interview with the subject and then a file review to cross-check information. The label 'psychopath' is applied to those who score 30 out of 40 on the 20-item checklist (although the figures can vary depending on which country the test is taken in), with 0 being applied if an item does not apply; 1 if it partly fits; and 2 being applied if this behaviour is characteristic of the individual concerned. The lowest one could therefore score is zero and the highest 40.

Most of us would score about 4 out of 40.

Another psychologist, Kent Kiehl, describes psychopaths as 'walking oxymorons' and has championed the use of MRI scans to show how the brains of psychopaths are different to those of 'normal' people. Specifically his work suggests that psychopathy is caused by defects in the paralimbic system in the brain – the regions which are responsible for processing emotion and inhibition. If they are defective, the individual will be aggressive, impulsive and irresponsible, have problems showing empathy and will also have poor behavioural controls; all redolent of psychopathy.

Kiehl's research suggests that it might be possible to treat psychopaths, to the extent that their behaviour could be controlled through alleviating or even repairing the paralimbic brain damage. This raises the whole issue of treatment and what we might be able to do to change psychopathic behaviour, or at least reposition that behaviour into a more suitable context.

It's at this point I want to introduce Noel 'Razor' Smith. Noel is my friend. He has also publicly discussed being clinically diagnosed as a psychopath, scoring 37 out of 40 on the PCL-R.

I first met Noel in the late 1990s, when he was a prisoner serving out his most recent sentence at HMP Whitemoor. We did not speak, as he knew I had been a governor and I knew that he was a 'face' – one of the prisoners who would frankly prefer to die than be seen talking with someone who had been in charge of a prison. We were on different sides of the fence. We met again a few years later in 2001, when he had been transferred to HMP Grendon and I was showing some visitors around the jail, in my capacity as chair of the charity The Friends of Grendon. That tour always ends with a lunch being shared between the visitors and some of the prisoners, and Noel joined me at my table. We smiled awkwardly at each other and then edged around each other's institutional history, until we eventually agreed on one thing – Grendon was a good place for Noel to try and make sense of his life. Noel then shared with the people at the table that since 1987 he'd only spent fourteen months outside of prison. He'd end up spending more than half of his life in prison, serving sentences for over two hundred bank robberies and other forms of violence, before being released from prison in 2010, aged fifty. I was one of the people who wrote in support of Noel receiving parole.

Noel is always quick to acknowledge that it was Grendon which got him back on the straight and narrow and, from that second meeting in 2001, I have developed a friendship with Noel that transcends our very different experiences of life and of prisons. My wife and I even attended his wedding. The theme of the wedding was 'skulls' and, even though we were the most conservatively dressed people there, both my wife and I regard this as one of the most memorable social occasions that we have ever attended.

Noel and I have spoken together about crime and punishment at a number of public events – at universities, at schools and at various academic conferences. We have become something of a double act and, after more than fifteen years of knowing Noel, I also conducted an interview with him for *In the Criminologist's Chair*, a programme that I presented on Radio 4. Noel's insights both in relation to himself as someone who has been through Grendon and as a man able to reflect on his offending life are invaluable. Below, I've used my written notes to flesh out what was only a thirty-minute broadcast, but I want to use these notes and the broadcast to further reflect on the themes which I have been discussing in this chapter about violence and psychopathy and, from the book as a whole, about the importance of childhood, relationships, education and the possibility of having prisons geared towards rehabilitation, rather than punishment.

My first question to Noel reflects my belief that you need to go back into the person's childhood to truly understand the adult, and what could be more important than discussing how we are named? I was also intrigued by what name Noel would prefer to be known by.

DW: You are called Noel because you were born on Christmas Eve 1960, but how did you acquire the nickname 'Razor'?

NS: When I was a teenager, I was in a Teddy Boy gang and we all had nicknames, mainly based on our chosen weapons. I used a cut-throat razor and so this name persisted into later years.

DW: Which name do you prefer to use now?

NS: It depends really. 'Razor' has become almost a nom de plume for my writing.

DW: OK, let me call you 'Noel'. Tell me this – how central has violence been in your life as an offender?

NS: Pretty central really. My criminal career started with violence and I went on to use violence. I went on to become violent.

DW: What are the attractions of the violent act in the moment that you are committing crime?

NS: The violence was mainly committed against other criminals. We classed it as a bit of a game. Gang fights – violence was a tool for rising up the criminal ladder. If people thought that you were game and able to carry out acts that others would baulk at you would gain kudos in the criminal world; you'd take a step up. It's all about power and making your mark in that sort of criminal area. You can be a criminal without using violence, but you are never going to reach the top that way.

DW: So what gave you the edge when you were being violent? How did you look and dress and act when you were going to use violence?

NS: That last thing – act – is right. A lot of violence is an act. You have to be convincing. You have to make people believe that you'd rather kill them than have the money. It's about being a good actor; about presenting yourself as a threat right from the start. Sometimes I'd wear extra clothes to look bigger. A ski mask – not just to disguise you but to strike fear into people from the beginning. You had to present a front to prevent people from tackling you. It was like an animal's display to frighten people away.

For me, one of his most interesting comments was Noel's assertion that he would be prepared to use violence that 'others would baulk at', as a tool to rise up the criminal career ladder. We can see the recklessness in his behaviour, given that this willingness to be violent might have drastic consequences not only for him, but also for those around him. Note too that Noel admits that this is all about getting to the top. He's prioritising his own needs. His description that this was like an 'animal's display' is also revealing. It suggests that when he was dressed and behaving in this way, he really was a predator; he was, or wanted to be, the 'top dog' – the one who was at the head of the food chain.

At this stage, I left to one side Noel's suggestion that the violence he had used was mainly against other criminals, as if this in itself justified what he had done, or that it was a 'game', as I was going to ask him specifically about the bank robberies that he committed. These clearly were *not* committed against other criminals, but members of the public.

DW: Of course criminally you are best known as a bank robber. Let's talk about you in the car driving towards the bank. So you are in the car – the bank hasn't yet been robbed – take us through that moment. How are people behaving and reacting? Is it exciting?

NS: Yeah, it's very exciting. There's a lot of tension in the car when you are on your way there as obviously you want things to go well. I would always check my gun thoroughly before I went in to make sure that it wouldn't go off accidentally. So there's a heightened sense of excitement, tension, but you've also got in the back of your head at this stage that if you walk away you can just walk away [from the robbery]. You haven't yet crossed the Rubicon, as that's when you have stepped into the premises. That's when you can't back out.

DW: After the robbery has taken place, what is the atmosphere like then?

NS: Well I always found it to be quite depressing afterwards because the actual act of armed robbery – when you are in there robbing the bank is ... you're very high. The adrenalin is pumping. But when you come out and you're in the car and you're safely away it's like being deflated.

DW: How much money did you make?

NS: I worked it out once that it was between £800,000 and a million. Obviously that was spread out over a thirty-five-year period. I probably could have earned the same amount of money if I had put my mind to something else and got work instead of having to spend all of that time in prison. It sounds a lot on the surface but you get it in dribs and drabs and the thing about stealing money is that once you've got it, it's not like you've worked for it, so you tend to spend it; you waste it. All the money has gone and that's your creed as a professional criminal. You spend it as easily as it came in. The money went very, very quickly.

What is clear is the thrill and excitement that Noel experiences, which some criminologists call 'the joys of transgression', when he is committing crime. There is tension but no real fear being expressed and so Noel doesn't walk away; he always crosses 'the Rubicon'. He would eventually admit to over two hundred bank robberies. Noel revealed that his role in the gang of bank robbers was that of being 'the frightener' – in other words he had to scare everyone into behaving exactly as the gang wanted. His heightened sense of excitement in this role can be contrasted afterwards with his description of becoming 'deflated' once the robbery had taken place. We didn't broadcast Noel's statement that committing armed robbery was like 'the best high ever' and 'more addictive than cocaine'.

Noel is also very honest about recognising that he could have earned the same amount of money by working legitimately and, if he had got himself an honest job, he wouldn't have had to spend so long in prison. However, he didn't learn from this mistake but continued to commit robberies. He also admits to simply wasting the money.

> DW: What did you do with the money that you got from the robberies?
> NS: Silly things really. I bought cars – lots of cars.
> DW: Why was that silly?
> NS: I didn't have a driving licence!

We also have to remember that Noel is recalling all of this as a much older man and after he has gone through five years of therapy at Grendon. That the average length of stay at Grendon is about two years gives us an indication of how badly damaged Noel must have been. He is now much more ambivalent about his past behaviour – perhaps we can see this ambivalence best of all in his suggestion that he always checked his gun so that it didn't go off accidentally. It's a statement that also seems to me to imply that Noel didn't actually want to use the gun at all, although we do not need to accept at face value that this is what he really felt at the time. What is important is that this is now what he wants to tell me. Might this also be about the development of empathy and a conscience?

We then discussed Noel's family background.

> DW: Can you describe for me the family circumstances into which you were born?

NS: My parents were Irish immigrants and my father
was a street fighter and a pub brawler. He was a very
violent man and he was a drinker – a very heavy
drinker. I was the oldest child. I have a brother two
years younger than me and a sister who is three years
younger than me.

DW: Have they ever committed any crimes? Have they ever
been to prison?

NS: No, they haven't. They're both 'straight-goers'. My
brother works for a housing association and my sister
is a housewife.

DW: So, there's something about your childhood that was
different. Something that prompts you to go onto
different paths.

NS: Dad used to go out every morning, as soon as the pubs
opened. He'd shine his shoes and away he'd go. My
mother would be working two or three jobs to keep
food on the table and a roof over our heads. So my
dad would go out. We lived in Balham and he'd catch
the 137 bus home every night. My dad could be very
difficult when he came in drunk, depending on what
sort of time he'd had. He could be violent. Sometimes
he'd throw his dinner up the wall. So my mother used
to keep me out of bed to engage him in conversation so
that when he came in drunk instead of having nothing
to concentrate on except his rage, it would be my job to
keep him engaged. I'd get him to talk about what it was
like when he was a child. That way he might eat his
dinner and then go to bed instead of slapping my mum
or wrecking the place.

DW: Were you successful?

NS: Sometimes. Other times he could be really, really
difficult and I would be sent to bed. I'd then hear the

shouting and the smashing and all of that and there
was nothing that I could really do about it.

DW: How did that make you feel?

NS: It made me feel quite helpless, really. I was only a
skinny kid at 12 or 13; I was like a rasher of bacon. I
felt powerless anyway. I used to get bullied a lot by
other kids at this time ... when I could engage my dad
in conversation I would feel good about it and when I
couldn't I was at a loss.

All of this information is powerful and revealing – the childhood
experiences of the man who would go on to commit over two
hundred bank robberies; moreover, robberies in which he would
play the role of 'the frightener'. Contrast that role with the child
who was a 'rasher of bacon' and who sometimes couldn't prevent
his mother from being beaten up by his drunken father. His helplessness is in marked contrast to the power and excitement that
he felt when, as an adult, he was in control of everyone during
the commission of the bank robbery.

Suffice to say that Noel regularly played truant from school
and left education while still functionally illiterate. It was while
playing truant with a friend that he was accosted by a group
of men who turned out to be an undercover burglary squad,
and Noel and his friend were beaten and forced to confess to
over sixty burglaries they didn't in fact commit. This would all
eventually be revealed at court and the charges were dismissed.
From then on, Noel was on the police's radar and had become
a 'marked man'.

DW: So how did you react to becoming a 'marked man'?

NS: Well, I thought that if the police want to incriminate
me in crimes that I haven't done, I may as well do
some. In my immature mind I thought that the best

form of defence would be attack. So I took the fight to the police, not just in committing crimes – stealing motorbikes and the like, but actually attacking the police. I'd ride up beside a police car and kick it and then ride off on my bike.

His tactic of 'defence' as 'attack' would result in Noel being sent first to a detention centre, then to borstal and eventually to prison. All told, Noel has been in some form of penal institution for over thirty-two years, more than half of his adult life. It took him a very long time to learn that this 'defence' was causing him more harm than good. Note also that this is the ultimate form of refusing to take responsibility for the life course that he had chosen. It wasn't his fault, as he explains it, but rather the police's responsibility that he would turn to a life of crime. Inevitably, Noel believed that he had been 'made' into a criminal, rather than having been born that way.

What prompted a change in Noel's behaviour was a tragedy which happened when he was serving a sentence in HMP Whitemoor in 2001. This is how Noel explained what happened:

NS: I was coming back from tea that day with a mate of mine – a Geordie fella. We looked up the landing and we saw a priest hanging about. There's a saying that if you see a priest or a vicar or an imam it's normally bad news. They come on the landing to deliver bad news. I jokingly said, 'There's someone in for a bit of bad news' and when I go up to the door it was me. My youngest son was nineteen years old at the time – Joseph – he'd been kind of following in my footsteps. He'd been arrested a couple of times, and the priest was there to tell me that my son had died in mysterious circumstances outside. Obviously I was devastated. It ripped my whole world apart. You've got to stop and think then. What's going on? I asked to go to the funeral and they told me no, I couldn't go to the funeral as I was too dangerous. I thought about that. I'd spent all these years building up this reputation as an ogre in the prison system and all it had done was mean that when it came time for me to ask them for a favour, it made it easier for them to say no. I wasn't allowed to go to my own son's funeral. That made me sort of think, what am I doing with my life? That was the catalyst that made me stop.

DW: So what did you do?

NS: My first instinct as a criminal was to strike back against the prison system but then I thought, I'm not going to do that. I started to look round at where I could change my life. It was then I found out that there's no real tangible rehabilitation in our prisons. The only thing I could find was Grendon.

This tragedy is the catalyst which encouraged Noel to stop offending. He wanted, he said to me, 'to give meaning' to his son's life. His reasoning above is the opposite of how he had reacted as a young man when he wanted to attack the police as a form of defence. Noel had finally learned that this type of behaviour was creating difficulties that caused him harm, rather than generating opportunities from which he or his family could prosper.

DW: What do you do now?

NS: I'm commissioning editor at *Inside Time*, the national prisoners' newspaper, and an author.

DW: Noel, two labels can be applied to you, neither of which describes me – you are a *Sunday Times* bestselling author, and you've been clinically diagnosed as a psychopath. Which label has been more helpful to you in your career?

NS: Of actual practical help I suppose being a psychopath

has helped me – I say 'helped', it hasn't really helped, it's put me in harm's way – but it gave me the sort of mindset to do the things that I did. I didn't have no conscience; I didn't have no thoughts for my victims; I depersonalised them and I suppose if you are talking about actual practical help, I suppose being a psychopath allowed me to rise to the top of the criminal tree and it got me into a lot of trouble. Being a bestselling author is kind of my alternative to crime. I get the same buzz off writing that I used to get from crime. Being an author has helped to keep me on the straight and narrow and certainly I'm over fifty now and so the psychopathy doesn't really come into it.

DW: But if we think about the classic psychopathic personality, it is someone who is going to be quite narcissistic; someone who will not be able to show empathy towards other people; someone who will love excitement, often putting themselves in danger and at risk. Those things seem to characterise our earlier discussions and so do you think that perhaps you've just repositioned that psychopathy? You get that narcissism and attention through writing, talking and broadcasting. Do you think that some of those things have disappeared, or have they simply been repositioned into something that is more favourable?

NS: Well I think you're right there. I do now get the same sort of buzz out of things that I used to get out of crime. I think it's just a matter of divergence. I was on a merry-go-round and didn't know how to get off and being a psychopath helped me with that as I had no remorse. When it came to violence, some people talked about stabbing, but I never had any compunction about it and so psychopathy helped me to progress in criminal terms and maybe I have really transferred it to something better. I still get impatient with people; I still get angry. The difference is that I have a cut-off switch. Whereas before I could go from nought to anger and from anger to violence in a very quick time, Grendon taught me to take time to think. A little stop. I get a good feeling from what I do – the writing I do, the work that I do. I get a buzz from that and I do not feel the need to use my previous personality. I think I have transferred everything.

DW: Do you think that you are fully rehabilitated?

NS: In as much as anybody can be rehabilitated. I haven't committed a criminal act in nearly twenty years now. I do still get the old feelings if I walk past a security van, or if a bank is opening up and I will look at my watch. I do think I'm truly rehabilitated. I think you have to want to be rehabilitated; you have to really want to change. Joe dying gave me the spur for that and ever since that I have wanted to change.

Finally I wanted to know if Noel had 'learned empathy'. In other words, if he had truly become empathetic about other people, or if instead he had simply, for example, managed to control his temper. I wasn't sure, in other words, if he was merely mimicking empathy, or if he did genuinely feel an emotional connection to other people.

NS: I don't think you can really learn empathy. If you haven't got it, you haven't got it. You become aware of it. It was explained to me what it is and you adjust your behaviour accordingly. I never cried when Lassie didn't come home; when the Titanic went down I just thought, the ship's sunk, that's it. I don't have those feelings that

other people have. I can feel an approximation of that
and adjust my behaviour accordingly.

Noel is explaining that therapy isn't some type of cure for psychopathy but, rather, it has allowed him to adjust his behaviour. While he is ageing, and this might also have played a role within the adjustments that he describes, repositioning the 'buzz' that he got from crime into his writing and work has allowed him to function in the world without reoffending. This has to be a major step forward not just for Noel, but also for society. Underneath all of this is still the same personality that is Noel 'Razor' Smith, but he can satisfy all the behavioural and interpersonal needs that go with his personality without damaging other people, or himself, or indeed robbing banks.

That leaves the affective part of his personality – the emotional dimension – to consider. This is the dimension of his personality which can be described as damaged and limited in relation to his emotional experience and responses. Noel didn't, as he put it, cry when Lassie never come home and nor did he see what the fuss was all about when the Titanic sank. We call all of this 'shallow affect'. In his case, Noel accepts that he has caused harm and that he has created victims, but he does not truly understand what harm is, why it should disturb him, or what it might have done to his victims. In other words, he has read the script and remembered the lines but doesn't actually know what those lines mean. However, could he perhaps learn to walk in another person's shoes and feel the pain that they might be experiencing, or perhaps take genuine responsibility for causing that pain? Can he have an honest emotional attachment to anyone else?

NS: I do understand that there is an emotional part of my
     personality that is missing but, once that has been

explained to me, I can feel an approximation to what it is that you feel.

This was as far as Noel was willing to go for, as he says, 'I don't have those feelings that other people have'. All he is willing to acknowledge is an 'approximation' of genuine feelings, rather than the feelings themselves. This seemed to be both a rather bleak but also an honest assessment of what Noel felt about this aspect of his personality. Genuine empathy is simply not part of the world of the psychopath.

I had no idea that one day during our public talks something would happen to make both of us reassess his conclusion.

For the past few years, I have chaired a variety of conferences aimed at A-level students and there is a session at the end of the day when I interview Noel. Noel will come onto a stage with a solitary chair for him to sit on, while I wander within the audience asking him questions, before offering the students their own opportunity to quiz Noel.

The questions that I ask always follow a set pattern, pretty much as described above: I ask Noel about his childhood; his schooling; his first experience of crime; what life in prison was like; why he wanted to change his life and how he went about doing that; and, finally, what does he do now?

Noel and I are very much an old double act by now but I try to keep things fresh by asking something that I haven't asked before. I once shocked Noel by asking him if he had ever engaged in situational same-sex behaviour while in prison – he hadn't. Once he shocked me by revealing that, when he was a child, his hero had been the fictional TV police officer in *Dixon of Dock Green*.

These exchanges aside, this session follows the set pattern so that we help the students to think about the conference theme by listening to an offender, rather than an academic describing his research. How has an offender experienced punishment and

what was the impact that that has had on him? Does he feel that
he was 'born' a criminal, or made into one through his experiences in his childhood?

One particular day the conference was in London, although
we had also spoken previously during the week in Birmingham
and Manchester. There were over a thousand students in the
audience. Noel had come on stage and, as he usually does, he
was holding the students' attention with his life story and his
honesty. Several students were taking notes. I heard one or two
gasp at what he described in relation to his bank robberies and
then most of the audience laughed when he acknowledged that
he would have made more money simply through getting a job.

So far, so good.

I then reached the point in the session where I asked Noel
about what had happened in Whitemoor in 2001, as a means to
get him to discuss why he had applied to go to HMP Grendon
and his experiences in therapy. Noel had discussed this part of
his story with me on hundreds of previous occasions.

'So, Noel, something happens when you are in Whitemoor
that is going to change the direction of your life. Can you explain
to the students what happened?'

'Yes,' replied Noel and then he stopped.

There was silence in the theatre; everyone was waiting for
him to continue with his story when I realised that Noel was
crying. Quietly at first and then louder, until he was sobbing
quite uncontrollably. I didn't know what to do, and neither did
the audience. We were all helpless, although in my mind I was
silently putting an arm around Noel to try and comfort him.
After all, I knew what had happened and so I was all too aware
that he was about to discuss the death of his son. I murmured
something inane into the microphone, urging him to 'take his
time' but this had never happened before and so I didn't really
know what I should say, or what I could do.

Time seemed to stand still.

Eventually Noel took a tissue out of his pocket, blew his nose and then wiped the tears from his eyes.

'My youngest son Joe . . .' he said and then he continued with the story.

The students in the audience gave Noel the warmest ovation that I have ever heard when he finished that afternoon, although he looked drained and was still visibly upset. He signed a few autographs and allowed the students to take photographs of their class with him before he left the stage.

I knew that something truly momentous had happened here and it was something that I had never previously experienced, either with Noel, or with any of the other clinically diagnosed psychopaths that I have worked with. It wasn't simply that Noel had told this story at hundreds of other conferences and had never cried before but more to do with the fact that somehow, on this occasion, the words that he had used to try to describe his son's death had hit home. This time he understood what the script actually meant. His words and what they conveyed seemed to connect to him in an authentic and deep way; this was not shallow affect. It was almost as if this was the first time that he fully recognised what it was he was describing and how what he was going to say seared into his very being. It was like a psychological dam had been burst.

I rushed backstage but before I could say anything Noel apologised for breaking down. I looked at him, still trying to find the right words to say, but all I managed was, 'What happened is called empathy, Noel. Don't apologise.'

CHAPTER SEVEN

Mass and Spree Murder

'The would-be-killer then transforms what
he initially senses as humiliation into rage.
Doing this binds the killer to his future. It
forges a momentary sense of eternal unity with
the "good"'

JACK KATZ, *Seductions of Crime*

It was a cold day for March and so, having driven over 350 miles, I was grateful to be checking into my hotel. The receptionist behind the counter tapped her computer screen, welcomed me to Dunblane and smiled warmly as she handed me my door key.

'Would you like a hot cookie?' she asked.

'No thank you,' I replied, as I was due to start filming a new documentary the following week and so I was watching my weight; it's one of the downsides of appearing on TV. I was about to turn away when I thought that she might be able to help me.

'Oh, one last thing,' I said, 'can you direct me to the memorial garden? I'd like to pay my respects to the children who died.'

The warmth in her manner disappeared almost instantly and her supervisor, who had been watching close by, glanced accusingly at the computer screen to see if he could recognise my name.

It only lasted for a moment and, after professional decorum had been restored, I was duly offered the directions to where I wanted to go. However, this brief exchange seemed to perfectly capture a sense I was given throughout the four days I was in Scotland. I was there to try to make sense of a dreadful mass murder on its twentieth anniversary but soon discovered that asking anything about the 'Dunblane massacre' was not something to be done – especially in Dunblane.

Understandably, what happened there in 1996 has left a deep scar on the community and, had the children who were murdered still been alive, they would by now have been leaving university, or working in Dunblane and getting on with their lives. I accept that whilst I might have perfectly valid criminological reasons for wanting to study what happened in Dunblane, these reasons should never be allowed to blind me to the fact that many children died and the lives of their parents were altered forever.

I hoped that I wasn't being insensitive at the hotel reception. However, given that 2016 marked the twentieth anniversary of the appalling shootings at Dunblane Primary School, when Thomas Hamilton – using four licensed handguns – opened fire, injuring seventeen people and killing sixteen children and their teacher, before taking his own life, I had come to Scotland to try and understand this mass murder – a mass murder that remains the worst in recent British history. Unsurprisingly it still has the power to shock today – perhaps because we have never really answered the questions that had brought me back to Scotland. Why had Hamilton chosen Dunblane, a perfectly ordinary setting for this most awful of crimes, and what might have motivated him to both repeatedly kill and then commit suicide? And, in the same way that I try to put single acts of violence or murder into context, I also wanted to understand the circumstances that led up to and may have prompted this mass murder. I also wanted to know much more about Hamilton himself. Was he an outsider – the lone predator – who waged war on an unsuspecting community, or was he instead much more embedded within the community that he targeted? This latter question is all the more relevant when we remember that violence makes perfect sense to the killer – no matter how senseless it might appear to us.

Trying to get to know more about Hamilton was not going to be easy, especially as he had committed suicide at the culmination of his murders. However, a 'psychological autopsy' is often undertaken after someone has taken their own life. This is a procedure which attempts to reconstruct the suicide's life through talking with surviving family members, friends and work colleagues and also analysing letters and other documents which they may have left, to try to make sense of their psychosocial situation immediately prior to their death. In this way, inferences can be drawn about the deceased's behaviours, thoughts and emotions.

I approached the anniversary by seeking to conduct something broader than a psychological autopsy. I wanted to conduct a 'criminological autopsy' of the events that had taken place and, in doing so, place Hamilton's suicide in a wider offending context. For me it is important to understand the psychosocial environment in which any mass murderer lived, as this is central in trying to comprehend why that mass murderer would want to kill as many of his family, or friends, neighbours and work colleagues as possible. So I wasn't just thinking about Thomas Hamilton in Dunblane but all the other mass murderers who succeeded him too, both in this country and elsewhere.

Here it might be helpful to differentiate between what we call 'spree' and 'mass' murder. Spree murderers are typically those men who kill four or more victims within a period of hours, or even days. The spree killer might also kill in different locations, travelling about to evade the police as he does so; but, crucially, there will be no 'cooling off' period, as we would expect with a serial killer. A mass murderer, on the other hand, will kill four or more victims within a single, destructive, killing episode.

What happened in Dunblane was therefore mass murder, committed by Thomas Hamilton, and it was Hamilton who was the primary focus for my criminological autopsy.

To do this, I drove the eight miles to Dunblane from Hamilton's house in Stirling, trying to imagine what he might have been thinking about on his twenty-minute journey from his home to the school. I walked Dunblane's streets and drank in its pubs; I spoke with a very few people who were prepared to talk to me; visited the memorial to the children and their teacher; and read and reread the Cullen Inquiry report – the public inquiry that was almost immediately set up to investigate the shootings.

This inquiry had been quick to paint a picture of Hamilton as abnormal; as entering the community of Dunblane like a perverted pied piper, as if out of nowhere, to suddenly steal the children from the community through their murders. He was a 'lone gunman'; insane; an 'oddball', with few friends, and thus largely unknown. The Cullen Inquiry did also point to systemic faults and failings which, for example, allowed Hamilton to legally own firearms. However, a sense that Hamilton was different, unusual or odd – that he was pathological – has endured as the dominant narrative about him and remains the explanation most likely to be given when the shootings are discussed, if they are discussed at all.

The picture that emerged from my criminological autopsy was very different, not just about Hamilton as an individual but also about his close association with Dunblane, a society he had been embedded in for almost two decades before the shootings.

All too often, in what the social psychologist Philip Zimbardo describes as 'the rush to the dispositional', we tend to link awful, violent, cruel behaviour to individual pathology. In other words we believe that the perpetrator is 'crazy'; 'odd'; 'not right in the head'; or that he just 'flipped'. We want to think that a violent offender like Hamilton is just not like us. Yet this narrative falls apart on close analysis. Placing all the responsibility on Hamilton, as tempting as that might be, fails to locate his crimes within a number of broader background factors which would, at the very least, include: masculinity; gun culture; and official approaches to the supervision of children at that time.

Explanations for the Dunblane massacre have largely over-emphasised the dispositional and the extraordinary and so they have failed to take into account just how entrenched Hamilton was in the community and therefore why he wanted to, in his view, punish that community by killing as many children as he could. Hamilton most certainly would not have seen himself as 'mad' at the time of these shootings – nor did he ever have any identifiable mental health disorder that would make violence more likely. Instead Hamilton considered himself as someone whose actions had a clear and justified purpose.

I know that many will find this type of reasoning objection-able and perhaps I therefore need to re-emphasise that I find his crimes deeply distressing. Nor am I trying to offer up excuses for his murdering. However, by re-considering what happened in Dunblane we might begin to identify patterns that will allow us to prevent other mass or spree murders in the future and that surely is something which we would all support?

Let's consider some of the facts.

In 1996 Hamilton had been running a boys' club at Dunblane High School since 1981, having been asked to leave the Scouts when he was in his early twenties. His club didn't have the most straightforward of histories. Permission to run the club on school property had been withdrawn in the summer of 1983, partly as a result of rumours that Hamilton had been asked to leave the Scouts because he was sexually interested in boys.

However, Hamilton appealed this decision to the ombudsman and a petition in support of him and his boys' club in Dunblane, signed by some seventy people, ended with the endorsement that: 'We are all proud to have Mr Hamilton in charge of our boys; he has a most activated, excellent quality of leadership and integrity and is absolutely devoted to his lads; above all he cares.' As a result of this local support, Hamilton continued to run a club in the town up until the time of his death.

As well as the club in Dunblane, Hamilton ran at least ten other boys' clubs at various points in time throughout central Scotland, all of which took place within local schools.

Boys paid a small amount of money to attend but these clubs might be better seen as 'loss leaders' that existed to drum up attendance at Hamilton's summer camps, where presumably he could make more money – and where he had greater opportunities to be alone with the boys. At the clubs boys played football and sometimes they were even allowed to shoot guns, although the main activity seems to have been gymnastics, where the boys would be asked to strip to the waist and wear ill-fitting swimming trunks, supplied by Hamilton. He took photographs and videos of the boys exercising in these trunks – to ensure, he claimed, that they were using the right muscles.

After the shootings, police found 37 video tapes, 445 slides, 542 photographs, 4,260 negatives – the majority of which were of boys with their tops bare – and a collection of swimming trunks at Hamilton's home.

We can get a glimpse of what life was like at a summer camp organised by Hamilton in July 1988, only because some things went wrong. During the camp on Inchmoan Island in Loch

Lomond, for boys who were nine years old, one boy became so unhappy that he had to be taken home. As a result, complaints about the camp came to the attention of the parents of the other boys and also to Strathclyde police, in whose jurisdiction Inchmoan was located at that time. PCs George Gunn and Donna Duncan duly visited the camp on 20 July. PC Gunn would later state that he found the campsite messy, with the sleeping bags of the boys damp to the touch, and he noted that the only food available was tinned or powdered. The thirteen boys who were in attendance seemed to PC Gunn to be cold and miserable but, crucially, no one accepted his offer to take them home. In conversation Hamilton also admitted to striking one or two of the boys as, he stated, they had been 'cheeky'.

However, no parent made a complaint against Hamilton, although he in turn would make a complaint against PC Gunn, whom Hamilton believed – wrongly as it happens – was a Scout leader and whom he suspected was therefore prejudiced against him. This complaint was later investigated, although this did not satisfy Hamilton who complained about the investigation into his complaint, which is why we know so much detail about what happened on the camp and which would later be referred to within the Cullen Inquiry. Hamilton plagued the officer so much that PC Gunn had to threaten to have him arrested and considered suing him for defamation of character.

There is also a second source about what happened on Inchmoan. Doreen Hagger was a mother of one of the boys who attended the camp. After her son complained to her, Doreen visited the camp herself and agreed to stay on to help Hamilton who had been single-handedly running all the activities. She was not impressed by what she saw and would later testify that Hamilton had had the boys rub suntan oil onto him, although she did not personally witness this taking place. However, she was so distressed by what she did see that on her return she went out of her way to draw attention to Hamilton's unsuitability to be in charge of boys. In particular, on 16 May 1989, in the company of her friend Janet Reilly who had also assisted at the camp, she assaulted Hamilton by pouring suntan oil and other substances over him as he left Linlithgow Academy at the end of one his regular boys' club meetings at the school.

Doreen wanted to be taken to court for assaulting Hamilton and, so as to garner as much publicity as possible, had arranged for a journalist and a press photographer to be present to witness the assault. To her great annoyance, Hamilton refused to press charges.

Hamilton was a paedophile. He wanted to be in charge of young boys so that he could groom and abuse them. At a time when paedophilia was largely hidden and when Jimmy Savile was still regarded as a much-loved celebrity who could 'fix it' for children, paedophilia was viewed as something which did not really happen, especially in places like Dunblane, or indeed at the BBC. In the same way that Savile was adept at hiding in plain sight and avoiding the label paedophile being applied to him, or his various activities being characterised as sexual abuse, Hamilton also successfully managed to avoid stigma attaching itself to him in any irrevocable way.

Hamilton did this by complaining to and about: the police, as with the case of PC Gunn; the Scouts; various schools; regional authorities; and through his constant letter writing to parents. In a pre-email age it was common for Hamilton to advertise his boys' clubs and summer camps by either hand-delivering letters within the community, or having schools put these letters into communications with parents. By some he may well have been seen as odd but not sufficiently so for his activities to be censured, his behaviour criminalised, or the community more generally to shun him and his activities.

The word which we should use here is 'silenced'. This is not just about the silence that comes from refusing to name – to label – what Hamilton's true intentions were but an official silence by the various organisations who failed to make public their private disquiet about Hamilton. In other words, to make public – loud and clear – his unsuitability to be in charge of children and to legally own guns. This official silence can be seen within the Scouts, the various gun clubs to which Hamilton belonged, a number of schools and the regional authorities which were for-mally responsible for the running of these schools, and within the police who granted firearms licences.

Only Doreen Hagger attempted to make public her pri-vate anxiety and, of course, in refusing to press charges against her, Hamilton silenced Doreen as effectively as he had silenced PC Gunn.

This private disquiet would only later emerge at the Cullen Inquiry, when it was too late.

By the time of the shootings Hamilton's boys' clubs were in serious decline. In Dunblane only five boys were left and a complaint about his club in Bishopbriggs had been made at the beginning of March – the month of the shootings. The Bannockburn boys' club had collapsed in January 1996, forcing Hamilton to write to the headteacher of the local primary school to complain about rumours that were circulating about him. In this letter he singled out Dunblane Primary School where 'even the cleaners' were 'spreading this poison'. Dunblane knew him best and therefore suspected the most.

Given the state of his boys' clubs, the summer camps that year were looking perilous and Hamilton, who had just reached the limit on his credit card, was £6,000 in debt. He'd been refused a bank loan. His life was spiralling out of control. On 6 March Hamilton telephoned the Scouts' headquarters to make one of his regular complaints and the following day, ever the fan-tasist, he wrote a narcissistic letter to the Queen in the hope that she could intervene so that he could 'regain my self-esteem in society'.

Narcissists are rarely passive and so the shootings, just a week later, allowed Hamilton to regain his self-esteem in a brutal and butch revenge on those whom he saw as damaging his reputation, which in turn frustrated his efforts to groom the boys he desired.

Now, more than twenty years on from the tragedy, it may seem that there is very little to learn from what happened in Dunblane. Times have changed; the world has moved on – especially as far as communication is concerned. A search for terms in the Cullen Inquiry, for example, found that mobile phones are mentioned just three times and the internet only once. There was only one telephone line into the school in 1996; mobile phone signals at the height of the shootings quickly became jammed; and there was only 'a line in the library that was used for the internet facility'. The internet was literally cornered in one room; locked up and kept under control. Letters being written by Hamilton are mentioned sixteen times and, in a pre-social media age, there is no Twitter or Facebook.

Compare all of this to the Norwegian mass killer Anders Breivik, whose 'manifesto' was spread widely online before and then after his horrific killing spree and who, as a killer, was adept at manipulating the image of himself on social media that he wanted other people to see. Despite these largely superficial and technological differences, there is for me much in Dunblane which is prophetic of the mass and spree murders which were to come, to the extent that Hamilton might be seen as the 'father' who begets Anders Breivik in Norway, Derrick Bird in Whitehaven and their bloody North American ilk.

Hamilton was desperate to order the world in a way which gave him power – perhaps even omnipotence. He saw this power as rightly his but believed that he had been frustrated in his attempts to gain authority by other people who had unfairly accused, shunned, or dismissed him. Often he interpreted this as a result of a conspiracy that prevented him from living a life less ordinary; a conspiracy that stopped him being a 'somebody'.

In Hamilton we see the perverted narcissism of all mass and spree murderers and also their desperate attempts to seduce you to their own way of thinking. Indeed, all of this is graphically echoed in the shootings carried out by the American spree killer Elliot Roger, a young man who had spent most of his life desperately trying to be cool, and who began to have 'fantasies of becoming powerful and stopping everyone from having sex'. Most especially it is seen in the following question which Rogers posted on the internet to justify his spree killings in California in 2014: 'Who's the alpha male now, bitches?'

Of course, this is simply another way of 'saving face'; of managing a sense of self and projecting a preferred image of how you would like others to see you. In this way, mass or spree murder becomes a perverted way of performing gender – a toxic, deadly form of masculinity.

Rogers, Breivik and the more recent mass and spree killers might use social media but Hamilton's letters, hand-delivered, often at night, were the forerunners of the web pages, Instagram posts and manifestos that are now routinely left behind by mass murderers and which are scoured after the event for explanation. Hamilton was the analogue troll who unleashed this particular bloody blueprint of death and destruction. He wanted advancement and success and with a gun in his hands he could play God in order to settle once and for all who was right and who was wrong, and so reorder his world to better suit his needs.

In truth, the minds of mass and spree killers haven't changed over the years; their motivations are remarkably similar. What *is* new is the speed and intensification of what they do – a development that has come with the internet being freed from its solitary line into the library to permeate almost everywhere. With the advent of the internet not only can the mass or spree killer get his personal manifesto – his excuse – out much more quickly and to many more people but also, having become so absorbed within social media, he comes to believe that his personal disappointments are much more intense than they might be, which in turn, propels him to take action. The result is therefore all too often the national tragedies that we see on our TV screens. After all, we have become so increasingly enmeshed with our virtual representations of ourselves, that the distinction between our virtual and physical selves continues to erode. That's ominous.

The good news is that in Dunblane one of the solutions to reducing the future incidence of mass or spree murder also emerges: what would have stopped Hamilton was to have made public what many suspected privately.

So far my focus has been on a British mass murder but what about our most recent spree murder?

I wondered how what I had discovered in Dunblane might compare with what had happened 150 miles further south, fourteen years later, and how the people of that area had made sense of the spree murder that took place in their community.

In June 2010 Derrick Bird, a fifty-two-year-old taxi driver, shot and killed twelve people, injured eleven others and then took his own life in what the local newspaper described as a 'killing spree' and a 'rampage throughout Copeland'. Copeland consists of six localities in West Cumbria centred on the towns and larger villages of the area including Gosforth, Seascale, Egremont, St Bees and Whitehaven.

Bird used two legally owned weapons throughout this 'spree' – a shotgun and a .22 rifle fitted with a telescopic sight.

The killings began in the early hours of the morning when

Bird drove to the house of his twin brother, David, shooting him eleven times. The motivation for this was described by the *Guardian* as 'an act of revenge for imagined family injustices,' and it characterised Bird as having 'a persecution complex'. He then went to the house of Kevin Commons, the family's solicitor, and killed him. By this point it was early morning and Bird travelled to a taxi rank in Whitehaven where he shot and killed Darren Rewcastle, a fellow taxi driver, with whom he had a long-standing grievance. Rewcastle had been accused of damaging Bird's car tyres. After driving around he attempted to shoot and kill three other drivers at the rank. On this point, the *Guardian* noted that there had been 'substantial tensions on the cab rank. Fellow drivers said Bird, who, like many cabbies in Whitehaven, worked for himself, had fallen out with several other drivers whom he blamed for stealing his trade.' Bird had also argued with other cabbies that week, 'over drivers taking fares at the back of the queue, instead of sending customers to the first cab on the rank'.

One of the injured drivers, Paul Wilson, would later describe how he had initially thought that Bird had fired a blank at him and that he was being a 'daft bugger', simply 'playing a prank'. He further described how when he had 'turned the corner, I noticed Derrick's taxi in the nearside lane coming towards me. I thought nothing of it and I carried on to the police station. He stopped next to me and called my name. I looked directly at him and I took a few steps towards him and ducked down to look in the passenger window. As I ducked to look at him, he fired. He called me over and shot me.'

Calling people to his taxi and then shooting them in the face was a recurring feature of Bird's spree.

From Whitehaven, Bird journeyed back and forth, shooting more randomly, and killed or injured those people that he encountered as he drove into the villages of Egremont, Thornhill,

Carleton, Wilton, Gosforth and Seascale. Finally, he travelled along the valley road, colliding with oncoming vehicles and a stone wall, before turning off the road signposted 'no through road' to Doctor Bridge, Boot. One of his tyres fell off, which brought the car to a halt. He then left his taxi and made his way on foot into local woodland, where he shot himself.

As the enormity of these events started to sink in, an editorial in the local newspaper struggled to capture a sense of the disbelief people felt and the unprecedented nature of what had happened in their community. 'People woke up yesterday to go about their normal day only to have their worlds shattered in the space of a few hours. Who could believe in our peaceful close-knit community such horror and devastation could occur?' The editorial was entitled 'Carnage in West Cumbria' and sought to draw a comparison; this was, the editorial explained, 'the worst mass shooting since Dunblane in 1996'.

I wanted to take a look at the differences between the two events and so, as with Dunblane, which I had studied before travelling to Cumbria, I drove to Whitehaven and walked in the town's streets, ate in its restaurants and drank in pubs, speaking with any local residents who were prepared to talk to me. I also hired a taxi in the town to take me to the place where Bird would eventually commit suicide, so as to imagine what he might have been thinking about on this forty-five-minute journey into the Eskdale Valley. Finally I visited the memorial to Darren Rewcastle, which his family and friends have created in the town.

What was immediately apparent was that many members of the public were very willing to speak to me about what had happened in 2010 – something at odds with my experience of Dunblane. However, what was common to both locations was emotion; the emotion that is central to small, face-to-face cultures where everyone knows each other and their business. There are comforts in this too and, as one person in Whitehaven described it, there's 'something nostalgic [about] playing pool with a pint, knowing someone you knew would walk past and acknowledge you at some point.'

I also describe what happened in West Cumbria as 'spree murder' and call Bird himself a 'spree murderer'. Spree is different to mass murder and so this is also an immediate criminological difference with what had happened in Dunblane. Bird's shooting spree took seven hours to unfold, during which time he fired in eighteen different locations, rather than just in one, and might best be seen as having three phases. The first phase related to the shooting of his brother and the family solicitor; the second to the murder of Darren Rewcastle and the shots that he fired at his fellow taxi drivers within Whitehaven; and, the final phase, to the more random shootings that took place outside of Whitehaven on his circuitous journey which would eventually end in Boot.

Of the twelve people who were killed by Bird, nine were unknown to him and it was clear that his experience as a taxi driver allowed him to evade detection. One police officer later commented, 'The fact that Derrick Bird had extensive local knowledge, was a taxi driver, was intent on causing as much damage as possible and the route and the amount of terrain he covered . . . made it incredibly difficult to find him.'

As has been alluded to above, there were a number of attempts to make sense of what had happened in the immediate aftermath of the shootings, then at the subsequent coroner's inquest into the deaths, and then again on the occasion of the first-year anniversary of the spree. This 'making sense' was essentially a binary process. In other words, what happened in Whitehaven and beyond was either to be explained through Bird's personal pathology, or through wider, more generic, cultural issues which sought to transcend an understanding based solely on placing responsibility onto Bird.

There was an immediate difficulty with putting responsibility onto Bird, for virtually everyone in Whitehaven that worked with him, or knew him, went out of their way to stress that he was 'a quiet fellow', or an 'ordinary bloke'. Mark Cooper, a friend and fellow taxi driver, described Bird as someone who 'owned his house and car. He paid his round in the pub. He was just like us. I've never seen him lose his temper with anyone or get angry.' Bird's two sons put out a press release in which they described their father as, 'The nicest man you could ever meet. He was a loving dad who had recently become a grandfather ... a loving and cheerful character and was well-known throughout the local community and the areas where he worked.'

As noted in a longer commentary by the journalist Jeremy Seabrook, this picture of Bird as an 'amiable, unassuming man with a quick smile' could be contrasted with a 'more complex picture' which began to emerge as various journalists started to dig a little deeper. This complexity was related to two issues in particular: speculation about Bird's mental health, and his willingness to engage in what was described as 'sex tourism' in Thailand.

In relation to the former, Bird was described as 'paranoid' and 'delusional', especially about his financial affairs. His doctor gave evidence at the coroner's inquiry suggesting that Bird was filled with 'bitterness, resentment and depression', which had led him to 'enact violent retaliatory fantasies'. The idea of 'retaliatory fantasies' may have been given some credence when it emerged that Bird had watched Steven Seagal's *On Deadly Ground* only hours before embarking on the spree, given that the film's plot is largely focussed on a lone gunman taking revenge. However, it is important to acknowledge that it was later revealed that he was not known to local mental health services and had rarely attended his own GP. Indeed, this idea that 'mental health' is often a cause of events such as this is a rather clichéd stereotype and we would all do much better to remember that people who have mental health issues are usually far more likely to harm themselves than attack other people. At the time, I suggested in the press that Bird's spree murders were 'a sadistic act of self-loathing'.

It was writer and journalist Joan Smith who raised broader issues related to spree murder and gender. Smith wondered why 'a very small group of men respond ... by killing people'. Smith was particularly keen to point out Bird's cruelty towards his victims and 'most important of all, [he] was a habitual sexual predator'. Her source for this statement was an interview conducted by the *Sun* with a bar owner in Pattaya, Thailand, who suggested that Bird had visited his bar and had become 'obsessed' with a twenty-two-year-old Thai woman. Smith argued that Bird's behaviour was a manifestation of his need for 'control, a fantasy-driven compensation for the slights and insults [he] perceived in everyday life.' She suggested that there was a 'widespread cultural imperative to normalise sex tourism by Western men' and, whilst this could have been seen as a generic statement about all Western sex tourism, Smith also concluded that 'there is something very seriously wrong with men like Bird'.

What is rarely given much prominence within this analysis is the wider financial pressures that Bird seems to have been under, not just because he believed that he was being investigated by HM Revenue and Customs but also because of increasing stresses at his place of work. There are echoes here too of Hamilton.

The *Guardian* quoted another taxi driver in Whitehaven who suggested that 'there had been a rise in tension at cab ranks in the town because of an increasing number of drivers and a decreasing number of jobs'. The same taxi driver also suggested that 'there are so many new drivers out there and not a lot of jobs. There have been fights over fares and accusations that some drivers are coming in from Preston and Blackpool to take jobs.' Bird's friend Neil Jacques suggested that the day before the spree Bird had wanted to 'talk about his money problems. He thought he was in proper trouble. He was bothered because of the tax demands, he could not cope. He had been doing the taxis for fifteen or sixteen years and he had never paid any tax.'

The day before the shootings, Bird said to a different friend that 'Whitehaven would be as famous as Dunblane' and another resident of the town had even suggested that Bird had, one by one, shaken the hands of his fellow taxi drivers and told them, 'There's going to be a rampage in this town tomorrow', although they had all 'laughed and didn't take him seriously'.

One of the questions that I used to start conversation while I was in the town was to ask about the plaque to Darren Rewcastle. This enquiry immediately allowed conversation to flow and did so without fail. Most people had a story to tell and were only too keen to share what they remembered of Bird and the fateful day in 2010. This willingness to talk to me may have been the result of never having been asked to speak about these events previously, as opposed to the worldwide attention that had been devoted to Dunblane. At the hotel where I stayed, the receptionist said that I was the first person ever to have asked about the shootings. Later, in the bar, I was recognised from a TV appearance and asked, 'You're that criminologist, aren't you? What you doing in Whitehaven?' They made no link between the events only seven years previously and why a criminologist might be visiting the town. Everyone I met told their stories in a pleasant and straightforward way. So much so that I did not once think about asking whether they had had counselling – Whitehaven just didn't seem to be that sort of place. The word to use here is perhaps resilience, although that also doesn't quite fit with what I experienced. A better description might be spirit, or attitude; an attitude which perhaps springs from being geographically located at the end of the line, rather than at the head of the queue.

It seemed important for this criminological autopsy to hire a taxi in the town and so I'd agreed to pay a taxi driver called John £70 to drive me to where Bird had committed suicide in Boot. I wanted to ride in a cab with a local taxi driver and discuss what had happened in Whitehaven, given that this had been Bird's trade and seemed to have been part of the psychosocial context in which the spree took place. Over the course of our ride, John gave me a glimpse into Bird, his psychological state and the culture of taxi drivers in Whitehaven, and I also glimpsed the isolation and beauty of the place in which this spree took place. John had occasionally gone fishing with Bird and described him as a friend and it was John who told me the most revealing story on our journey.

John described a meal that Bird had had with some of his friends in a local restaurant. One of the friends had gone to the loo and removed a small toilet block of disinfectant from the lavatory and placed it on the table in front of Bird. He told him it was a mint. Bird had picked it up and put it in his mouth, chewing it for a few seconds before spitting it out.

Everyone else had laughed but not Bird.

In the face-to-face culture of the town, where everyone knows everyone else, Bird knew that this story was going to be told time after time, until he could no longer bear to even hear the story mentioned. He was ashamed that he had fallen for the prank; he had been humiliated. As John explained, 'You could blend in and disappear in London, but not here. If someone runs away from my taxi without paying their fare they will eventually get back into my taxi. Everyone knows everyone. We're close even though we don't all know each other.'

A number of the people that I spoke to told other stories which suggested that Bird had felt picked on by family, friends and customers. Another taxi driver, for example, told me about an incident with a passenger where Bird had had teeth knocked out, after his passenger had tried to run off without paying his fare.

As we journeyed further into the countryside, we passed a number of hill-walkers and four campsites. I asked John why Bird hadn't shot more people. John replied that he thought that his friend simply 'ran out of ammunition', which suggests that some of the shootings might have been opportunistic. Just at that moment we passed some more walkers and John joked, 'They're giving way to me as they see the taxi stripes and they're thinking the last time I saw a taxi driver up here he had a gun! I'm surprised they haven't run for cover.'

I asked John if he thought that Bird might have been making a point; perhaps trying to take revenge on the people whom he thought had, in some way, wronged him. John replied, 'I don't think that he was trying to achieve anything. I just think he lost his mind. He had a mental list – a paper list has never been found – and was going after his brother, solicitor, Darren and some of the other drivers.'

Like most other people that I spoke to, John was being asked about these matters for the first time and so can be forgiven for appearing contradictory in how he analysed what had happened. After all, suggesting that Bird wasn't trying to achieve anything and then targeting very specific people implies two different things. So too John thought that the people of Whitehaven are, 'Friendly. I can say "hello" and they would say "hello" back. We are just calmer people here,' without realising the irony of that statement.

There were further contradictions. John thought of Bird as 'a loner, although he did mix with people,' and 'I think of it [the spree shootings] as evil what he's done, but he was a normal person before that.' His conclusion about Bird was that 'he was just an ordinary bloke who flipped,' and as a result 'he got Whitehaven recognised for all the wrong reasons.'

Finally, John had an opinion about the police. 'The police didn't want to catch him; they were scared. We are a small town with no armed response. This kind of thing doesn't happen here. Our police are just village blokes that we all know.'

The abiding sense that I got from my criminological autopsy of the events at Whitehaven was of contradiction, both about the place and about Bird himself. Bird was a loner but also someone who you could go out with for a drink; an ordinary man, who seemingly went on sex tours of Thailand. Whitehaven was a place where people were close but didn't really know each other; where duping a colleague into eating lavatory detergent was simply seen as a bit of a joke, rather than bullying; where people were willing to talk but had actually never been asked; a place that was calm but had also produced a horrific spree murder.

These spoken contradictions were in marked contrast to the silences and therefore the public certainties of Dunblane. There the rush to the dispositional had created a clear, unambiguous answer as to the cause of mass murder – Thomas Hamilton. Woe betide anyone who might want to discuss that conclusion further, for that might open up different possibilities and exactly the same contradictions that I found being expressed in Whitehaven.

There are other differences too. For one thing, Whitehaven has never become defined by Bird's killing spree. The press describe what he did as 'The Cumbria Shootings', in contrast to how Dunblane is remembered. What Bird did was fragmented – it was a spree; Hamilton's murders were concentrated in one small space.

And, of course, Hamilton also largely targeted children, whereas Bird killed adults.

And what about Bird and Hamilton as men? What can we learn from them about mass and spree killers?

First, both of them killed using legally owned firearms and neither was seen to have been so odd as to have had their shotgun licences revoked. Neither Bird nor Hamilton were known to mental health services. Here, though, it is worth noting that our already tough gun laws were strengthened even further in the wake of Dunblane and the Firearms Amendment Act came into force in December 1997. Second, both Hamilton and Bird were part of the communities in which they murdered and they both seem to have harboured grudges against a number of people or institutions which then prompted and shaped what they did. These were not alien 'others' who entered Dunblane and Whitehaven but embedded members of their local communities.

For me these grudges are key.

Hamilton and Bird wanted advancement and success, like all the more recent mass murderers, but what they experienced or imagined (especially in Bird's case) were set-backs and disappointment, often through their own, all-too-obvious inadequacies.

Not so with a gun in their hands.

With a gun they could play God so as to settle, once and for all, who was right and who was wrong; with a gun they could take revenge on the communities they had grown to hate; with a gun they could save face.

As they would both have seen it, theirs was righteous slaughter which served to reorder their world in a way that better suited who they thought that they were and what they were entitled to. Hamilton and Bird committed these murders themselves and for their own warped reasons, but I've also encountered men whose deadly services could be hired.

CHAPTER EIGHT

Hitmen and a Hitwoman

'Hitmen occupy a secret world, an underworld, where they make business transactions with others wishing to conduct themselves "beyond the pale."'

LAURIE CALHOUN, *The International Journal of Human Rights*, 2002: 9

I am sitting in a café, drinking a cup of tea which is brewed so strongly that I involuntarily grimace every time I put the mug to my mouth.

It's the type of café that most people would walk past, rather than enter; more of a caff, really. It's not unwelcoming but it has an air about it that suggests that there will be trouble if you actually go inside and, as it happens, I am the only customer. Inevitably it was suggested as a good place to meet by the person that I have come to interview.

He's late and I'm now starting to worry that he might not show.

I bring the mug of tea to my mouth once more but only mime drinking its contents. The proprietor looks over at me and I fear that he guesses that I'm not really drinking anything at all. I put the mug back down on the table.

The interview I'm about to conduct has taken several weeks and hundreds of phone calls to set up. I have spent that time vouching and assuring and endlessly guaranteeing that I am just an academic who is interested in asking a few questions about contract killing. Nothing more. The main guarantee I've had to give is that I'm definitely not a detective and that everything said in the interview will be off the record.

I haven't asked permission from the university's ethics committee to conduct the interview, as I am more or less certain that none would have been given. I've taken the view that it is easier to ask for forgiveness than permission.

I look out of the window, hoping that my interviewee will arrive soon, and then look back at my watch. I'll give him ten more minutes.

The mug of tea seems to be staring back at me, gloating in triumph.

Then, unobtrusively, suddenly, I'm taken by surprise and he's sitting beside me. I hadn't seen him enter until he was literally pulling up a chair at my table. It was only later that I realised that this was part of his professionalism; a skill that he has perfected in his trade.

'Another mug?' he asks.

'Thanks,' I reply, dreading that it would have been offensive to have refused.

He looks over at the proprietor and shouts, 'Bring them over won't you, Del?' Del nods and seconds later two mugs of the same offensively strong tea have been left on the table.

'OK,' my informant says, getting down to business, 'you want to know why the doorstep?'

And so begins one of the most fascinating encounters of my life. An interview with a hitman.

I did indeed want to know why the doorstep seems to be one of the most common sites where a hit will take place. Is there something psychological going on here, or is the choice of location merely picked for practical purposes? A doorstep is what we call a 'liminal space' – it's a boundary between the interior, private world of home and family and the external, public reality of the person's life in the community and the world beyond. The doorstep exists on the edge of these spaces and therefore occupies an ambiguity that might suggest that the hit is personal or, alternatively, intended to make a much more public statement about the victim.

For the next hour I am offered a masterclass in the choice of location for a hit. No tape recording was allowed but when the hour was up my frantic scribbles had filled my notebook with inky smudges. I used the train journey back home to decipher what I had written and flesh out from memory some of the things that we had discussed.

We started with the doorstep:

DW: Why would some hitmen commit their hits in the street and others on the doorstep of the person they're targeting? Why would they commit the hit on their doorstep? Why would they decide to hit them on the doorstep as opposed to going into the house?

HITMAN: That's pretty easy to answer. If you're going up to your doorway, you've got your back to the street, so it's a simple matter of slipping in behind somebody fumbling for their keys, concentrating on their door, then two in the back of the head and you walk away. If you go into the house, you might leave forensics, if you're on the doorstep, bang – simple. It's like the Jill Dando case: straight in the head, walk away. And that's the way you do it; you do it like that because that's the one moment that somebody feels at ease. It's their own home: they're going through a familiar ritual; getting their keys out, they're not looking at what's behind them – it's a perfect moment. The ones on the street are mainly done for show because somebody wants to send a message of what happens if you mess around.

DW: Is it therefore less risky to do it on the doorstep?

HITMAN: Oh definitely, definitely, you're not out on the street, especially if somebody lives in a residential street because it's a simple matter, you slip in. You follow them down the street and slip in off the street ... boom boom. Done. You know. And then you walk away because people might hear the noise and think it's a backfire or it's anything else, could be a car tyre bursting. So it's the fact that they are very comfortable where they are so they're not going to be suspecting of it, unless you're me because when I'm going to my door I'm always looking around, but that's experience because I know. And that's the reason for it: it's quick and easy and you know that they are going to be distracted; they're not going to be on the ball and they're going to feel quite safe because they're on the verge of entering their own property so that's why.

DW: You mentioned Jill Dando; she was only shot once in the back of the head, not twice. Do you think that is significant?

HITMAN: I do yeah, I mean if I was asked to comment on that I'd say the gun probably failed to go off the second time. It was very unusual ammunition as well, homemade ammunition, so you can easily get a misfire round. So I should imagine it was supposed to be two ... that's ... You know ... that's the way to do it, two shots.

DW: Do you think the Dando hit was done by a professional, master-hitman?

HITMAN: I do yeah, I do.

DW: What makes you think that?

HITMAN: Well the fact that it was on her doorstep, as I've explained that's the way it's done. The fact that she was shot in the head. I mean … an amateur might shoot them in the body, might be a bit squeamish, one in the body first to see how it goes. That was someone who has killed before. Someone who has just walked up and boom. Probably tried for the second shot, couldn't get it and just walked away. And that's the way I see it. I've been in jail with hitmen and loads of people who have done hits and most of them you know quite professionally. The idiots are the ones who drive around in cars and spray machine guns out of the windows and things like that.

DW: Of those professional hitmen that you know, how did they train to become hitmen?

HITMAN: You do it through a combination. You start young. This is how you become a hitman if you sort of going this route. When you're in prison you can get hired to do hits in prison. People do them very cheap, not necessarily killing people but giving people some serious damage. The favourite in Parkhurst and places like that was to wait till the target was in the shower – couple of geezers with a spike and stab him as many times as you can. It's called tea bagging – not the same as the tea bagging you hear about out here but that's what it's called because you leave them with a thousand perforations. If you're doing hits in jail for a drug dealer then when you get out, the next logical, progressive step is that they already know you, you know them. Word spreads that you're willing to do that for money so that's how they get their training – when they're in jail. Most of them that I know, that's how they've done it. They become reliable; they keep their mouths shut; they know how to get rid of the evidence, because don't forget when you're in a prison, if someone gets stabbed right, you've got to get rid of the weapon, you've got to get rid of all of the forensics, clothes and everything. So what you do is you go around, and you have people who you hand your jumper to and they'll get it out and rip it into pieces out that window onto the wire – boom. The knife goes down the toilet, whatever. So it's ... it's ... the essence of it is prison ... what you do in prison, if you're good at it you can do it outside – see what I mean?

DW: Why do some hitmen leave their gun at the site of the hit?

HITMAN: Because then they are untraceable. If you get caught with that gun, you're tied to that hit. That's why if you go and get some guns to do an armed robbery and you go to an armorer they will say, 'Do you want clean or dirty?' Now that means do you want a gun that has been used in something that may come back on you if you haven't got an alibi. Or do you want a clean gun, which costs more. So if you can, say, get two revolvers and one of them has been used in six different shootings and you get caught with that revolver in your hand – you're down for those six shootings unless you've got a very good alibi, so that's why they leave the gun. The gun is always a throwaway or it might have been something that has been used over the border – so you just leave it – it's not worth the money taking it with you because you're looking at a life sentence as opposed to £500 for the gun – so you just drop it and leave it! If you get caught with it, that's it.

In one hour I'd discovered more than I'd thought possible about hits and hitmen.

But how did I get here?

It's strange the roads that life can take us on and, in this case about hitmen, it really *was* a road and a particular place: Spaghetti Junction. On my drive into Birmingham City University I have to leave the M6 at the infamous Junction 6. As I progress down my exit, slowly spiralling around the various, confusing, intertwined roads there is a billboard which has been carefully placed, so as to maximise the number of drivers and their passengers who will catch sight of what's on it. For several months in 2007, it advertised a movie called *Hitman*, starring Timothy Olyphant.

My journey through Spaghetti Junction ensured that I saw that poster day after day after day. Even so I had no further information about the film and, to be honest, I had never even heard of Timothy Olyphant.

Several of my students went to see the film and when I asked about it, they explained that the movie was based on a Danish video game of the same name – most of them had gone to the movie because they were already big fans of the game. The protagonist in both the game and the film is Agent 47 and it was this character that was being played by Olyphant. His image as that character dominated the billboard.

It was this image that had initially caught my attention. It was very deliberately stylised: Agent 47 wore a black suit; black leather gloves; and a white dress shirt, coupled with a red tie. The character was bald (or at least had a shaved head) and had deep, penetrating blue eyes. He carried a silver gun in each of his gloved hands. The design conveyed an impression of glamorous professionalism – it suggested a man who knew how to get the job done and with style.

I started to wonder, Is that what hitmen are really like? How close were they to the portrayal of the professional, trained, criminal undertakers like Agent 47 who, acting on behalf of an organised criminal network – or indeed as part of a government agency – ruthlessly pursued their targets and, like Canadian Mounties, 'got their man'?

It wasn't as if this was an unusual trope. Hitmen have become familiar figures in crime films, TV drama, popular fiction and video games – they seem to be everywhere, carrying out these fictional hits within smoky rooms, bars and casinos frequented by gangsters, well-hidden from everyday members of the public. What I wanted to know was how this really compared with the criminological reality and so I set about researching the real world of contract killers, hits and hitmen.

There were immediately a number of obstacles.

As the American philosopher Laurie Calhoun observes, hitmen 'occupy a secret world', which presents a number of challenges for any academic who wants to research this type of offender and the circumstances in which they operate. Perhaps as a result there has been comparatively little academic research into hitmen, or the phenomenon of contract killing.

This did not deter me. I knew that there had to have been murders of this kind, as research by a variety of criminologists into organised crime in the UK had long established a link between violence – including lethal violence – and illegal trading networks. Still, my task was not going to be an easy one. So, along with some of my PhD students and colleagues at Birmingham City University, I embarked on a journey to discover something of the reality of contract killing (now called 'targeted attacks' by the police) in Britain.

Our first task was to define what we meant when we said that someone was a 'hitman'. After debating this to and fro, we eventually settled that a hitman was someone who had accepted an order to kill another human being from somebody who is not publicly acknowledged as a legitimate authority regarding 'just killing'. Using this definition allowed us to avoid philosophical debates about whether, for example, soldiers or state executioners should be considered as hitmen. It's an important debate but one which would have clouded the research we were setting out to undertake. The definition also implies a distance between the victim and the perpetrator – a distance not present in conventional homicide or murder, where there is usually a prior relationship between victim and perpetrator.

In our research we discovered only one British 'hitwoman' and so we retained the gender-specific description of hitman.

After deciding on how to define a hitman, the next step was to look at newspapers so as to build up a sample of people that had been described as 'hitmen' and convicted of contract killing, or attempting to carry out such a killing. Eventually, our research produced a list of twenty-seven cases of contract killing committed by a total of thirty-six hitmen (a number of hitmen worked with an accomplice) active in Britain from 1974 to 2013.

Somewhat controversially, given the ethics of conducting academic research, we also used our own extensive networks of offenders, ex-offenders and those who work, or have worked, as part of the criminal justice system to gain access to those with direct knowledge of contract killings. I would go on to conduct a small number of off-the-record interviews with these informants, so as to provide a means of triangulating the information we had gathered.

All of this means the results which we generated related only to those hitmen who had been caught and so the hitmen who remained at large might present a very different profile to that which we produced. It should also be remembered that we only looked into British hitmen and so it is perfectly possible that there may be differences abroad and at odds with the typology of hitmen that we developed. Unless otherwise stated, the research below refers to British examples and we consciously excluded hits conducted in Northern Ireland.

And, despite all the difficulties involved and the 'ifs' and 'buts' of what we could produce, this was exciting research. It felt like we were explorers drawing, as best we could, the contours of a new, undiscovered territory.

We also tried to discover what might have motivated the hit. However, even after looking through our sample in some detail, it was difficult to be precise as to what might have motivated each of these hits, though where a motive could be discerned, the majority seemed to have been the result of a business dispute of some kind, especially contracting the hit to remove a successful rival. The motivations that we could establish for the other hits included: disputes within gangs or, more formally, 'organised criminal networks'; using the hit as a mechanism to rise up a gang hierarchy; domestic disagreements between divorcing husbands and wives; cases of mistaken identity; or, more broadly, the hits related to 'honour killings'. Of course, it was very rare for the hitmen themselves to discuss who had commissioned them, or why they had been commissioned in the first place.

So, what did we find?

At a general level, far from the media portrayal of hits being conducted inside smoky rooms frequented by members of an organised crime gang, they were more usually carried out in the open, on pavements, sometimes as the target was out walking their dog, or going shopping, with passers-by watching in abject horror. Hits emerged from and took place within the suburbs, not the criminal underworld beloved by fiction. Often the victim and the hitman lived in the same locality and indeed this lack of geographic mobility on the part of the hitmen was one of the most common reasons why they were brought to justice.

After gathering our wealth of research, we also attempted

to construct a typology of British hitmen. Typologies can be used to better explain the phenomenon that is being discussed, although they are also fraught with difficulties. There can be and often is 'seepage' between one type and another; different academics looking at the same material might not agree with the classification adopted; and there needs to be a willingness to update these types based on the discovery of new evidence. However, we hoped that our typology would be seen as a starting point for further discussion.

We decided that the information that we had collected suggested that there were four different types of hitmen whom, again after much deliberation, we decided to call: the Novice; the Dilettante; the Journeyman; and the Master.

We gave these labels considerable thought, as we wanted to capture accurately the skills and experience shown by the different hitmen that we uncovered. We also recognised that some might see these descriptions – especially that of being a Master – as glorifying murderers. That was not our intention. These labels that we have given to the hitmen are being used as they express the patterns and characteristics of the different types of hits that took place and the crime scenes that were created. We also noted that many of the cases that were reported upon involved someone carrying out a hit for the first time, for which we'd use the description Novice. By this we mean that the hitman was a trainee, or a beginner. However, this should not be interpreted as implying that the hitman was unable to plan the hit, or carry it out successfully.

Let's consider a few of these Novices in detail. They include the youngest hitman that appeared in our research. In 2010, teenager Santre Sanchez Gayle, who was fifteen years old at the time, killed Gulistan Subasi and was paid just £200, despite having been promised £2,000. He undertook the hit so as to prove himself to his fellow gang members.

Sanchez Gayle had carefully planned the hit and had left no forensic evidence at the crime scene. He took a taxi to the house where his victim had been staying, executed the hit and then returned home, again in a taxi. The taxi driver later described Gayle as being 'normal' on the journey away from the murder. According to the senior investigating officer attached to the case, the police initially viewed the murder as being the work of a 'professional'. All of this may have been because Sanchez Gayle was not unaware of the world of crime – two of his elder half-brothers were in prison for unrelated murders and he himself was a member of the gang called the Kensal Green Boys and had the street-name 'Riot'.

In fact, Sanchez Gayle was only caught because he bragged about the murder to his friends, who then reported him to the police – he was subsequently sentenced to a minimum of twenty years in prison for the murder.

The Novice categorisation also included the only female 'hitwoman' we came across in our research. Te Rangimaria Ngarimu, a Maori woman living in London, was contracted to murder Graham Woodhatch, a roofing contractor. This hit seems to have been motivated by a business dispute. She was paid £1,500 – having been promised £7,000 – and shot Woodhatch while he recovered from an operation at the Royal Free Hospital in North London. Ngarimu had tried to carry out the hit the previous day but, having failed, returned to the hospital disguised as a man and was successful. Immediately after the shooting, Ngarimu fled to New Zealand and though her flight aroused the police's suspicions at the time, they had no forensic evidence against her and she was not arrested.

It was only after a visit to her local church in New Zealand and against the advice of her lawyer that Ngarimu returned to Britain to confess to her role in the murder and was subsequently sentenced to life imprisonment. It remains unknown why a multi-lingual, devout Christian who held several degrees, who had never been in trouble with the police, agreed to the commit the hit although, as with Sanchez Gayle, perhaps the fact that she was paid less for carrying out the hit than she had been promised reveals an underlying naivety.

Next let's consider the Dilettante, who is often much older than the Novice when planning, or conducting, the hit and seems to have decided to do so for a range of reasons. The label Dilettante was used to imply that this type of hitman does not necessarily come from an offending background, belong to a gang, or work for a government agency and only seems to have decided to accept a contract as a way of resolving some form of personal crisis. More often than not this personal crisis was financial. As such the Dilettante dabbles and dips into the culture of contract killing, but not necessarily with any enthusiasm, or indeed with much skill.

The case of Orville Wright perhaps best illustrates the Dilettante. Wright, who had previously worked as a legal clerk in Jamaica, was offered £5,000 to carry out the murder of Theresa Pitkin by her former lover. Wright broke into Theresa's flat in North London wearing a balaclava and brandishing a knife. However, after speaking to his intended victim, Wright decided he could not go through with the task of killing her. Described by the judge at his trial as 'a hitman who lost his nerve', Wright's inability to complete the hit displayed the incompetent and dis-organised nature of his involvement in contract murder. This also helps to explain why Wright was only jailed for two and a half years. From the details of the case described above, we can presume that Wright's intention was to use a knife against his victim. This again displays a difference in technique as often the Dilettante, unlike the other hitmen in our sample, could not gain access to firearms.

Like Wright, Paul Cryne was also a Dilettante hitman. Cryne

was jailed for life in 2010 for the murder of Sharon Birchwood. Cryne had lived a high-rolling lifestyle in Thailand throughout the 1990s, after receiving a £500,000 insurance payout. However, his excessive spending eventually caught up with him and, while on bail for suspicion of carrying out another contract murder, Cryne managed to accumulate a debt of £11,000. At this point, he seems to have met up with Sharon Birchwood's ex-husband, Graham, through the expatriate community in Thailand, and accepted the contract to kill her. Sharon Birchwood's death would allow her ex-husband to inherit £475,000. Contracted for £30,000, Cryne flew back to the United Kingdom and strangled Birchwood in her home, leaving her 'cruelly trussed-up with parcel tape and electrical cord'. Cryne was apprehended after leaving forensic evidence at the scene of the crime which the police matched to his DNA sample, taken after an arrest for a crime he had committed many years earlier.

Finally, the case of Richard Austin and Carlton Alveranga throws further light onto Dilettante hitmen. Having been contracted and instructed through gangland connections, in March 2006 Austin and Alveranga were driven to the Brass Handles pub in Salford, Manchester, where their two intended targets were watching a football match. A witness would later describe the pair as 'appearing reluctant to go inside', although they did continue into the pub, each armed with a handgun. According to news reports, Austin fired six bullets, five of which hit their targets. During the hit one of the guns jammed and the crowd inside the pub disarmed the pair and then fired back at them. As a result, Austin and Alveranga 'staggered outside and collapsed' – both later died of their gunshot wounds.

Each of these three cases of the Dilettante hitman shows clearly this type of hitman's general lack of success. Often they fail to kill their intended target; they may use different methods to attempt the hit from the norm, generally because they are unable to source a firearm; any firearms they do get hold of can be faulty; they get 'cold feet' – and they are always caught.

The Journeyman classification has some parallels to the Dilettante, in that they're not especially exceptional performers. However, they are capable, experienced and reliable which, in some instances, means that their hits can remain undetected for a lot longer than with Novice and Dilettante hitmen. This description fits John Childs. Childs was also the most prolific hitman that we uncovered, although I suspect that very few people have ever heard of him and we do have to take some of his confessions on trust. Between 1974 and 1978 Childs carried out six murders – I cannot think of a serial killer convicted of a similar number of crimes who would have escaped public attention.

Childs was an outlier in our research in many ways. In Childs' killings, for example, we found the only child victim of a hit. In 1975 he not only murdered his intended target but also his target's son, for fear that the boy would be able to identify Childs as the killer. Unlike the majority of the victims in our sample, the bodies of his victims were never found and we therefore only have Childs' account of how these hits were carried out – if they were carried out at all. It may well be, for his own personal reasons, that Childs has exaggerated how many hits he conducted, as a perverted way to garner some offending kudos. However, if we are to believe him, Childs would take his victims to his house in London, dismember and then finally burn them. In 1980 he was sentenced to life imprisonment, having initially been arrested for a series of security van and bank robberies.

The hitman team of David Smith and Roger Vincent could also be described as Journeymen. Smith and Vincent were sentenced to a minimum of twenty-five and thirty years respectively for the murder of David King. Known as 'Rolex Dave', King was described as being a 'well-known underworld figure with many enemies'. Displaying some of the most obvious characteristics of Journeyman hitmen, the hit executed by Smith and Vincent was well planned and organised. The police believe the motive behind the murder was related to organised criminal activity. It was assumed by his killers that King had become a police informant, after a case held against him for importing 14kg of heroin had been dropped in 2002. When King left his local gym on the morning of 3 October 2003, Smith and Vincent were waiting outside in a stolen Peugeot Boxer van and ambushed him. Vincent fired in excess of twenty-five rounds from an AK-47 Kalashnikov machine gun, killing King instantly.

After the shooting, Smith and Vincent fled the scene, burned the van and then proceeded to escape in another pre-arranged vehicle. It was during this change in getaway vehicle that Smith and Vincent made the mistake that would ultimately lead to their apprehension. Police found a plastic glove in the second van and were able to identify Smith via a palm print. From this they were able to track over 100,000 mobile phone calls and collect over 1,200 witness statements. During their sentencing, the judge stated that the hit was 'a thoroughly planned, ruthless and brutally executed assassination'.

There are a number of characteristics in this case that iden-tify Smith and Vincent as Journeymen. First, a gun was used to shoot their victim and it was a much more dangerous and unpredictable weapon than that used by any other hitman in our sample. Second, the crime scene was organised, in that the hitmen knew where their intended victim would be and ensured that they were able to get away from the hit leaving as little forensic evidence as possible. Their target was well known to criminal networks in the area and thus the contractor's motives undoubtedly had roots in organised crime. So too we should note that Smith and Vincent were apprehended due to local intelligence, the discovery of a glove with a palm print and as a result of eyewitness testimony.

The oldest hitman we uncovered was sixty-three-year-old David Harrison, whom we also described as a Journeyman within our typology. In summer 2010, Harrison travelled to the Staffordshire home of Richard Deakin, where he proceeded to shoot the skip hire boss in the chest and leg while he slept. It was quickly established that the motive for this attack was not robbery, given that valuables within the house were left untouched. Described as a 'bull-necked, toothless, career criminal', Harrison was soon under police suspicion for the murder. Harrison made a number of fundamental mistakes that led to his conviction. These mistakes included mobile phone records that placed him at, or near, the murder scene on three separate mornings prior to the hit; police discovered £26,000 in banknotes at his second home, all of which were dated within two weeks of the murder and which are presumed to have been his payment; and, in a further search of his home, police uncovered newspaper cuttings about the murder.

After Harrison was sentenced to life imprisonment, a casework lawyer from West Midlands Crown Prosecution Service's complex casework unit stated that: 'This has been an important prosecution where a professional hitman and his driver have been convicted of a cold and calculated murder, depriving two very young children of their father.'

Harrison's case, like that of Vincent and Smith, demonstrates many of the characteristics that we would expect from the Journeyman. First, his method of executing the hit is consistent with our expectation that he would use a gun, though the sawn-off shotgun that he used to kill Mr Deakin was never recovered. Second, the crime scene was organised, with little or no forensic evidence found. It is unclear as to why this hit had been contracted and police were unable to establish a definitive motive at the time. The final characteristic of the Journeyman hitman is the fact that Harrison was already involved in crime and, quite apart from this hit, he was suspected of having used a crossbow bolt to kill another target.

Finally, we come to the Master category. This one remains a mystery, as we didn't uncover anyone within this last classification, suggesting that the Master hitman is not easily caught. Indeed, I have to assume that the man we met at the start of this chapter was a Master hitman. What we can do is glimpse how a Master hitman operates when carrying out a hit, and the murder of Frank McPhee in Scotland in May 2000 is a good place to start. McPhee, popularly described as a 'gangland boss', was killed by a single shot to the head from a .22 rifle with a telescopic sight outside of his house in Maryhill – just 500 yards from the Maryhill Police Station. It is widely believed that McPhee was killed by a hitman to prevent him from becoming involved with the sale of drugs in Northern Ireland. McPhee's killer has never been brought to justice, but cases of this kind did throw further light onto the characteristics and patterns of behaviours associated with our other three types, even if it didn't help us to establish the identity of this Master hitman.

From my discussions with a network of informants, it was clear that such Masters do indeed exist and it was alleged that they would often come from military or para-military backgrounds, though this is impossible to verify with any certainty. These Masters, by virtue of evading justice, exist in the shadows – almost like ghosts – and it has therefore been impossible to build up any concrete picture of them as individuals, as opposed to the picture that I have been able to present of the types of hits that they might execute.

It would appear that one of the major reasons that they evade justice is that these Masters travel into the community where the hit is to take place and then leave that community shortly afterwards. As such, local intelligence about the hit and the hitman is minimal. This is an important consideration, for it was local intelligence which, by and large, brought most of the British hitmen in our sample to justice.

In one sense therefore our typology is based on failure – the only hitmen we can accurately describe are those that have been apprehended and then prosecuted. It is impossible for us to say to what extent these hitmen are characteristic of those who evade justice. Almost certainly they will have more sophisticated methods for carrying out hits – it might even be the case that some hitmen are so adept as killers that the deaths of their victims do not even raise suspicion and are thought to be the result of natural causes. It's impossible to verify these conjectures but, as this is theoretically possible, it makes it extremely difficult to determine whether or not the incidence of contract killing is stable, getting worse, or indeed falling.

What emerged as crucial in our discussions was motivation. The hitman was primarily motivated by cash, although a small number of our hitmen were members of gangs, or organised trading networks, and so could establish their reputations as reliable and competent if they carried out a hit. However, the gang or the illegal trading network was also in business to generate an income. For the individual hitman, if he wanted to make as much money as he could, he had to be professional. Being professional, above all, meant not getting caught. Here was an important difference between hitmen and serial killers. The hitman was extrinsically motivated – his motivation was not the same as the intrinsically motivated serial killer. Understanding this allowed me to think more about how the successful hitman might psychologically reframe his intended target into being 'cash' or 'just money', rather than as another sentient human. These were not people who were being shot; they were not 'victims'; they were 'targets'. When I asked the Master hitman in the café about all of this, he simply smiled, sipped a little more of his tea and replied, 'It's business'. The successful hitmen were what

Professor Steve Hall calls 'criminal entrepreneurs', or 'criminal undertakers' who were able to reframe their intended victim as someone – something – less than human.

In that sense, could we regard Novices and Dilettantes as criminal entrepreneurs? Did their reputations develop in prison or the community, or did they have different reputations and motivations altogether? Were they also able to psychologically reframe their targets in the same way as Journeymen and Master hitmen? Thinking about these questions allowed me to go further into the world of effective and unsuccessful contract killers.

I wanted to understand what our Novice and Dilettante hitmen – Sanchez Gayle, Ngarimu, Wright or Cryne – could tell us about psychological reframing. I wanted to see if they reframed their actions so as to be able to execute the hit and therefore engage in a process whereby their victims were depersonalised and simply became 'targets' or just 'money'.

We can consider all of this best by contrasting the cases of Wright and Sanchez Gayle. Wright, 'the hitman who lost his nerve', clearly could not reframe Theresa Pitkin as just money – a process that seems to have been destabilised when he engaged his intended victim in conversation. Wright spent time with Pitkin and therefore got to know her as an individual. Sanchez Gayle, on the other hand, was the consummate professional and, if the taxi driver is to be believed, was coldness personified. He also shot his victim as she came to the door, a hallmark of hits. If he hadn't bragged to friends, who knows if this would just have been the first hit of a Master hitman?

The cases of Ngarimu and Cryne also both offer us further insight into the reframing process. Ngarimu, our only hitwoman, was unable to maintain this reframing on her return to New Zealand. In her native country, where she seemingly re-established her faith and, perhaps just as importantly, where she was physically removed from the pressures that had first led to her accepting a contract, she could no longer sustain the idea that her hit was just 'cash' and not another human being. Reframing would therefore seem not to be a once-and-for-all process but rather something that needs to be constantly managed. For Ngarimu to have done that she would have needed to engage in further hits so that this process became embedded into her working, or 'professional' personality.

On the other hand Cryne, while successfully executing his hit, nonetheless did so using a method – stabbing – which indicated unfamiliarity with guns, or an inability to gain access to one. The manner in which he carried out the murder precipitated his arrest. However, he does seem to have viewed his target as just 'money' and to have successfully depersonalised her as a target.

At first glance, only Sanchez Gayle appears to have come from an offending background and to have engaged in this reframing process. Neither Wright nor Ngarimu would appear to have had criminal records, although Cryne had committed a much earlier offence which had led to his DNA being kept on the national database. More tellingly, what seems to have driven each of them to the hit was their need to generate income. Yet Wright was unable to achieve his objective, perhaps because he spent some time talking with his intended victim which prevented any psychological reframing from taking place. As a result, his intended victim quickly regained her individuality, rather than remaining just money.

Thinking about this further, British hitmen do not exist solely, or perhaps even primarily, within some secret, criminal underworld. Rather, they are often part of that community in which their hits take place. Indeed, this reality is one of the major reasons why they are eventually apprehended.

Nor were all of the hits in our sample particularly professionally carried out. Dilettante hitmen in particular changed their minds; they got cold feet and could, in extreme circumstances, become the victims of their intended targets themselves. The Journeyman hitman could be successful over a long period of time, although thankfully he would eventually be caught – largely due to the intelligence that was built up about his activities and through developments in forensic science. The importance too of police informants cannot be underestimated.

Hits in this respect were not unusual and extraordinary but rather commonplace and ordinary. So, too, the motives for a hit being contracted were mundane. Frankly, the motivations to pay a hitman the relatively small amount to carry out a murder were depressingly banal and misogyny was never far from the surface. Husbands and wives fell out with each other, or wanted to gain early access to life insurance policies, and all too often it was the ex-husband who wanted his former wife or partner killed. Business partners wanted to go their separate ways; business deals fell apart; and young male gang members wanted to impress other, older male gang members with their bravado.

As far as I could see, the life of your average a hitman is far more banal than the life of Agent 47 would lead you to believe.

Chapter Nine

Interviewing Murderers and Other Violent Men

'Real empathy; real not phony. Not just calling a guy by his first name, or shaking hands, or giving him a cup of coffee and cigarettes and going through all the standard procedure of putting a guy at ease. That's important but there had to be real empathy which, impossible as it may sound, lacks judgement. They [serial killers like him] have a particular view of the world that you have to discover.'

American serial killer Ted Bundy in one of his final police interviews

The Colston Hall in Bristol was filling up rapidly, as I sat backstage with Dean Strang and Jerry Buting eating crudités. Strang and Buting had been the lawyers who had unsuccessfully defended Steven Avery on a murder charge in 2007 – a defence which had been brought to the public's attention through the documentary series *Making a Murderer*. Avery had previously been exonerated, after spending almost two decades in prison, from guilt for a violent crime. However, despite

Strang and Buting's best efforts, he was then convicted along with his nephew Brendan Dassey of murdering Teresa Halbach.

It seemed that almost everyone had an opinion about Avery's guilt or innocence once the documentary was aired on Netflix and Strang and Buting's dogged, albeit fruitless, defence of their client had turned them into the unexpected stars of the series.

Strang and Buting now wanted to use their personal popularity to discuss not only the Avery case but also miscarriages of justice more generally and the broader failings of the American judicial system. I joined them as moderator for a number of nights of the tour they used as a vehicle for getting those discussions out more widely and so I got to know them well. By the time we reached Bristol, we had hammered out what we thought was a good first half to the event before we would open the floor to audience questions. I had a range of questions that would get the pair talking and also posed one or two awkward ones relating to the partiality of the series.

One of my set questions related to the police interviews of Brendan Dassey.

Dassey was Avery's sixteen-year-old nephew, an introverted teenager attending special education classes at his high school because of his low IQ. Despite this, he was questioned by the police on four occasions over a forty-eight-hour period, without legal representation, or an adult guardian being present. During his ordeal, Dassey would eventually confess to local detectives Tom Fassbender and Mark Wiegert that he and his uncle had murdered Halbach – a confession he later retracted. He explained to his mother that he'd only confessed because Fassbender and Wiegert had 'got in my head' but by that point it was too late.

I usually gave this question to Strang.

'Dean, the police interviews of Brendan Dassey were one of

the standout moments of the series. How typical is this style of interviewing in the US?'

I liked this question as it opened up a number of different areas which we could cover. Most immediately: the differences between police interviewing techniques in the US and the UK; confessions and their use; false confessions as a feature of mis-carriages of justice; and the broader issue of how we might tell if someone is lying, or telling the truth.

It seemed to me that Dassey's confession was something that we would have called in this country a 'coerced-compliant confession', which would therefore have rendered it useless in a British court. As Fassbender and Weigart conducted all four interviews without a guardian or legal representative being present, this would also have made this confession ineligible. Dassey's conviction, as far as I was concerned, had therefore been a miscarriage of justice.

I was less convinced – and unquestionably less certain than Dean and Jerry – about Avery's innocence, especially as his past history of offending and unsavoury behaviour seemed to have been ignored within the documentary.

'That's right, David,' Dean would reply, 'what we see in these interviews are a number of aspects of the Reid technique.'

John Reid was a former police officer in Chicago who became a polygraph expert in the 1940s. He believed that he could get even the most recalcitrant suspect to confess – not through the common tactic at the time of beating the suspect (sometimes called 'the third degree') but through a technique he'd developed, alongside his self-taught understanding of human psychology. This technique is now widely taught to police officers in the US as the best way to interrogate suspects.

Reid's technique has two phases. First there is an interview to determine if the suspect has a case to answer, based on whether the police officer believes that the person is lying or telling the truth. The second phase involves the nine-stage Reid method of interviewing. These nine stages, which don't need to be used in order, or even all carried out, are:

- Direct, positive confrontation
- Theme development
- Handling denials
- Overcoming objections
- Procurement and retention of the suspect's attention
- Handling the suspect's passive mood
- Presenting an alternative question
- Having the suspect orally relate various details of the offence
- Converting an oral confession into a written confession.

It is perhaps the first of these stages that reveals the crucial difference between what happens in the US and the approach here. The Reid technique is predicated on being accusatory, rather than investigatory. As such, American police officers will confront their suspect with the details of the case and the evidence they have against them at the start of the interview. Crucially, though, that evidence does not have to be genuine – American detectives are allowed to lie. They may state that they have found the suspect's DNA or fingerprints at the crime scene, or that there are witnesses who have identified the suspect as being the culprit. None of this needs to be true.

The second stage of 'theme development' then involves the detective suggesting more palatable reasons as to why the suspect might have committed the crime – even if they did not – as excuses that they might latch on to, as the interview progresses, to explain their behaviour. These excuses might include the detective suggesting that, 'We know you didn't mean to do this', or perhaps, 'You had put up with so much and then something just snapped'. This will go on for many hours, until eventually the interviewee cracks and 'confesses', even if that confession might be for a crime that they did not in fact commit. The suspect signs the confession, often because they want the interrogation to stop and perhaps in the belief that a later retraction of that confession will sort things out. It usually does not.

There are three different types of false confession: voluntary false confessions; coerced-compliant confessions, such as the one suggested above; and coerced-internalised false confessions, when an innocent suspect actually comes to believe that they *are* guilty of the crime, although they have no memory of committing it.

Innocent people might volunteer false confessions as the result of a desire for notoriety; the product of underlying mental health issues; or to cover up for the real culprit. This type of false confession happens on a surprisingly regular basis, which is why police in the UK will often keep back certain details about how the crime was committed, so as to be better able to determine if the person 'confessing' to the crime is legitimate.

The coerced-compliant false confession, on the other hand, happens when the person being interviewed knows that they didn't actually commit the crime but offers the confession in order to avoid the pressure and stress of being interviewed further. The person making this type of false confession is often submissive in the face of authority and so is easily manipulated and persuaded by the police to confess, wrongly believing that the truth will emerge later. They prioritise getting out of the interrogation at that moment, too worn down to fully consider the consequences.

We see aspects of the various phases of the Reid technique throughout the police's interviews with Brendan Dassey, resulting in what appears to me to be a coerced-compliant false confession. At the time, Dassey was an immature teenager, seemingly only interested in animals and Wrestlemania. He was pulled out of school by the detectives, who repeatedly pressed Dassey to give what they called the 'right answers' to their questions. It seems clear to me that, because Dassey didn't know what those right answers might be, he repeatedly changed his story over the course of the interviews. It becomes increasingly obvious that the detectives were asking him leading questions and feeding him the answers that they wanted him to give. Here's a typical example:

FASSBENDER: Did he [his uncle Steven] say why he wanted you to do that?

DASSEY: No.

WIEGERT: Which knife did you use?

DASSEY: The one he stabbed her with.

FASSBENDER: How many times?

DASSEY: Once.

FASSBENDER: Are you sure about that?

WIEGERT: So Steve stabs her first and then you cut her neck? [Dassey nods.] What else happens to her in the head?

FASSBENDER: It is extremely important you tell us this for us to believe you.

WIEGERT: Come on Brendan what else?

[Pause]

FASSBENDER: We know, we just need you to tell us.

DASSEY: That's all I can remember.

WIEGERT: All right, I'm just gonna come out and ask you. Who shot her in the head?

DASSEY: He did.

FASSBENDER: Then why didn't you tell us that?

DASSEY: 'Cos I couldn't remember.

By this stage of the interview the two detectives wanted Dassey to describe what injuries Halbach had sustained to the head. Brendan had first suggested that her hair had been cut and that she had been punched. These were not the right answers. That's why Wiegert, almost in exasperation, tells Dassey that Halbach was shot in the head – and, in accordance with the Reid technique, once Brendan had orally repeated what the detectives had told him, it would then reappear in his written confession, as if he had voluntarily provided this piece of incriminating evidence.

The police interviewing of suspects in this country is governed by the Police and Criminal Evidence Act 1984, which is universally known as PACE. It originated from a 1981 report and introduced a whole raft of new procedural requirements to govern the conduct of interviews and enhance the rights of suspects. It was thoroughly disliked by many detectives at the time, who had by then developed their own tried and tested ways of ensuring that suspects 'confessed' through oppressive questioning, bullying, lying and even physical force. These new PACE safeguards included the formal tape recording of all interviews; the right to have a solicitor present; and, the right to say nothing at all to the police.

The goal in all of this was to eradicate false confessions. In the preceding decades these were rife. Many convictions of people believed to have been planting bombs on behalf of the Provisional Irish Republican Army (PIRA), for example, were overturned in the 1980s and 1990s in high-profile miscarriage of justice cases. These confessions were attributed to pre-PACE abuses. It was also at this time that the successful appeal on behalf of The Bridgewater Four was carried out. In all of these cases suspects seemingly 'confessed' to the crimes that they were being interviewed about and then convicted of, even though they were actually completely innocent.

My knowledge of false confessions emerged through my

encounters with Stefan Kiszko in the Acute Psychiatric Unit (APU) at Grendon in 1988. At the time Grendon operated this small unit as a national resource to cope with prisoners who had developed mental health issues but who might not need to be sectioned under the Mental Health Act. The APU was managed on a day-to-day basis by the hospital principal officer, Stan Smith, and it was Stan who suggested that I should have a 'quiet word' with a new reception that had just been sent to us from HMP Wakefield. As far as Stan was concerned, 'Something's just not right.'

Stefan Kiszko had been convicted for the murder of eleven-year-old Lesley Molseed in 1976. Lesley had gone missing from her home in Rochdale in October 1975 and her body had been found three days later on Rishworth Moor. She had been brutally stabbed twelve times and her killer had then ejaculated on her clothing and her body.

At the time of her disappearance, Stefan was just twenty-three and after his arrest confessed twice to having murdered Lesley – once orally and once in writing. He was grossly overweight, had no friends and lived at home with his mother. He had no previous convictions and was working as a tax clerk. Stefan's pride and joy was a Hillman Avenger car that his mother had bought him and he had an unusual habit of collecting car registration numbers. He was regarded as rather eccentric. Stefan confessed to Lesley's murder after three days of questioning without a solicitor present and later claimed that the confession had been bullied out of him. It would emerge that the police believed that Stefan fitted the profile of the type of person that they thought was likely to have killed Lesley and sought evidence that could 'prove' his guilt, ignoring anything that would point to another suspect. This is called confirmation bias – investigators prioritise only that which confirms their beliefs, downplaying, or completely ignoring, anything to the contrary.

An element of xenophobia may also have fed into this confir-mation bias. Stefan and his family were Eastern Europeans and, as I have discussed, it is often easier to imagine that murders such as the one that he confessed to would be committed by an alien 'other', rather than by someone from within the local community.

As soon as he was able, Stefan retracted his confession, pleaded not guilty at his trial and continued to maintain his innocence even after his conviction. It was all too late. As a convicted child killer, Stefan did not have an easy time in prison and was regularly attacked by other prisoners. He spent a great deal of his sentence in solitary confinement and was given the nickname 'Oliver Laurel' by the other prisoners: he had the body of Oliver Hardy but the voice of Stan Laurel. His high-pitched voice was the by-product of a condition he suffered from called hypogonadism. This medical condition occurs when the body does not produce enough of the hormone testosterone, which plays a key role in masculine development during puberty. In Stefan's case, quite apart from the fact that he had a high voice, this condition also meant that he could not produce sperm. The police knew this at the time of their original investigation but suppressed the evidence as sperm had been found in the semen left by Lesley's killer. At his trial the judge had also placed a great store on the testimony of four schoolgirls, who had given evi-dence that Stefan had exposed himself to them just days before Lesley's murder.

Stan went off to unlock Kiszko's cell and I sat down at a desk to quickly read through his file. The entries were, to say the least, odd.

I noted that Stefan had started to hear voices and that he believed that the then-popular BBC Radio 2 DJ Jimmy Young was communicating with him through the airwaves and, he claimed, Barry Manilow was recording songs that he had written. This had resulted in Stefan being transferred to the APU and also provided a context to understand, or assess, some of his claims about innocence, or guilt. I saw that as well as hypogonadism, he had been diagnosed with Klinefelter Syndrome, which meant that he had been born with an extra X chromosome. Typically men are born with two different sex chromosomes (X and Y) and women with two of the same (X and X). From the notes it was also clear that Stefan had continued to maintain his innocence, to the extent that a psychiatrist at another prison had suggested that he was suffering from 'delusions of innocence'.

Frankly I wasn't certain what to make of all of this information, or indeed what to expect of Stefan himself. However, I trusted Stan's judgement and so was more than happy to see if there was anything that I could do.

Stan knocked at my door and then ushered a large, shuffling man inside, whom he introduced as Stefan. I directed him to take a seat. Stefan seemed to wheeze himself into the chair and it looked to me as if he was about to cry. He didn't appear at all well. I asked him how he was and whether his mother had been able to visit, as it was a much longer and more complicated journey to get to Grendon than to Wakefield from their home in Rochdale. Stefan shook his head and then Stan prompted questions about Lesley's murder. In his soft, high-pitched voice, Stefan again denied any involvement in the crime.

I really didn't know what to do.

'Look Stefan, let me have a word with one of the prison's psychiatrists, to see if there's anything that he might be able to suggest.'

Stefan looked unimpressed and, frankly, I didn't know what help a psychiatrist would be able to offer.

'I will also have Stan arrange for you to make a phone call to your mother.'

I looked at Stan and he nodded; Stefan appeared delighted by this news.

Stefan got up to go and, as he was about to leave, I suggested to him, 'Perhaps you might like to stay at Grendon and go onto one of our units that specialises in working with sex offenders? Wouldn't that be better than going back to Wakefield?'

Stefan looked as if he was about to cry again and, in retrospect, I made matters worse when I added that, 'In due course we might even be able to get you parole but, of course, only if you admit your guilt.' I was actually thinking more about his having exposed himself to the four schoolgirls, which seemed to me to have been forgotten, as much as I was thinking about the murder of Lesley. In fact the evidence that the schoolgirls had provided at the time had made quite an impression on the trial judge.

Stefan just shook his head and then left with Stan.

I did get one of the prison's psychiatrists to speak with Stefan, but he merely reminded me about the previous psychiatrist's diagnosis concerning 'delusions of innocence', which had been recorded on the file. Of course I had worked with prisoners who had proclaimed their innocence before, but I trusted Stan and the more that I looked at the evidence that had convicted Stefan, the more I became uneasy. There was something clearly at odds with what Kiszko had been convicted of and the man who had been sitting before me who continued to maintain his innocence.

I felt helpless and confused. I wasn't in possession of all the facts and so I couldn't be certain of Stefan's innocence, but I knew that I did want to help.

Meeting Stefan would initiate and then cement my interest in the problems faced by those men who might indeed still be innocent after conviction. These prisoners were caught in a dreadful Catch-22, which involved them having to admit to a crime that they hadn't committed, if they ever wanted to gain parole. On the one hand, we were offering them the prospect of being released but, on the other hand, threatening them with spending even longer inside if they refused to acknowledge their guilt. Political scientists call this a 'throffer' – the coupling of a threat with an offer. Having looked into this area in some depth, I believe that there might be as many as a thousand prisoners still caught up in these circumstances.

At the time, once a suspect had been charged and convicted there didn't appear to be any way of reversing that decision; it seemed to me that the whole criminal justice system almost conspired to keep perpetuating the same, original error. In Stefan's case, that guilty decision was seen as simply his own perverted reality – a reality that then needed to be managed. My offer of staying at Grendon was intended to be a kind gesture of support, given that it would have been less stressful for Stefan than life in solitary confinement at Wakefield. However, in the end, I was just another official who was maintaining an unfair and inappropriate status quo.

Through the tireless campaigning of his mother and his solicitor Campbell Malone, Stefan was eventually released after an appeal in 1992. The four girls who had given evidence against Stefan at his trial and had make such an impression on the judge admitted that they had made all their evidence up 'for a laugh'. The following year Detective Superintendent Dick Holland, the senior officer in charge of the original investigation, and the forensic scientist, who was by then retired, were charged with 'doing acts tending to pervert the course of justice' by suppressing evidence that would have demonstrated Stefan's innocence. Stefan claimed his confession had been beaten out of him and that Superintendent Holland had assaulted him, repeatedly stating that, 'I'll get the fucking truth out of you one way or another'. Holland had also fed Stefan information which only the police and the actual murderer could have known, in much the same way as the American detectives had done with Brendan Dassey, so as to make any subsequent confession that Stefan made much more credible to the jury.

This case against the two officials was eventually dismissed, because it was suggested that the passage of time made a fair trial impossible.

The actual murderer was a taxi driver called Ronald Castree, who had abducted and sexually assaulted another young girl, just days before Stefan's trial for Lesley's murder in 1976 – and for which Castree was fined just £25. Two years later he also abducted and indecently assaulted a seven-year-old boy, close to where Lesley lived. On that occasion he was fined £50. In 2006, a DNA match from the semen taken from Lesley's clothes would prove that she had in fact been abducted and murdered by Castree. He was duly convicted of her murder in 2007, although he too now maintains his innocence.

Sadly, all of this came too late for Stefan. On release he had spoken of his desire to travel and settle down, but he died just eighteen months later, aged forty-one.

Cases such as this prompted the introduction of PACE and it was without doubt an important initiative. However, a small number of government-funded studies in the years following the new tape recording of interviews revealed that the police were still surprisingly inept at interviewing suspects, especially those who denied the offence. There still seemed to be too much emphasis being placed on extracting a confession, largely by presenting the suspect with the information that the police had at the start of an interview and hoping that this would lead to an admission of guilt. That approach worked on occasion but only if the evidence that the police had at these initial stages was particularly strong. If their evidence was weak and the police showed their hand to the suspect at the start of the interview, this allowed guilty suspects to grasp the strength of the case against them and plan accordingly. PACE had succeeded in discouraging inappropriate or illegal tactics being employed by the police but had failed to offer them alternative and more effective procedures.

As a result, a new national five-day police interview training programme was introduced in the early 1990s, informed by psychological principles. The ethos of the training was to shift police interviews away from being confession-driven to interviews which were investigatory. Such an approach now involved the police listening to what a suspect said, as well as gathering information and preparing their interview questions from other evidence that might have been collected. It also became clear that the more successful police interviewees were those able to establish some rapport with their suspect, rather than those who attempted to bully or threaten. It was soon established that the police should interview suspects as if they were interviewing witnesses.

The mnemonic PEACE is used to describe this new, investigatory, information-gathering interviewing procedure. PEACE stands for:

Preparation and Planning
Engage and Explain
Account
Closure
Evaluation.

The stages of this procedure are self-explanatory but what is less obvious is how these stages are accommodated within an approach that treats the interviewing of suspects as if the police were interviewing witnesses. As unlikely as it might seem, especially if we were to base all of our understanding about police interviews on how they are portrayed in the media, research suggests that most suspects will be polite and co-operative. However, they will react differently if the police react negatively towards them, by making accusations, or appearing hostile and aggressive.

This all sounds very hopeful but there remain problems with PEACE as an interviewing technique. Most obviously, while it might be possible to establish rapport with some suspects, those who have a psychopathic personality will not necessarily respond to this. And, given that about a quarter of the prison population is made up of people who would fit the criteria for being psychopaths, it stands to reason that the police and prison staff will encounter many more such people in the course of their day-to-day dealings than most other professions. My own experience of interviewing people who have psychopathic personalities is that it is impossible to establish genuine rapport with them and that their most typical response within an interview is to exercise their right to say nothing at all – they are silent and uncommunicative about their crimes.

However, even if most of the serial killers and murderers that I've interviewed were 'silent and uncommunicative' about the murders that they had committed, this did not mean that they hadn't plenty to say. What most preferred to discuss were matters that interested them, rather than issues that I might have wanted to pursue. Dennis Nilsen was unusual in that he genuinely wanted to talk about the murders he had committed, partly, I believe, because he was still trying to work out for himself why he repeatedly killed. Other murderers and serial murderers were often masters at dissembling and obfuscation but still pleased to be the centre of my attention. As this implies, using information collected through interviews is rarely enough to build a case against a suspect that will stand up in a court of law. That's why it is important to gather information from as many other sources as possible.

However, there is one final issue that needs to be considered. If someone is prepared to talk to you, how do you establish if they are actually telling you the truth?

Many people will not really have noted, or even questioned,

that the Reid technique has two phases. Most concentrate on the second phase of the nine-stage interview technique. Somehow the procedural technicalities of the second phase blind us to what happens in the first phase. This is a mistake as the first phase is equally important, as it is predicated upon a number of commonly held, but erroneous, assumptions about how to detect deception.

During this first phase, the interviewing detectives will attempt to assess if the interviewee has a case to answer, based on previous responses to questions about the crime. These detectives are taught to base their assessment on a number of verbal and non-verbal cues that people might give off when they are being interviewed. Such cues would include, if they are guilty of the crime, not looking the detectives in the eye; looking away when questions are put to them; shifting uneasily in their seat; or performing a number of self-grooming gestures which aim to provide a form of self-reassurance.

Many students will describe these and other cues to me in the belief that they are good indicators of lying, or of truth-telling. I've overheard heated discussions about whether looking down and to the left or smiling too widely implies guilt and sincere declarations that a firm handshake is indicative of honesty. After many press conferences that I have attended it is commonplace for journalists to express their belief that it was 'obvious that X was lying', or indeed being honest, based on their firmly held belief that they can spot a faker, by looking for a number of 'tell-tale' signs – their 'tells'. Contrary to this, I've also heard people describe how they instinctively trust 'attractive people' but tend not to believe people who are 'ugly', overweight, black or Muslim. I hope that we're past the point where we consciously determine guilt based on these sorts of factors, although events in the news constantly remind me that we are not.

The reality is that, unsurprisingly I hope, none of these

gestures, cues or tells are necessarily indicative of honesty, or falsehood. Many might be the by-product of nerves – indeed, most people would be nervous when being formally interviewed by the police. Nor does everyone use these gestures or cues when they are nervous or lying. In reality, some people – yes, including those people who are physically attractive – do not find lying difficult, or stressful. Despite what many people believe, and some American detectives are trained to watch out for, there are no uniform verbal or non-verbal cues that might differentiate a truth-teller from a liar. Cues might exist, but they vary from person to person and situation to situation.

By and large it is very difficult to determine if someone is lying or telling the truth. This makes my work all the more difficult. Frankly I'd be very be grateful if there were an accepted number of gestures, cues or tells that I could use in every situation, irrespective of the individual that I'm interviewing.

How then do you go about attempting to understand if what someone is telling you can be relied upon? First, in common with the findings of a number of research studies, you need to work on the assumption that lying is much more taxing on the memory than telling the truth. Telling the truth merely involves retrieving and reconstructing a memory of something which has happened. However, if you are lying you have to invent new stories, or at least develop those which you have available to you in your memory, to accommodate the lies which you want to tell. The story still needs to be plausible so that it doesn't contradict what has been said previously, or which is already known to whoever is conducting the interview. This places greater burden on the memory and that burden gets greater the longer the lie persists. In technical jargon, there is an increase in the 'cognitive load'. As a result, and this is what is important, responses to questions become slower, often spoken with hesitancies and, in extreme cases, speech errors that the interviewee then has to correct.

This is why it is essential to seek out new information in interviews, as opposed to going over familiar ground, which is my second piece of advice. An interviewer who seeks to ask the same questions time after time is only asking the interviewee to repeat what they have already said and so the story has become fixed in their memory – be it the truth or a lie. On the other hand, an interview which is investigatory will be looking for new information and challenging statements which do not fit with what is already known or has been stated. Asking questions which seem to come out of left field can often unnerve an interviewee and make them feel less confident if they are telling lies. And, when they are less confident, they begin to slip up in their answers.

A good way to find a left-field question in an interview is to come at issues from new or surprising angles. This is where my training as an historian has been helpful to me. Historians are taught to make connections between seemingly disparate sources of evidence and to spot discrepancies, or make broader links that aren't initially obvious. In doing all of this, it also helps to have a good memory, or to keep a very full written account of questions and responses. I have been in the habit of keeping a reflective diary for over forty years, noting down snatches of conversations, descriptions of meetings, particular words that were used by an interviewee, as well as times, dates and places where the interviews have taken place. If someone was to look at these entries they may be struck by how often I mention the weather at the time that I conducted the interview. This isn't just a casual, quintessentially British observation – I record it so as to ask the interviewee what the weather was like when we last met in our next meeting. It's surprising how often answers to this simple question allow you to gain a sense of how reliable the interviewee is about other matters.

Third, it is also essential to learn the art of good conversation management. By this I mean it is important to learn how to keep the interviewee on topic, rather than allowing them to wander off into areas which might be of interest to them, or which they would prefer to discuss. This is timewasting. They are 'laying out, while simultaneously covering up' – a description ascribed to the serial killer Fred West. Often good conversational management is achieved by clearly spelling out at the start of the interview the areas that you want to discuss and reminding your interviewee of those areas if they start to drift. Once you've done this, any obfuscation and deliberate muddying of the waters becomes very suspicious.

Finally, in line with research about good police procedure, I use what is known as the 'strategic use of evidence' (SUE), adopting the principle that it is best to reveal evidence that you have gathered at the end of your investigation, rather than, as with the Reid technique, at the start. There are a number of reasons for SUE. Most obviously, offering a suspect all of your evidence straight away merely allows a liar to invent a more plausible alibi. Accomplished liars can quickly accommodate what you have uncovered into a narrative of their own invention. More than this, if you are genuinely engaged in an investigation, you need to listen to what your interviewee tells you and then seek out evidence that will confirm or deny what has been said. That takes time and, no matter what your suspect has been accused of, empathy.

At the end of all of this you do eventually have to weigh up what has come out of the interview and come to some sort of conclusion.

One way I have found to go about that is to compare what has been said by the interviewee with the stories and existing narratives already told by people in similar situations. Murders share a surprisingly common number of features. There is, of course, a subjective element in drawing conclusions in these circumstances but I have found that there are often points of comparison between and similarities with many of the murderers' stories I have heard. Most, for example, as I have described are filled with tales of shame and of losing face, and the resort to murder is to regain a sense of personal autonomy. A smaller number of more troubling narratives are dominated by feelings of 'righteous slaughter'; of the killers using murder to try to reorder a world in which they have felt powerless and ignored. Of course these narratives each have a unique context which is personal to the murderer. Sometimes that context is dominated by addiction to alcohol, or to drugs. Sometimes sexual fantasy, misogyny, or flawed masculinity create the background to the murder that is committed. At other times the context is simply immaturity and making awful choices with tragic consequences. Finally, it is also important not to forget psychopathy and the risk-taking, chaotic and irresponsible behaviour that goes with this personality disorder.

In these ways I try to make sense of who is lying and who is telling me the truth, rather than relying on a confession.

The sheer scale of the stories of those who falsely confess should make American law enforcement think very carefully about continuing to use the Reid technique. Some measure of the scale that we are dealing with here can be gleaned from the fact that recent estimates by innocence projects across the United States have identified over three hundred cases of wrongful convictions based on false confessions. The Reid technique may indeed have been an improvement on what existed previously but the approach has clearly had its day. American detectives need to adopt an investigatory, rather than an accusatory, style of interviewing, or the numbers of false confessions will continue to grow. There's no justice in that, either for the victim, or for the wrongly convicted – and worryingly it also allows the guilty to go free, with every likelihood that they will commit further offences.

Even so, spotting when someone is lying remains a very difficult thing to do. Some liars are simply too good at lying, to the
extent that it's doubtful if they even know themselves what is
true and what is invented. Lies become incorporated into their
memory, making it all the more difficult to use the popular,
uniform and constant cues or tells that are routinely described
in newspapers and magazines about spotting a liar.

And isn't that the problem with all the frenzied speculation that has been generated by a documentary like *Making a
Murderer*? The issue really isn't whether we can tell if Avery is
lying or telling the truth, which reduces this important case to
something akin to a superficial parlour game and takes all of our
attention away from a botched police investigation, flawed interviewing techniques and how guilt or innocence is established.

So what should we do?

PEACE as an investigatory style of police interview is clearly
the way that we must proceed. This will still occasionally produce wrongful convictions – we are all fallible – but not to the
extent that we have seen in the past in this country and continue
to see in the US. We also need to be less focussed on 'confessions'
and use the many developments in forensic science to build a
case, based on all the evidence that can be gathered when a crime
has been committed.

I have spent nearly forty years interviewing people accused of
all kinds of violent crimes and remain aware that my investigatory and empathetic style of interviewing might not deliver the
truth in every situation, but I remain convinced that this is the
best method to adopt. I use this style with every offender that I
interview and try not to be deflected by either charm, or threats.
I would have to use all of this experience and more besides when
interviewing another convicted murderer called Bert Spencer.

CHAPTER TEN

Theory into Practice:
Interview with a Murderer

'Because you can't trust if a psychopath is telling
you the truth, you have to carefully review all of
their files in order to be able to verify everything
that they say. If you catch them in a lie, you have
to be willing to call them on it and see how they
respond. Just sit in the chair closest to the exit –
in case you piss them off.'

KENT KIEHL, *The Psychopath Whisperer:*
Inside the Minds of those without Conscience

It all started simply enough, with an email from the author Simon Golding. He was getting in touch to ask if I would write a foreword to *Scapegoat for Murder!* This was a true crime novel he had written, which had the intriguing subtitle, *The Truth about the Killing of Carl Bridgewater.* Even if you have to be a certain age to remember the awful murder of thirteen-year-old Carl Bridgewater, shot in the head at point-blank range as he was delivering newspapers, it was an eye-catching title.

In September 1978, Carl's murder at Yew Tree Farm in Staffordshire attracted national headlines, which in turn put the local Staffordshire and neighbouring West Midlands police forces under considerable pressure to find the culprit. By February 1979, four men, who would become known as 'The Bridgewater Four', were charged with Carl's murder. Their convictions would eventually be overturned on appeal in 1997, although by that date one of the four – Pat Molloy – had died in prison.

No one has ever been successfully convicted of Carl's murder and so the case remains unsolved.

One of the original suspects in the Staffordshire police's investigation had been a local ambulance driver called Bert Spencer, who drove a make and colour of car – a blue Vauxhall Viva – that had been seen at Yew Tree Farm on the day that Carl was murdered. As a result, he'd been interviewed several times but had a cast-iron alibi. He claimed that he had been working at the local hospital all day on the day when Carl was murdered and his secretary, Barbara Riebold, could vouch for his whereabouts. There may indeed have been a blue Vauxhall Viva seen at the farm, but it wasn't his.

But there were other things quite apart from his car that had tied Spencer to the murder. He collected and sold antiques and the murder was clearly part of a robbery that had gone wrong; he owned a shotgun; he knew Yew Tree Farm well, as he occasionally worked there; and he and his family had once lived only a few doors away from the Bridgewaters. Perhaps Carl had interrupted the burglary on his paper round and had recognised his killer?

However, Spencer did have his cast-iron alibi, so his name quickly faded out of the investigation. The police lost interest in him as a suspect, especially after they had arrested The Bridgewater Four and extracted from them two 'confessions' to the murder, albeit in dubious circumstances which would only later come to light and which would see the cases against them being quashed. However, their exoneration would have to wait for nearly twenty years; in November 1979, in a gross miscarriage of justice, The Bridgewater Four were all convicted of Carl's murder at Stafford Crown Court. The police had got their men and seemingly justice had been done.

Case closed.

Imagine the police's surprise when, just a few weeks after the trial verdict, a murder was committed at Holloway House Farm, which neighbours Yew Tree Farm. That night Spencer, who was at a party at the farm, murdered his friend and some-time employer Hubert Wilkes, shooting the elderly farmer in the head in exactly the same way that Carl had been killed. Spencer was convicted of this murder in June 1980, although he has always claimed that he could remember nothing about what happened that night, or anything that would make him want to kill the man whom he saw as his friend and as a 'father figure'. In spite of these claims, Spencer would spend over fourteen years in prison before being released, although I personally never encountered him whilst he was imprisoned.

Sadly, murders happen all too regularly and other notorious cases would dominate the headlines in the years to come and even after the release of The Bridgewater Four. Over time, Carl's murder slowly became just another footnote in the history of miscarriages of justice and I doubt if many people outside of his family and friends would remember much about the young Scout whose life was cut short. It is even more doubtful that anyone thought much about Bert Spencer and the part that he may, or may not have played in Carl's death.

Spencer, now in his seventies, out of prison and living in Norfolk, deliberately changed all of that by re-opening this can of worms and deciding to speak to Golding about the case. Spencer, it seemed, didn't want the case forgotten at all but remembered. In particular, he stated to Golding that he has been scapegoated for Carl's murder for all of these years and that he felt that this scapegoating has coloured much of his life. After all, Bert claimed, the stigma of being suspected of being a child killer is hard to lose, even if it was hard to think of anyone, beyond a small circle of people, who actually discussed the case at all.

I certainly knew very little about Carl's murder but, as far as I could tell, Spencer did not seem to have been scapegoated at all. Rather, to my mind, there were difficulties with his alibi – 'rubbing points' – that didn't make sense to me and needed to be clarified, and so too the original police investigation seemed flawed. These rubbing points suggested to me that Spencer still had a case to answer and, contrary to his claims, he appeared to have benefited, most especially through the police's determination to wrongly convict four innocent men. I told Simon all of this when replying to him to say that I would consider writing the foreword but I needed to know more about Spencer before I did so.

'OK,' came the reply, 'why not interview him yourself and come to your own conclusion?'

I agreed but on one condition – I wanted to film the interviews in order to generate as much publicity for this cold case as I could.

Even so, I knew that interviewing Spencer wouldn't be as straightforward as it sounded. Over the years I've got used to the games that murderers can play and when all was said and done that was exactly what Spencer was – a convicted murderer. Some murderers are experts at using silence about what is important and garrulousness only about trivia; they bully and threaten, while others deceive through flattery; some are narcissistic; and others have an ability to display surface emotions which clearly do not reflect genuine feelings. In other words, they can be manipulative, conning and cunning.

However, the chance to find out what kind of murderer

Spencer is was an opportunity I couldn't miss, especially as our discussion might also shed some new light on Carl's murder.

In my initial negotiations with Bert, I explained that I would come to an honest conclusion based on my reading of the case. I would do this based on how he explained the rubbing points of his alibi and further research that I would undertake based on evidence gathered at the time of the original police investigation. I also gave him an assurance that I would tell him, as I put it, 'man to man' what I had concluded. I was going to put in practice my investigatory and empathetic style of interviewing.

Soon enough I would judge for myself if Golding's book should have had a question mark, rather than an exclamation mark, as part of its title.

During the process of setting up the interviews, Channel 4 agreed to film them in a documentary that would eventually turn into *Interview with a Murderer*. Initially we didn't have a title for the documentary and Bert suggested that it should be called *The Spencer Factor*, in homage to the Jason Bourne movies. There was obviously some risk in us filming, especially as the hope that a human, psychological chess game between myself and Spencer would emerge might never have happened. He could easily have refused to speak to me after we had met for the first time but my instinct made me doubt that that would be the case. I rather thought that he would play to the camera and, in doing so, open himself up to greater scrutiny.

A few weeks later I found myself in a car being driven by the documentary's director, David Howard, to where Spencer was now living. As we drove into the village, I didn't need to be told which his house was. I spotted it immediately.

'That's it,' I said.

David looked at me and smiled, as if I had developed some kind of telepathic powers, but everything that I had read about Spencer suggested narcissism and so, of course, his front garden was going to stand out from the others in the street. While every other garden was simple, with neat, trimmed lawns, Bert's was crammed with various pottery figures of animals and what looked like angels; a pram that he'd painted white; a little wooden bridge; and various pots and pans holding assorted plants, all scattered about here and there.

Look at me, the garden was saying, *and look at the person who lives inside this house.*

Sometimes crime scenes reflect the personalities of their creators; sometimes gardens do as well.

This seemed like an obvious talking point to me but Spencer was always particularly annoyed by me asking questions about his garden, even more so after the documentary aired. I have reflected on his anger about this matter a great deal. Why become so angry about *that*? After all, his garden comes at the bottom of a very long list of other things that he might have got angry about. Perhaps it has something to do with the fact that everyone can look at the garden for themselves and form their own opinion. In that respect it's not something that Bert can control, unless of course he changes how his garden looks. Or perhaps it's merely because he had never made this connection for himself and therefore he felt outmanoeuvred by my observations about how his garden might have reflected the underlying personality of Bert Spencer.

Spencer must have spotted us coming into the village, for he and his current partner Christine were waiting to meet us as I stepped out of David's car. Both Bert and Christine looked the picture of rural domesticity, standing by the front garden in their matching green Barbour jackets. It was as if I had entered Ambridge. I think that that was the picture that Bert wanted to paint.

'Ah, you must be young David!' he said, grasping my hand firmly.

'Yes,' I said. 'Thank you for agreeing to speak to me.'

'I've heard a lot about you,' Bert replied, before adding, 'and some of it was good!'

This type of joshing and faux bonhomie would continue as Bert led me through his house, followed by Christine who was, in turn, followed by the cameras, and then the rest of the crew brought up the rear. The house was a one-bedroomed bungalow, with a kitchen and a sitting room that was dominated by a television. This room was also filled with bric-a-brac that Spencer had collected over the years and on the walls he had hung a variety of his own paintings, including one of a vibrant, growling tiger. He had a back garden where he grew vegetables.

I was in no doubt that Bert had indeed heard a lot about me and had probably also gone out of his way to look me up; he struck me as someone who would carefully prepare for this meeting. However, I had too. I had read and reread everything that there was to find about the Bridgewater case and I knew exactly the questions which I wanted to ask. Above all, I had thought long and hard about the first question I would ask about Carl Bridgewater.

However, before we got to that, as is my habit, I first wanted to know about Bert's childhood. This could be seen as a way of developing rapport between us, although my suspicion was that Spencer wasn't the type of person with whom genuine rapport could be established. Rapport is about creating a connection – about developing empathy with each other – and I wasn't sure if someone like Bert was capable of empathy, given what he had done to Wilkes. In fact by now I was pretty sure that Spencer was your classic psychopath.

My main intention was to try and discover if this behaviour had been learned through his upbringing, moulded by shared experiences with his father, brothers and friends; or if Bert's propensity towards violence was more innate and was therefore

the result of genetic, biological, medical and psychological factors. Talking about his childhood was also a way of increasing
cognitive load and establishing a baseline of Bert's verbal and
non-verbal reactions when he was under very little stress.

The good news was that Bert was keen to talk; the human
chess match was on.

Bert was in the garrulous category of murderers and, though
his willingness to speak was exactly what we'd hoped for, sometimes it was difficult to keep him on track. My conversation
management skills were constantly being put to the test. More
than once I would have to bring him back to the original question, as he set off yet again on a weird, convoluted story that
seemed to be designed to actually avoid answering what he had
been asked. All of this was obfuscation; deliberately creating
a smokescreen that I was going to have to pierce in order to
uncover the truth.

In this first meeting Spencer related an extraordinary story
from his childhood, about an incident that clearly still made
him angry and which seemed to me to be both revealing and
significant.

Bert had been taken into care at an early age and described
living in a dormitory at what were then called Dr Barnardo's
homes. It was obviously a difficult place to live and he described
how he had got out of bed one morning and, while he was washing his face, the boys he shared the dormitory with had switched
the mattress of his bed with one belonging to another boy who
had soiled it during the night. Bert had then been punished for
wetting the bed and was still angry at how unfair that punishment had been.

He told this story as if it had happened yesterday. He spoke
about it with passion and with anger but it just didn't ring true
to me. It seemed to have been constructed to create an impression on the listener; it was a far-fetched story, told so as to act

as a mirror for later developments in his life. I tried to question him on this, asking if he was sure that the truth wasn't as simple as him wetting the bed and assuring him it was nothing to be ashamed of. Spencer was adamant that one of the older boys in his dormitory had switched the mattress with the younger, weaker Bert. No matter how many times I asked about the likelihood of this having occurred in the way that he described it, Bert would not be shifted from the story he told. It was a story of wrongful conviction, with Spencer as the victim.

And that was essentially how Bert preferred to see himself: the victim; the put upon; the undeservedly criticised, rather than the culprit. He was an innocent man, not really a convicted murderer.

Later I wondered if this would be why he continues to claim that he struggles to remember anything about the murder of farmer Wilkes – to acknowledge what he had done would disrupt his presentation of self; the reality that he has committed murder would unsettle his firmly held fantasy that he is incapable of doing wrong, or behaving in a way that is unacceptable. He talks instead about being drunk at the party when farmer Wilkes died, or drugged and having an 'out of body' experience on the night that he committed a murder for which he was convicted in a court of law. His version of events would eventually expand to accommodate a theory that he was protecting his first wife, Janet, from Wilkes's sexual advances. I would later interview Janet as part of the documentary, although at the time of this first interview I had no idea that she would eventually agree to speak to me.

I had thought very carefully about my first question concerning the murder of Carl.

I wasn't expecting Bert to admit to the murder and I already knew what his answer to the direct question, 'Did you kill Carl Bridgewater?' would be. Bert had been asked that question hundreds of times and, by now, he would have developed a response. I needed another way in; a left-field question. I wanted to get a sense of Bert's recollections of the time around Carl's murder in a way that he hadn't already been asked about.

After cups of tea, sandwiches and breaks in filming, we edged closer and closer to the question, until finally I asked, 'So Bert, where were you when you first heard that Carl Bridgewater had been murdered?'

'I was at home,' he said. And then he immediately changed his story. 'No, I was at work.'

The man whose life was supposedly transformed by being falsely accused of Carl's murder couldn't even remember where he was when he first heard that Carl had been killed! From that moment onwards I concluded that Spencer was a liar – his speech hesitation and then his correction had given the game away to me.

Why couldn't he immediately recall where he had been when it would have been so important?

Perhaps it wasn't momentous because he didn't need to be told that Carl had been killed; perhaps because he was already all too aware that Carl had died, since he was the culprit?

During all of our later interviews it was abundantly clear that there was very little that Bert said which could be relied upon. He would downplay everything which counted against him and deliberately obfuscate most of the crucial details, so that it was difficult to see the wood from the trees. Spencer wanted to paint himself in the best possible light: in his mind he was a defender of women and a saviour of children; he loved animals; he worked hard; and he was loyal to his family and friends. He didn't like it when I put it to him that in fact he had killed his 'best friend' and 'father figure' Hubert Wilkes. I'd also uncovered police reports that he had hit his first wife so severely that she feared for her life. He then admitted to me that he had had an affair, which he later claimed was merely a 'fling', and I had to remind him that these very interviews that he had agreed to had come about precisely because he is still widely suspected of having killed a child.

At the end of that first day's filming we said our goodbyes and made our way to the little car park at the bottom of Bert's road. My head was spinning but David wanted me to sum up the day on camera. It would take the crew a few minutes to get ready, allowing me a few precious moments to gather my thoughts.

The camera zoomed into my face and I was about to share what I had thought of this first interview, when I pointed behind the crew and said, 'Look!'

They all turned around.

It was Spencer.

He had followed us down to the car park but he wasn't alone. He was carrying a large, docile dog which he claimed had become lost, so he was going to take it back to its rightful owner. It was a bizarre piece of theatre for our benefit. Like an appreciative audience, we watched attentively as Bert placed the dog in the back of his car and then disappeared into the dark, presumably to drive the dog to the other side of the town.

'There goes Bert,' I said, no longer worried about how to sum up this first day of interviews, 'dog lover, child lover, killer.'

I was helped in my research into Spencer and the Bridgewater murder by a small group of my Masters and PhD students who assisted me in painstakingly going through the various documents, newspaper accounts, court and police reports to see if we could make sense of what had happened on the day that Carl had been murdered. In these papers we also uncovered a seemingly banal issue concerning Bert's previous convictions. Bert had been convicted of an offence prior to the murder of farmer Wilkes – for office breaking and larceny, after stealing a cashbox from the office of a friend's girlfriend, for which he had been fined £25. I asked him in one of our later interviews what age he was when he committed this crime. His reply again offers a good insight into Spencer and the picture that he wants to paint for us.

'I was eighteen,' Bert assured me.

'Eighteen?' I queried.

'Yes,' he replied.

I asked a third time and got the same answer.

It was a serious offence but, at the age of eighteen, it can be dismissed almost as a boyish prank that went too far. It is a youthful indiscretion; a fleeting misjudgement that can be put down to the immaturity of a teenager, rather than something which might reveal a broader pattern in someone's life.

That was certainly what Bert wanted me to believe, although what he didn't realise was that I had checked with the courts and this incident had taken place in late 1964. At that time Spencer was married, had a child and was twenty-five years old. It would be very difficult indeed for someone to confuse when he had committed this crime given these family circumstances. So too there is a world of criminological difference between a twenty-five-year-old committing this type of crime and a youth of eighteen. It suggests someone who has an eye for a criminal opportunity and who is prepared to seize it if the occasion presents itself, no matter the costs if they are caught. Once again, Bert wanted to paint a particular picture of himself and of his past that best fitted his interests. It was another version of the soiled mattress story.

This small lie underpinned my view of the Bert Spencer that I came to know: shallow, manipulative, narcissistic and disingenuous.

It also made me think again about the murder of Carl which, at this point in making the documentary, was never far from my mind. That too was committed by someone who had an eye for a criminal opportunity and who was prepared to seize it, no matter what the consequences.

Of course, it might be suggested that this lie about his age when he stole the cash box, along with the others that Spencer told, was simply a feature of the forgetfulness of a man in his seventies and so I wanted to see if I could make sense of Bert in a broader way by conducting a P-SCAN. This stands for 'Psychopathy Scan' and, whilst I was at Grendon, I had been trained to administer this assessment tool and had done so on hundreds of occasions. The P-SCAN is completed by awarding scores based on police and other reports about the person, previous convictions that he might have had and any interviews which have been conducted. The subject does not need to be present for the P-SCAN to be completed. I actually conducted the P-SCAN on Bert after returning to my hotel room on the night of the first interview, about half an hour after Spencer had rescued the lost dog, although I wouldn't reveal the results of that scan until our final interview. It took me an hour to complete the scan and, while I will not give the actual scores, Bert came out in the 'high' range.

What does this mean?

If someone scores highly on the P-SCAN, it does not indicate a clinical diagnosis of psychopathy but it should give cause for serious concern. It suggests that the person will have many, or most, of the features that define psychopathy. This person is likely to be egocentric, callous, cold-blooded, predatory, impulsive, irresponsible, dominant, deceptive, manipulative, and lacking in empathy, guilt or genuine remorse for socially deviant or criminal acts. This person would be mainly concerned for himself and with exerting power and control over other people. They are capable of violence and intimidation to get what they want but their actions lack the emotional colouring that characterises the violent acts of others.

The score, while significant, did not necessarily mean that Bert had been involved in the murder of Carl Bridgewater. However, think about these descriptions and how they might apply to someone like Spencer, who has been convicted of one murder and is widely suspected of another. Look for patterns in his behaviour and keep all this in mind as I take you on a journey back to where Bert had once been a near neighbour of the Bridgewaters. And remember too that there was still the cast-iron alibi for Bert's movements on the day that Carl was murdered to contend with, although unexpectedly, Bert took me to the woman who had provided that alibi.

Bert's secretary at Corbett Hospital, where he worked at the time of Carl's murder, was Barbara Riebold. It had been Barbara who had made a number of statements to the police explaining that Bert had been at the hospital all day. What Barbara said was important, as it established an alibi for Spencer – put simply, if he had been at the hospital, he couldn't have been at Yew Tree Farm within the time frame in which Carl had been murdered.

I had been able to uncover all of Barbara's statements with the help of my students. In Barbara's final statement she had admitted that Bert would often take a lunch break. This break was usually about 1 p.m. but sometimes it could be a little later and therefore it was conceivable that he had left the hospital sometime in the early afternoon. Still, the murder occurred late in the afternoon so it wouldn't necessarily have coincided with Bert's lunch break, if he had indeed gone out of the hospital for lunch at all that day. Nonetheless, this was one of the rubbing points that I wanted to pursue, though I didn't expect to be able to get access to Barbara. As with many of the events in the documentary, it was an extraordinary set of circumstances that would allow me to meet this key witness and speak with her.

David had arranged to take us back to film in Wordsley where Bert and his daughter and first wife Janet had once lived. The

Bridgewaters had been near neighbours of the Spencers and Barbara Riebold had also lived nearby. The Spencers had first moved there when Carl Bridgewater was five and had then moved again to another property close by, five years later. The Spencer and Bridgewater children were friendly and sometimes all of them would play together in the streets.

This trip to Wordsley allowed me to undertake a rather extraordinary criminological autopsy in the company of Bert. In particular I was able to see for myself how close he had once lived to Carl and his family. Think about your own neighbours and how you might have got to know them and the lives of their children if you had lived next door to each other for five years, especially in a close community such as Wordsley. Spencer, however, claimed that as he had always used the back door to his property, he would never have seen the children playing at the front of the property out in the streets. This seemed rather fanciful but when I put that to Bert he was once again adamant on an illogical point. He claimed that he had never really met Carl at all and he certainly couldn't remember him. Even in the unlikely event that this was true, it didn't mean that Carl might not have remembered and recognised Spencer.

We also returned to Holloway House Farm, where Bert murdered Hubert Wilkes, and then made our way on to Yew Tree Farm, where Carl was murdered but which has since been converted into flats. On the path outside, Bert recited some lines about his name being linked to Carl's name in the form of a prayer. I was rather taken aback by all of this and asked him, 'What do you think Carl would say if he could reply?' Bert wasn't sure, mumbled something and then asked me what I thought Carl would say. I suggested 'He might say you killed him.' This didn't please Spencer at all and if looks could kill the documentary would have ended there and then.

Despite the results of the P-SCAN, I had thought all of this might be rather distressing for Bert. He was, after all, returning to the places where he had lived prior to his own murder conviction and the murder of Carl. It would have been natural for him to have felt stress, or to have been troubled by what he was doing. Quite the reverse. Spencer was clearly enjoying every minute and seemed to especially relish filming in the streets, with a camera crew tagging behind him. There were the inevitable stares of passers-by and the curtain-twitching of people in their homes to get a better view of what was happening. The filming was causing quite a stir.

I pointed out to Bert that I was flabbergasted by his nonchalance about being back in the street where he had once lived beside the Bridgewaters, especially as he claimed that his association with the murder of their son had had such a major impact on his life. Spencer replied that he was simply enjoying how much better and improved everything in the area seemed to now be. By this point he was gesturing rather grandly and the pitch of his voice had risen dramatically.

Then something unexpected happened that would prompt an extraordinary turn of events.

I was recognised.

A man emerged from his house and said, 'Excuse me, Professor Wilson, I just want to say that I love your shows.'

I thanked the man and we briefly discussed the programmes that he had seen me present. During this conversation, Bert stood by my side and, to put it charitably, was very uncomfortable with attention being devoted to me. It was clear that he did not want anything to detract from his 'starring role'; this was *his* documentary – *The Spencer Factor*, as he had originally suggested. As I think he saw things, there was room for only one star and that star was Spencer. How could he regain control? How could he ensure that everyone's attention would turn once again to him?

Imagine my surprise when Bert interrupted my discussion with my chance admirer and suggested that we should all see if we could locate Barbara? She had, of course, lived on the same street as the Spencers, after they had moved from the street where they had been neighbours of the Bridgewaters.

'Is she still alive?' I asked incredulously.

'Well, let's see,' replied Bert and off we went. This was going to be interesting, although it seemed to me to have been offered as a way of Spencer re-establishing control of the documentary and what, or perhaps more importantly who, was to be filmed.

Bert remembered that Barbara lived at 'double the number' of his address – he had been number 42 and so Barbara was at 84. We walked together up the street and all the time I was filled with a sense of disbelief that Spencer was taking us to the house where his former secretary and the provider of a crucial alibi had lived. Did he realise how important this meeting might be? We reached number 84; there was a car in the drive.

'Someone's home,' said Bert.

He knocked on the door and a young woman answered. Spencer recognised her as Julie, Barbara's daughter. Bert explained who we all were and why we were there and then asked, 'Is your mother in?'

She was.

We were invited into the house.

I could hardly believe what was happening and, turning to David, whispered, 'Oh my God!'

Barbara met us in the doorway but quickly returned to her chair; she was by this time quite frail physically. Her mind, however, was still as sharp as a tack and she and Bert happily reminisced about old times. I stood in the corner of Barbara's living room, taking it all in.

'Oh, Bert,' she said, 'it's not starting all over again, is it?'

'Not to worry, Barbara. It's different this time. I've written a book to show a lot of people why they were wrong in all of those allegations,' was his response.

As should be obvious, this wasn't true. Simon Golding had written the book and, while it might have been about Bert's life, it was not an autobiography. Bert's explanation was sufficient for Barbara to feel that she could discuss what had happened on the day that Carl had been murdered. Even so, I had to get Bert to allow me to ask Barbara questions without him constantly interrupting what she said. For me, his interruptions served as a way of guiding Barbara as to how he would like her to answer. Perhaps for the first time, I was firm with Bert and told him he should be quiet and let me ask questions.

Bert turned to the camera and mimed zipping his mouth shut. That was my cue.

'Barbara,' I said, sitting near to her, 'the one part from your witness statements that I would like you to clarify is that you say that you don't know if Bert could have gone home for lunch on the day Carl was murdered. You suggest that he took his lunch between 12 p.m. and 1.30 p.m. Did Bert take lunch that day?'

'I suppose . . . you are going back a few years now,' she replied. 'I usually went for my lunch between 1.00 and 1.30. There would be various times he was missing. He could have gone for lunch on that day. Yes.'

I turned to Bert, ignoring the statement, 'There would be various times he was missing' and asked him, 'So, did you go for lunch that day?'

BS: I don't know.
DW: You don't know? You don't know?! You've been
      scapegoated all these years for murder and you don't
      know if you went home for lunch on the day that Carl
      was murdered?

BS: Now listen to me. I didn't have a set pattern. I was all over the place. My phone never stopped ringing.

DW: Well if you didn't have a set pattern and you were all over the place you could have been there at four or five!

BS: Will you listen. I didn't go home for lunch. You'll have to believe me. You can't disprove it.

This was all captured on camera and, on screen, you can see me become exasperated at Bert's obfuscation, as well as becoming increasingly worried that Barbara Riebold had let a film crew into her house and now there we were, at the beginning of a heated argument with someone that she clearly thought highly of. I was embarrassed.

Yet one thing was abundantly clear – Bert had no cast-iron alibi at all. All it had taken to demolish that alibi had been to ask the person who had provided it whether or not Spencer had taken lunch on the day in question. It was a breath-taking moment, made all the more extraordinary by Bert's throwaway line that he couldn't remember if he had taken lunch that day, only to then have a change of heart and then state that, in any event, I would have to believe him as I couldn't 'disprove' it. It was yet another demonstration of his speech hesitation and error.

As astonishing as all of this was, speaking with Barbara Riebold didn't even mark the end of interviews with key players in this story. Through good research and diligence on the documentary team's part, we were able at a later stage to interview Bert's daughter Jannell. She didn't want to appear on camera but was prepared to admit on tape that she had always felt that her father had been at Yew Tree Farm on the day that Carl was murdered, although she could offer us no definitive proof. She also said that she had heard her father discuss burglaries with farmer Wilkes.

Armed with the information that I had been able to gather

from my research about the murder and in particular with the revelation that Bert no longer had a watertight alibi, I prepared to meet with Spencer for one last time. I had carefully thought about what I wanted to say and, with David and producer Rik Hall, I had drafted out a script to guide how we wanted this last interview to play out. Most importantly, I had to memorise an order to the information with which I wanted to confront Bert and so had reduced this to A, B, C, D and P:

A was for alibi and specifically what Barbara Riebold had told me.
B was for bending the truth – Bert's lies to me on numerous occasions.
C was for connections to Carl, Hubert Wilkes, burglaries and antiques, based on what Jannell had said.
D was for the death of farmer Wilkes and the connection to the way in which Carl was murdered.
P, inevitably, was the P-SCAN.

As it transpired, this last exchange has proven to be the scene in the documentary that most people watch over and over again.

As well as this interview plan, I was going to show Bert the crime scene photographs to see if that might prompt a reaction from him, although we would not show the images on camera. I didn't really have much faith in this as a tactic as Bert had been an ambulance driver and would have encountered distressing scenes in the past. However, it would remind him that what we had been discussing for months was about a real human being who had been brutally murdered.

The venue for our final meeting was at Stoke Rochford Hall in Lincolnshire; a splendid but rather incongruous setting for our filming. Bert and Christine had driven down the day before and were to spend a few days in the hall after filming too. Before our final showdown, Bert and I had photographs taken together which would serve to publicise the documentary. One thing I was very clear on was that I did not want to be photographed shaking his hand and so I said to the photographer that I wanted to be seen behind Bert's shoulder, almost as if I was his conscience.

The time before the final filmed interview was difficult and I was laden with layers of ethical issues I had to think through very carefully. Spencer had little idea about what I was going to say and I found that it was difficult to make polite small talk with him and Christine – I felt as though I was about to ambush them both, even if I had promised to tell Spencer 'man to man' what I had concluded. Bert, on the other hand, was clearly enjoying himself, as he always seemed to when he was the centre of attention, but I wondered what he would be like after I had suggested to him that I believed that there was enough evidence for the police to re-open the case. Far from him being scapegoated, it seemed to me that there was a case to answer.

When we were finally sitting opposite each other, I had to calm my nerves and follow the script I had memorised.

'Bert, I want to thank you for allowing me to interview you not once but on many occasions over the last six months. We have been in conversation for about thirty hours in total. I also want to thank you for inviting me into your home and for allowing me to accompany you on a trip back to the Midlands where you once lived. At the start of all of this you said to me that you wouldn't run and you wouldn't hide and I pay tribute to that. Of course, the access which you afforded me comes at a cost and I know that I rather annoyed you on occasions, especially by my observations about your garden.'

Bert had been rather enjoying what I had to say up until this point but I then struck a very different note.

'You also said that you wouldn't lie to me. I can't acknowledge that. You've lied to me on many occasions and I want to explain to you how those lies, what Barbara Riebold told me and all my other research has helped me to come to a conclusion about you and the murder of Carl Bridgewater.'

From then on I followed my script, with Bert simply staring at me, until I ended with the results from the P-SCAN. I explained to him what a result that falls in the high range suggests and, looking him in the eye, I said, 'and all of that fits you to a "T"'. Spencer immediately shot back, 'It fits you to a "T" too, you bugger.' This exchange still makes people laugh but is in itself a demonstration of psychopathy – Bert is merely mimicking what I am saying; he was stealing my language. If he has no genuine emotions of his own and therefore no form of words to express that emotion, he would simply have to use mine.

I pushed on and then suggested, 'This is you Bert. You are not some kindly, old, grandfather figure. That's your shtick and I see through it. And, in the absence of you having an alibi, because you were there when Barbara Riebold said she can't verify your movements on the day that Carl was murdered, I think that there's enough evidence for this case to be re-opened.'

There were some brief further exchanges but the showdown was complete and I left the room saying that I was going to present my evidence to the police. After I had left, Bert turned to the camera and said, 'This psychopath needs a cuddle.'

Then he smiled, as if he was both a devil and a clown.

As it happens, I needn't have worried about how Bert would react after the showdown, for he and Christine had a very jolly meal in the restaurant discussing over drinks what I had said with the rest of the team. Call that what you like – a lack of insight; surface emotions; no remorse; a failure to take responsibility for his actions; psychopathy – but, frankly, what I had said seemed to have made little or no difference to him whatsoever. He wanted to party the night away with David and Rik in attendance.

This final showdown was intended to be the end of the documentary but then, with little warning, Bert's first wife Janet agreed to be interviewed. She still uses the surname Spencer. We had been in contact with Janet from the very outset of the film but she had firmly and politely turned down our request for an interview. Now, as the documentary was beginning to be edited, she had changed her mind.

We have no idea what brought about this change of heart, though Janet suggested on camera that she wanted to speak because it had been 'long enough' and she wanted to tell her own side of the story. I did wonder if, through the grapevine, she had heard what Bert had been arguing and what Jannell, her daughter, had said on tape.

Janet said she believed that Spencer had killed Carl and that she now wanted the case to be re-opened. She had come to this public conclusion slowly and painfully but with pieces of private evidence that she revealed to us for the first time and which were truly extraordinary.

Janet said that Bert had admitted to her that he hadn't been at the hospital for all of that fateful day, as he said he had had 'stomach problems'. She also claimed that when she had come home from work she had found Bert washing a green jumper – a piece of clothing she had never seen before, which he was hanging on their washing line and which, by implication, he must have been wearing at some stage during the day. Spencer never did the washing and this was why it struck her as especially odd. Janet said that she never saw that jumper again. She also said that Bert had told her that he had also disposed of a shotgun on the day after Carl had been murdered and had then hidden a bag of stolen antiques near Prestwood. He later warned Janet that she should never discuss any of this with anyone and she hadn't – until now.

On the night that Carl was murdered Janet said that Bert was 'out of sorts'; that he 'wasn't his normal jovial self', and that she confronted him directly after the murder had been reported on the news. Spencer had gone off to bed early and later Janet herself climbed the stairs and went into their bedroom. Bert wasn't asleep. She told me:

> I just said to him, 'Please God, please tell me you had nothing to do with that murder, you know?' Bert replied, 'No, I didn't. But don't you think they'll be after me? It's on my patch.'

Clearly troubled by that reply, Janet had then suggested that someone at work would be able to vouch for him but it was then, she said, that Bert revealed that he hadn't been at the hospital for all of that day because of his stomach problems.

I asked Janet if, given all that she knew, she thought that Spencer had killed Carl. Slowly, hesitatingly, I watched her weigh up the jumper, the stolen antiques, the disposal of the shotgun and the fact that Bert hadn't been at the hospital all day, as he had claimed, and she replied, 'Well, you know, it's hard to say but deep down, yes. I probably ... yes, I do.'

It is difficult to describe my feelings on finishing that interview but, most of all, I felt relief. It seemed to me that months of hard work had at last paid dividends. I had found someone close to Bert at the time of Carl's murder who had come to the same conclusions that I had – an outsider, re-examining the case many years later. But there was one last problem. We had to give Bert a right of reply to everything that Janet had said.

By this stage in the making of the documentary, Spencer was no longer speaking to me. He was, in fact, doing everything he could to tarnish my reputation. One of my favourite claims that he made was that he thought that I must be a drug addict, as I didn't eat much and had dilated pupils whenever I spoke to him. However, because of this animosity, it was left to David and Rik and the rest of the team to drive once again to his home and put to him what Janet had told us. Bert did not take things well. He threatened 'kamikaze action' against Janet, saying that he would take her 'down with him', as she had been part of a process that had seen four innocent men being sent to prison.

He said, 'Hear this. I will never, ever be a scapegoat for the murder of Carl Bridgewater for you, or any other idiot who comes forward with allegations.'

The documentary was a resounding success and alongside the positive critical reception, we were nominated for various awards. The first was The Broadcast Awards and on the night of the awards we were all nervous, not only because of the event, but mainly because Bert had demanded an invitation. He had contacted David because, as he saw it, this was his documentary. David explained that it was actually Channel 4 who invited people and so Spencer had then suggested that he would write personally to Jonathan Ross, who was hosting the event.

Here was yet another echo of Spencer trying to re-assert control over the proceedings and another reminder of the personal characteristics of the man whom I had come to know; a man who did not realise that virtually everybody in the country who had watched the documentary suspected him of being guilty of the murder of Carl Bridgewater.

As it happened, Bert didn't make it along that night.

We had all practised our best gracious-loser smiles but when the golden envelope was opened, the result was that *Interview with a Murderer* had won. We bounced up on stage and, even though I wasn't supposed to, I took the opportunity to say a few words.

'We are all very grateful for this award, thank you ... The biggest award would be to have this case re-opened by the Staffordshire police because then, at long last, we might get justice for Carl and his family.'

Parting Thoughts

In 2017, after five years in therapy, 'Big Al' was at last leaving Grendon and he'd invited me to his farewell celebration on C wing, in my capacity as the chair of the charity The Friends of Grendon. It's the tradition at the prison that if someone successfully completes therapy and is moving on, they are allowed to invite family and friends to share a meal on the wing with the rest of the community. As you sit drinking tea and eating cake, one by one the prisoners will stand up and say a few words of encouragement and support to the person who is leaving.

The rest of the community had decorated C wing's meeting room with some bunting and a few balloons and, on one of the walls, they'd pinned a photograph of Big Al and his partner, who had died while he was in the jail.

I was about to grab a piece of cake – I had no upcoming filming commitments – when Big Al spotted me and took me by the elbow to have a quiet word.

'Thanks for coming,' he said. 'I really appreciate it.'

'Well, thanks for all the help that you've given to The Friends of Grendon over the years,' I replied. 'Do you know which open prison they're sending you to?'

Big Al was moving on from therapy but he wasn't being released. As a convicted murderer he was to be 'tested' in open conditions before being allowed back into the community. He told me where he was being sent to and he asked me if I would like to visit. I readily agreed and promised to stay in touch.

I was about to try for a second time to get a piece of cake when Big Al looked around the room and then, almost as if he was sharing a secret, said to me, 'It's all changed hasn't it? It wasn't like this in my day.' I thought at first he was meaning the people who come to Grendon but, as evidence for his statement, he said, 'Look at that murder in America.'

'Which one?' I asked. 'There have been a few!'

'You know, the journalist who got shot on TV,' replied Big Al.

Big Al was about my age and from London's East End. He liked to think that he was an 'old-fashioned gangster', with the supposed values that went with a 'criminal code'. Inevitably he could trace his criminal activities back to the days of the notorious Kray twins – Ronnie and Reggie – and rumour had it that he'd been a close personal friend of Reggie at one time.

The murder in America that he was referring to had been the shootings of TV reporter Alison Parker and a photojournalist and cameraman called Adam Ward in Roanoke, Virginia, by a former employee of their TV station called Vester Lee Flanagan two years earlier. It had clearly preyed on Big Al's mind. Parker could be seen and heard conducting her interview live on air, when suddenly there was the sound of gunshots, followed by screams. Ward dropped his camera and briefly captured an image of Flanagan holding his pistol. Flanagan posted a short video of the murders onto his Twitter and Facebook accounts, before they were suspended.

The idea of posting live videos of yourself carrying out your crimes was not something that Big Al could get his head around. It just didn't seem right to him and was, from what he was suggesting, indicative of how things had changed from his day.

Although I didn't tell him so, I remain to be convinced that things have changed that much at all, especially as far as violence and murder are concerned. Big Al's criminal mentors, once the 'most dangerous men in Britain', were very able manipulators of their own media image, even to the extent of having journalists regularly follow their exploits so that they could be better reported upon. They went as far as commissioning John Pearson, Ian Fleming's biographer, to write their own biography in 1967, which would eventually be published as *The Profession of Violence*. The Krays, just as much as Vester Lee Flanagan, were violent men who wanted to control the narrative about who they were and what they did, even if the type of media that can now be used is more instant, capable of going 'viral' and therefore reaching a much wider audience.

This sense that I have that violence and murder haven't really changed at all does not chime well with a growing mountain of books that want to discuss the decline in murder and violence. I doubt very much that this is close to being achieved, even if I can accept that as a species we are slowly becoming more 'civilised'. As wonderful as it is to imagine that there will come a day when people will not do awful things to each other, sadly the continuities between Big Al's times and the present day seem as real and as tangible as ever. Young men will still lose face and want to regain it through being violent and some will, as a result, commit murder; there will still be disgruntled employees, like Vester Lee Flanagan, who will take deadly revenge for ill treatment, actual or perceived; far too many men, both young and old, will still want to hurt their female partners and their children; and, in the absence of genuine employment opportunities, violence will remain a commodity that can be sold to the highest bidder. Being violent – being a criminal undertaker – will remain a career option for too many young men, with all the dreadful consequences that go with this toxic lifestyle.

Meanwhile, we will remain as fascinated as ever by serial murder. We will be both repulsed and entertained by the latest gruesome case and be encouraged to delve ever deeper into the psychology of the killer, in the hope of discovering 'why he did it'. Allowing responsibility to fall solely on the serial killer seems a much easier thing to do than actually tackling the circumstances in which people fall victim to serial murder. After all, as I have explained, if we really wanted to reduce the incidence of serial murder in our community, we would challenge homophobia; give a voice to the elderly; help young people who run away from, or are thrown out of their homes; and have a grown-up debate about how we monitor and police those young people – usually women – who sell sexual services.

This might all seem almost utopian. A naive, idealistic plea, which is never going to become embedded in our culture by being translated into public policy. And yet, if it is idealistic and naive it is a still a conclusion which is based on my experiences of working with violent, murderous men and realising that they are ultimately not monstrous 'others' but all too obviously are made of real flesh and blood and, all too often, are the perfect embodiment of our culture and of one type of masculinity. The message from my work is clear.

Violence, murder and serial murder tell us something about ourselves, our values and what we might call our civic society. For too long we have created a culture of 'us' and 'them', where the gap between the 'haves' and the 'have-nots' grows wider and seems on the verge of widening still further. Is it any surprise that the victims of violence, and all too often deadly violence, are women who are usually also poor and disadvantaged?

We don't need to accept this; we really don't, even if there are precious few signs that things are actually changing, or that we are about to adopt policies that might actually work.

Policies that work?

As I have argued throughout, murder and serial murder do not make much sense when viewed as isolated acts of violence. Context is everything when trying to explain individual murderers, or those who want to kill again and again and again. I also know that violent men do not respond to political rhetoric that promises to be tough on crime. Nor do they seem all that bothered about how many officers walk the beat, or what new powers might have been given to the police in the hope of combatting the latest crime that has hit the headlines. None of this works because these men can often use violence on the spur of the moment and with little regard for the consequences. When their violence is planned and thought through, too many of them still find that it is rewarding – it is an effective means of achieving what it is that they want. Violent men are also, in my experience, invariably egocentric and exploitative – especially of women – and often seem to be impelled to violence because of their own inadequacies and low self-esteem. In other words, they are violent because they don't really know what else to do.

This is the deadly, male, mix that creates the context in which violence occurs in our society.

So, of course we need to continue to invest in the rehabilitation of men who have been convicted of violent crime but we also need to tackle the circumstances – the context – in which their violence occurred in the first place. Often that context is about young, immature men fighting with each other, or about gangs and organised crime, because they have nothing else which they regard as important in their lives. It really is about the economy and jobs and security and feeling fulfilled. However, there is another context too. Whether I have been describing murder or serial murder, invariably this other context is misogyny – a pernicious cultural prejudice that views women as less than equal and therefore not worthy of the full protection of the state. That's why two women a week are murdered by their partners or ex-partners. That's 104 women every year, plus all those women who remain imprisoned within a violent relationship.

Tackle this and we really would make our country safer.

All of this was going through my mind when, at last, I managed to get a piece of cake and sat down, listening as one man after another wished Big Al every success in the years to come. When it was my turn, I wished him well too and then arranged a date when I could visit him again.

A Guide to Further Reading

This guide is not intended to be definitive. Rather, it aims to introduce the reader who has been interested in the issues which I describe to other books which have both influenced my thinking and/or which push my analysis a little further. As fits with the style of the book, I have not included peer review articles or government reports within the guide. More specialised sources can often be found within the bibliographies of the books that I am going to cite, and the really interested reader might also want to consider enrolling on a psychology or criminology course at their local university. I can also recommend the distance learning courses of the Open University. There are, of course, a number of books cited within the narrative of the book itself, especially in those chapters concerning psychopathy and serial murder, and these should not be ignored, although I have not always re-cited them here.

For those who do not want to read, or have read much of this material before, can I recommend that you visit your Crown Court and get a sense of how a trial operates? This is a really good way to begin to see how crime can have devastating consequences in our community. You might also want to join The Howard League for Penal Reform, or volunteer for New Bridge.

But let's start at the beginning.

There has been surprisingly little rigorous academic attention paid to murder, to the extent that Fiona Brookman, in her *Understanding Homicide* (London: Sage, 2005) has gone as far as to claim that the subject has suffered from 'academic neglect'. This remains a good introduction to the subject and can be augmented by using Shani D'Cruze, Sandra Walklate and Samantha Pegg's *Murder* (Cullompton: Willan, 2006). More recently Elizabeth Yardley has produced a more contemporary take on the subject in her *Social Media Homicide Confessions: Stories of Killers and their Victims* (Bristol: Policy Press, 2017).

For a more historical view about murder – which fits into the hypothesis that there has been a long-term 'decline in violence' – see Pieter Spierenburg, *A History of Murder: Personal Violence in Europe from the Middle Ages to the Present* (Cambridge: Polity, 2008) and Steven Pinker's *The Better Angels of our Nature: A History of Violence and Humanity* (London: Penguin, 2011). A similar theme appears in Richard Bessel's *Violence: A Modern Obsession* (London: Simon & Schuster, 2015), and the origins of this idea are, of course, in Norbert Elias's great work *The Civilizing Process* (Oxford: Blackwell Publishing, 1994).

If homicide has suffered from academic neglect, studying serial murder, especially in the UK, has fared no better. As an accessible text, my own *A History of British Serial Killing* (London: Sphere, 2009) remains the popular introduction to the subject and, of course, there is a plethora of 'true crime' books about specific serial killers. For example, I particularly value Brian Masters' *Killing for Company* (London: Arrow, 1995) about Dennis Nilsen, and Gordon Burn's *Happy Like Murderers* (London: Faber & Faber, 1998) about Fred and Rose West. However, I would seek to push the interested reader into more theoretical territory. Two accessible and serious accounts include Laurence Alison and Marie Eyre's *Killer in the Shadows: The Monstrous Crimes of Robert Napper* (London: Pennant Books, 2009) and David Canter's *Mapping Murder: The Secrets of Geographical Profiling* (London: Virgin Books, 2007). I also continue to use Elliott Leyton's *Hunting Humans: The Rise of the Modern Multiple Murderer,* which was originally published in 1984 but has been re-issued several times by different publishers. In the USA there are a great many books about serial murder that can introduce the serious student to more theoretical territory, although I repeatedly return to James Alan Fox and Jack Levin's *Extreme Killing: Understanding Serial and Mass Murder* (Thousand Oaks: Sage, 2005).

Readers might also like to consider why we are so fascinated by serial murder and serial murderers by consulting Scott Bonn, *Why We Love Serial Killers: The Curious Appeal of the World's Most Savage Murderers* (New York: Skyhorse Publishing, 2014) and D. Schmid, *Natural Born Celebrities: Serial Killers in American Culture* (Chicago: University of Chicago Press, 2005).

The more serious student will also want to consult some introductory texts related to forensic and criminal psychology, especially as the issues which I raise about, for example, offender profiling, police interviewing and false confessions would most immediately be found within books from this academic branch of psychology. A few good starting points are Ray Bull et al., *Criminal Psychology* (Oxford: Oneworld, 2009); Adrian J. Scott, *Forensic Psychology* (London: Palgrave, 2010); and Peter Ainsworth, *Psychology and Crime: Myths and Reality* (Harlow: Longman, 2000).

Two good launching pads for those who are interested in truly understanding psychopathy are James Fallon's *The Psychopath Inside* (New York: Current, 2013), especially as Fallon himself fits the clinical diagnosis of psychopathy, and Kent Kiehl's *The Psychopath Whisperer: Inside the Minds of those without a Conscience* (London: Oneworld, 2014). I quote some of Kiehl's work in Chapter Six.

I have shared a number of my experiences of working with

murderers and the things that they say about murder. I have not offered a single 'grand theory' of murder but, rather, have suggested that there is a complex interplay between the 'faulty individual' and the 'faulty social circumstances' that permits murder. What might be 'faulty' about the individual? Students wishing to pursue this further in explaining murder might consider the contributions from three different branches of psychology: psychoanalytical psychology; evolutionary psychology; and, finally, social learning and cognitive psychology.

The foundation of psychoanalytical and clinical psychology is the work of Sigmund Freud and his suggestion that the workings of the mind affect personality and behaviour – including criminal behaviour. Two introductory books about Freudian theory which I have found useful are: Stephen Frosh, *A Brief Introduction to Psychoanalytic Theory* (London: Palgrave, 2012) and Michael Kahn, *Basic Freud: Psychoanalytic Thought for the Twenty-First Century* (New York: Basic Books, 2002). The really motivated student might also want to consult the work of Slavoj Žižek and Jacques Lacan to see how they have incorporated Freud's ideas more generally into their own understanding of politics and society. For a criminological perspective that uses psychoanalytical theory, try Steve Hall, *Theorizing Crime and Deviance: A New Perspective* (Thousand Oaks: Sage, 2012). Hall's work, often written in conjunction with his former colleague Simon Winlow, remains the most exciting and innovative approach currently being undertaken in criminology in this country and I have used a number of his/their ideas in the book, especially related to 'criminal undertakers'.

Freud viewed criminal behaviour as the product of some mental conflict, which can often be traced back to problems in childhood. As I have explained, he suggested that there were three core aspects of the human psyche: the id, the ego and the superego. The id contains the unconscious, primitive biological drives for survival, such as aggression and sex, and is said to work on a 'pleasure principle'. In other words, it seeks to avoid pain but both satisfy and enjoy these primitive drives, without regard to how others might suffer, or the negative consequences that might flow from following these primitive urges. The id is also the site of the 'death instinct' – a willingness to self-destruct. The ego is the real 'self' that also controls the drives of the id by responding to the needs of others, and conforming to what is expected of an individual as a result of social convention. The superego, which like the ego develops throughout childhood, is that part of the personality which has internalised the moral and ethical rules of society, largely by the child being socialised by his parents or carers. Freud – who had quite a bit to say about violence – suggested that criminal behaviour was either the result of mental disturbance, or the product of the offender's weak conscience.

A more modern application of Freud's psychoanalytical approach can be found in James Gilligan's *Violence: Reflections on our Deadliest Epidemic* (London: Jessica Kingsley Publishers, 1999) based on his interviews with violent men in his capacity as a prison psychiatrist. For Gilligan the internal mental conflict that is the key to understanding why some men use lethal violence is shame and loss of self-esteem. He suggests that violent men have often themselves been the objects of violence in the past – especially in their childhood – and that, as a consequence, they experience feelings of embarrassment, powerlessness and worthlessness. So, in a situation where they feel that their self-worth is being challenged, and in which they also reason that there is no other way to diminish that sense of shame, they will use violence to rebuild their wounded self-esteem. Peter Aylward harnesses some of these ideas in his work when trying to explain why Thomas Hamilton attacked Dunblane in *Understanding Dunblane and Other Massacres: Forensic Studies of Homicide, Paedophilia and Anorexia,* (London: Karnac, 2012).

One of the major criticisms of the psychoanalytical approach is that it is difficult to prove. We cannot directly observe the id, the ego or superego and nor can we actually prove (or disprove) that they exist – despite attempts to do so through, for example, psychoanalysis, ink blot tests or dream analysis. How then can we be certain that they play any role at all in shaping an individual's behaviour? We might also criticise psychoanalytic psychology for being overly deterministic. In other words, everything is explained by internal conflicts and tensions within the individual's psyche, and thus, for example, environmental factors are overlooked.

The basic premise of evolutionary psychology is bound up with biological assumptions that human existence is primarily determined by genetic adaptation and inheritance. In other words, that human behaviour has ancient biological origins and that the behaviour of humans has thus undergone a process of natural selection to ensure that the adaptive 'selfish genes' which ensure reproductive success are passed on from one generation to the next. 'Proximate' accounts within evolutionary psychology suggest immediate causes or factors as to why an individual might respond to a given situation, while 'ultimate' accounts look much more historically into our evolutionary past for an explanation. So, would murder be an adaptive or a maladaptive strategy to ensure that one's genes are passed on from one generation to another? Would killing parents or one's children make sense from an evolutionary psychological perspective?

David Buss in *The Murderer Next Door: Why the Mind is Designed to Kill* (London: Penguin Books, 2005) uses an evolutionary psychological approach to explain that murder is evolutionarily functional and, as such, a normal trait in human beings which is inherently logical, especially as it is a behaviour that is advantageous to reproduction. At the most obvious level, for example, the killer survives and is thus still able to reproduce, while his victim perishes, effectively ending this genetic line. So too the killer – should he wish – would be able to sexually possess his victim's mate, and will also through the murder have scared other would-be killers by his behaviour. In turn, Buss suggests, this will make him more attractive to even more potential mates, given that he will be able to provide protection from other predatory men. Indeed, so great are the advantages of murder that Buss questions why there are so few.

A less enthusiastic but still evolutionary approach can be found in Martin Daly and Margo Wilson' *Homicide* (New York: Aldine de Gruyter, 1988). They suggest that murders are usually the result of young men trying to gain dominance over other young men, or women trying to gain independence from pro-prietary partners. As such, murder is not pathological but rather a strategy to survive in situations where resources or breeding opportunities are scarce. In keeping with the idea that murder is a strategy for ensuring the survival and continuance of the kill-er's genes, Daly and Wilson suggest that homicide will occur less often between individuals who are genetically related and point out that, while most murders take place within families, such killings occur between spouses, who are of course not geneti-cally related. They also theorise that children are more likely to be killed by step-parents rather than biological parents, who do not have a genetic relationship to these dependent children but who may be seen by the step-parent as a drain on resources in the household.

Unfortunately for Daly and Wilson, evidence from this coun-try does not support this theory. For example, just over 90 per cent of children who are murdered are killed by a biological parent and only some ten per cent by a step-parent. So too Buss's theory that murder makes genetic sense is rather undermined by his own observation that there should be more rather than fewer murders. If murder was an adaptive, as opposed to a maladaptive, evolutionary strategy, then it would be much more common than it is, which further suggests that if humans have progressed biologically without resorting to murder in great numbers then we should view murder as a pathological and not a normal trait in human behaviour.

Social and cognitive psychology is concerned with how behaviour is affected by social situations and focuses on the immediate, interpersonal dynamics of those situations that produce violence. As such the focus is not so much on the individual and his personality but rather on how external factors affect human behaviour. Particular attention is paid to how people process information and why they might perceive some situations as ones in which they will have to use violence. I have found the work of Jack Katz to be important in shaping my understanding of how some situations lead to murder. His *Seductions of Crime: Moral and Sensual Attractions In Doing Evil* (New York: Basic Books, 1990) analyses the situational and 'foreground' factors of violence, and he pays particular attention to the emotional or psychological state of the murderer at the time of the murder. In other words, what it feels and means to kill and what is achieved as a consequence. Katz describes different emotional levels that are involved in the 'typical murder', such that the killer commits an 'impassioned attack', or a 'righteously enraged slaughter' of a victim who has humiliated the attacker. Thus, through this slaughter the killer can defend his sense of 'good' against 'evil' by transforming his humiliation into a rage that will prove fatal. In this way, Katz argues that violence is not senseless but has meaning and value for the attacker.

I mention a number of prisons and describe some penal history within the text. I used my own *Pain and Retribution: A Short History of British Prisons,* (London: Reaktion Books, 2014) throughout and, in relation to HMP Grendon, I cite Elaine Genders and Elaine Player *Grendon: A Study of a Therapeutic*

Prison (Oxford: Clarendon Press, 1996). In those sections about Grendon where I mention the case of Stefan Kiszko, a recent book by Michael O'Connell, *Delusions of Innocence: The Tragic Case of Stefan Kiszko* (Winchester: Waterside Press, 2017), is a very good starting point. I also mention Eamonn Carrabine's *Power, Discourse, Resistance: A Genealogy of the Strangeways Prison Riot*, (Aldershot: Ashgate, 2004). A recent book by another former prison governor – John Podmore – called *Out of Sight, Out of Mind: Why Britain's Prisons are Failing* (London: Biteback, 2012) is also useful. From a prisoner's perspective Erwin James's collection of *Guardian* columns, written while he was still an inmate, are of great interest. The collection is called *A Life Inside: A Prisoner's Notebook* (London: Atlantic Books, 2003).

I drew attention to the fact that a number of the offenders that I describe in the text have written their own accounts of their lives and Erwin James is no exception. His memoir is called *Redeemable: A Memoir of Darkness and Hope* (London: Bloomsbury, 2016), although I have drawn attention to the fact that Erwin does not really discuss the two murders that he committed in the memoir – something which I quizzed him about on Radio 4's *In the Criminologist's Chair*. Noel Smith has produced two excellent autobiographies: *A Few Kind Words and a Loaded Gun: The Autobiography of a Career Criminal* (London: Penguin, 2005) and *A Rusty Gun: Facing Up to a Life of Crime* (London: Penguin, 2010). Bert Spencer was the focus of Simon Golding's *Scapegoat for Murder: The Truth About the Killing of Carl Bridgewater* (Beeston: DB Publishing, 2016). I first became aware of the details of this case by reading the late Paul Foot's excellent *Murder at the Farm: Who Killed Carl Bridgewater?* (London: Penguin, 1986).

Credits

Page 3.   Søren Kierkegaard, *Notebook IVA*

Page 11.   Hannah Arendt, *Eichmann in Jerusalem: A Report on the Banality of Evil*, Viking Press, 1963

Page 39.   Alan Sillitoe, *The Loneliness of the Long Distance Runner*, 1959

Page 63.   T. C. N Gibbens, *Violent Men: An Inquiry into the Psychology of Violence*, 1992

Page 89   James Sharpe, *A Fiery & Furious People: A History of Violence in England*, Random House, 2016

Page 118.   Professor David Canter, *Mapping Murder: The Secrets of Geographical Profiling*, Virgin Books, 2007

Page 127.   Malcolm Gladwell, "Dangerous Minds: Criminal Profiling Made Easy," *New Yorker*, 2007

Page 170.   Jack Katz, *Seductions of Crime*, Basic Books, 1990

Page 192.   Laurie Calhoun, 'The Phenomenology of Paid Killing', *The International Journal of Human Rights*, 2002

Page 235.   Kent Kiehl, *The Psychopath Whisperer: Inside the Minds of those without Conscience*, Oneworld, 2014

Acknowledgements

I would like to thank my former colleagues in HM Prison Service who took the time to discuss with me the various issues which I raise within the book. I would especially like to thank Professor Michael Brookes (now also a colleague at Birmingham City University), Dr Eric Cullen, Jacquie Wolstenholme, Frank Flynn and Martin Lomas, now HM Deputy Chief Inspector of Prisons, and also Mark Fairhurst of the POA. I would also like to thank Dr Jamie Bennett, the governor of HMP Grendon, Richard Shuker and James Hole, Carole Roe and Dame Katherine Grainger of the Friends of Grendon. Noel Smith and Erwin James also kindly gave up their time to speak to me informally and more formally in the Radio 4 programme *In the Criminologist's Chair* and I would like to thank Jolyon Jenkins who was editor of that programme. There are other ex-offenders and prison staff who helped me in relation to the book but they would prefer to remain anonymous.

Academic colleagues at Birmingham City University (BCU) have also been very helpful and encouraging, especially Professors Elizabeth Yardley, Craig Jackson and Donal MacIntyre and also Emma Kelly, Dr Sarah Pemberton, Dr Mohammed Rahman, Lukas Danos, Dan Rusu and Liam Brolan. The students at BCU continue to inspire me to think about the issues that I write about within the book in new and exciting ways and I look

280 MY LIFE WITH MURDERERS

forward to teaching them every Thursday. I would also like to pay a special tribute to my doctoral students both past and present.

My friends Neil and Sue Foster, Erik and Kathy Daley-Skon, Brian and Elizabeth Taylor, Ross and Jane Collins, and Peter and Linda Lee-Wright are always encouraging and have helped in different ways, at different times, in smoothing my move from prison back into academia and the media. Alan Brown very generously continues to give up his time to ensure that I stay fit and Justin James has helped me on numerous occasions when I have to do something that is potentially dangerous. He also accompanied me on my trip to Dunblane.

I would like to thank the Chairman of BRUFC, Julian Cook, as rugby remains an important part of my life, despite the stresses and strains of supporting Northampton Saints.

In the media my agent Jacquie Drewe is always a stalwart and redoubtable fighter on my behalf, as are her assistants Hollie Wilson (who went off to travel the world just as I finished writing the book) and Emma Power. I would especially like to pay tribute to the very talented David Howard and Rik Hall of Monster Films, who are pushing true crime documentaries into uncharted territory in this country, Chris Shaw, and Rob Coldstream – formerly a commissioner at Channel 4. Dean Strang and Jerry Buting were wonderful companions 'on tour' and I have enjoyed discussing psychopathy with Jason Watkins, Claudia Lewis, Ashley Gething, Emilia Fox and Freddie Fox, Sam Rowden and Jess Rampling in the course of writing the book.

Gordon Wise at Curtis Brown is rightly regarded as one of the best literary agents in publishing and I am pleased to count him as a friend. I would like to thank my many friends at Little, Brown, especially Sophie Wilson and my editor, Rhiannon Smith, who believed in this project from the start and has always been an enthusiastic supporter.

Finally, my children Hugo and Fleur and now their respective partners Suzie and Tom remind me every day what it is to laugh and to love.

My greatest debt is of course acknowledged within the dedication at the start of the book.